Win or Learn

MMA, Conor McGregor and Me:
A Trainer's Journey

JOHN KAVANAGH

With Paul Dollery

Foreword by
Conor McGregor

PENGUIN

IRELAND

PENGUIN IRELAND

UK | USA | Canada | Ireland | Australia
India | New Zealand |South Africa

Penguin Ireland is part of the Penguin Random House group of companies
whose addresses can be found at global.penguinrandomhouse.com.

Penguin
Random House
UK

First published 2016

007

Copyright © John Kavanagh, 2016

The moral right of the author has been asserted

Set in 12.25/15 pt Bembo Book MT Std
Typeset by Jouve (UK), Milton Keynes
Printed in Great Britain by Clays Ltd, St Ives plc

A CIP catalogue record for this book is available from the British Library

ISBN : 978–1–844–88381–3

Win or Learn

To Mam and Dad
Thanks for making me believe in myself

I earn my living from coaching people how to fight. It may come as a surprise, therefore, to learn that until I was in my early twenties, I was terrified of fighting. I hated arguing, shouting, violence – all forms of conflict, basically. That's not unusual, of course, but to be honest, I was a bit of a wimp – or, as some of the kids in school liked to tell me, a pussy.

I was raised in Nutgrove Avenue in Rathfarnham, a suburb on the south side of Dublin. My sister, Ann, had already been on the scene for two and a half years by the time I arrived on 18 January 1977. James, my brother, came along much later.

We lived in a cul-de-sac and most of the other kids in the estate were girls, which meant that I spent much of my time alone. There was one other boy but he was a lot older than me, so I was hardly ever allowed to play with him. While Ann was off with the other girls, I was hanging around with various local creepy-crawlies. From quite a young age I loved Spider-Man, and I was extremely interested in real spiders. (I still am: I have a tarantula beside my desk in my office. Don't worry, he doesn't wander around the gym at his leisure or anything – I keep him in a tank.) One of my favourite hobbies was feeding spiders. I'd go looking for ants and then throw them into the webs to observe the spiders as they ate them. That was my thing.

When I did try to hang around with Ann and her friends, I'd quickly be sent on my way. I was a boy and they were all girls, so I was seldom anything other than a source of irritation to them. Every once in a while, though, I'd get a tap on the shoulder and be told, 'John, you're going out with her now.' As the only boy of a similar age in the area, I was sort of shared around among the girls as a token boyfriend. Unfortunately for me, this wasn't due to my irresistibility: it was just a case of them lacking options.

My parents say that I was an easy kid to deal with, but Ann and James were a bit wild. I'd describe myself as similar to my mother – calm, introverted. It's difficult to get me riled up. Ann and James share more of my father's characteristics. He's got a fiery temper, to say the least.

I was bullied quite a bit in school, and Ann was usually the one who came to my rescue. She always had my back. The main bully in our school was a boy called Steven. He was the kind of guy who'd steal your lunch, or your money on the rare occasion that you actually had any. Ann spotted Steven giving me some grief one day. She made a beeline for him and attacked him with an umbrella. That was the end of me being bullied by Steven. Hell hath no fury like a Dublin girl with a brolly who sees her little brother being picked on! But Steven wasn't the only bully. I was never really in a proper fight: I usually just ran from it. When I did get punched, I wouldn't hit back.

Even though we had different personalities, Ann and I were always very close. One day Ann was walking along a steel fence that separated our garden from our neighbours'. She fell and took a nasty bang – and I cried more than she did. Whenever I'd be given something – even if it was something as simple as a biscuit – I'd always ask, 'What about Ann?' I wouldn't take anything unless there was some for Ann as well. We were very tight.

My dad and I were never close when I was growing up, and it wasn't until I was in my late twenties that I started to form any sort of a relationship with him. Along with my mam, my dad did a brilliant job of raising us and I wouldn't change a thing, but he was loud and aggressive and revelled in shouting and arguing, whereas I was the exact opposite. My dad wouldn't shy away from standing up to ten people; I was frightened by the prospect of standing up to one, never mind an entire group. He'd make me watch *Match of the Day* – probably in the hope that I'd come to share his passion for soccer – but I absolutely despised it. The theme tune still drives me mad when I hear it now.

But the years have changed our relationship significantly. Now, I would honestly say that he's my best friend. As we grew older, we probably began to understand each other better. Even now, though, he loves to have an argument. If we're both sitting together quietly, he'll often just manufacture an argument. That's his nature. My dad and James are constantly bickering. They're rarely in each other's company without disagreeing over something silly. I can't fathom how people can thrive on stuff like that – it just seems tiring to me – but for them it's different.

It's similar to how I feel about Brazilian jiu-jitsu: I enjoy that as much as they enjoy having a row.

Moving out of the family home when I got older definitely had a positive impact on my relationship with my dad. When you move out, you finally start to see your parents for the human beings they are. Until then, they're just your parents.

Apart from my dad arguing with whoever was in his vicinity about whether the sky is blue, we had a pretty standard Irish family home. My dad is an amazing man. He was the manager at the sports complex at De La Salle College – where I went to school – and later he became a builder. He's very independent and self-motivated. If I've got an entrepreneurial spirit, that's probably where it came from. My dad has no plans to retire. He has said many times that he'll be carried off a building site. He loves it. He'll never stop.

Looking at what he did with his family as we were growing up, I have so much admiration for him. He was incredibly hard-working, so while we weren't a wealthy family, we were never left short of anything we needed. The flip side of that was that we were never given money. Other kids used to talk about getting pocket money and I thought that was amazing. We never got that. Ever. Getting money for doing nothing, that sounded too good to be true. And in our house it was.

I was always kept on my toes by my dad. Never once, as a kid, did I get to have a lie-in. And if I ever made the mistake of saying there was nothing to do, he would quickly have a list of duties for me to take care of, whether it was washing clothes or cutting the grass. From the time I turned fourteen I'd often go out and work with him on the weekends and during school holidays.

I was definitely a mammy's boy, though. My mother was a calm, reserved, quiet character who never got upset, so I was able to relate to her much more easily. She did some cleaning jobs but, like many Irish mothers in those days, her priority was to keep the household running smoothly. When I was in secondary school, every lunchtime I'd come home and she'd have my toasted ham-and-cheese sandwich ready. I'd eat that while watching *Neighbours*; that was my routine for my little forty-five-minute break. I loved that. My mam and I would barely say anything to each other but that's the way we liked it: peace and quiet. It was perfect – unless my dad came home early. Then *Neighbours* would have to go off because we weren't allowed to watch TV before 6 p.m. My dad cared little for Jason and Kylie's wedding as long as there was homework still to be done.

Not that we were given much, since for my last couple of years in primary school at De La Salle, we didn't actually have a teacher. The principal oversaw our class but he would be in and out of the room throughout the day, so most of our time was spent alone in there. It seems crazy in retrospect – I suppose it was because of cutbacks. Left to our own devices, we'd clear the desks out to the sides and play Royal Rumble. I was the guy on the door, keeping an eye out in case the principal was on the way back.

When I went into secondary school, I was in the lowest stream of students. I had done terribly in the entrance exams because I'd spent my last two years of primary school messing around. I wasn't outstanding academically, but I was pretty good when it came to studying and applying myself. I wasn't one of the cool kids, but I wasn't part of the nerdy group either. In fact, I was mostly on my own, or with my best friend, Derek Clarke. Derek and I both started keeping tarantulas.

When my father was in his late twenties, he started doing a little bit of karate. It was the first time he had trained in anything other than soccer. He had been a good goalkeeper back in his day and he also refereed in the League of Ireland. Soccer was undoubtedly his passion, but he knew from quite early on that I wasn't interested.

I was four years old when my dad brought me to my first karate class. There were clubs near to where we lived, but instead we made the journey to a club on Sheriff Street in the north inner city because that was where my dad had trained. It was a twenty-kilometre round trip from our house, and we didn't have a car, but my dad would put me on the crossbar of his bike and we'd cycle there and back. The place was run by an old-school Japanese instructor: a classic sensei kind of guy with a real mystique about him. In the early 1980s, most people in Dublin hadn't come from any further afield than Mayo, so to see a Japanese man was quite unusual.

I started going to the karate classes two or three times a week. I loved it right from the beginning, but not because I was learning how to punch and kick. What I enjoyed most about it was the quietness. The serene atmosphere. When I attended the classes, I never saw it as the beginning of an education in fighting. The sequences – repeating patterns – seemed more akin to dancing than fighting. What I was actually doing didn't really matter. It was the environment that was important. I was never thinking: *I'm learning to fight here because that's what I'm going to be doing for the rest of my life*. I liked quiet time and the karate classes afforded me plenty of it.

From the start, the instructor told my dad that he saw something unique in me for a child so young. I was able to concentrate entirely on the class without being distracted. When I'm asked by parents what age a child needs to be to start training, I always tell them it's better to just bring the child down to see how they get on, because everyone is different. I could focus on a sixty-minute karate class when I was four, whereas my concentration on other things might not have been so great. A very traditional karate class isn't easy for a child to focus on; but it suited me perfectly.

When I got bullied as a child, my knowledge of karate didn't really help. I never found that it was a good form of self-defence. Learning karate in a hall doesn't prepare you for the pressure of being involved in a fight on the street. When physical altercations broke out, I froze. It's similar to a response you sometimes see in nature when an animal is being preyed upon. Animals often freeze, in the hope that their attacker will just go away. For all the good karate did me when people picked on me, I may as well have been learning ballet.

I continued to train in karate throughout my childhood, and became increasingly competitive. At twelve, I was awarded my black belt. As I entered my teens, I started training under a new instructor in the evenings at the hall in De La Salle College. There, I was awarded my second-degree black belt. At the age of fifteen I became an All-Ireland Kenpo Karate champion at the National Basketball Arena in Tallaght. I trained extremely hard for that and I was very proud of the achievement at the time. There was even an article about it in the local newspaper, including a big picture of yours truly. For a long time afterwards, my granddad carried the article around in his wallet and he'd show it to everyone he'd meet.

When I was eighteen, I was introduced to an instructor from a different club. He seemed kind of cool. He was a big guy who wore a red karate suit, whereas we all wore black. I was sort of mesmerized by him. When he said I'd be welcome to train at his club, I didn't hesitate to take him up on the invitation.

One morning, my karate instructor at De La Salle arrived in the hardware shop where I had a weekend job. He had found out that I was also training elsewhere and he wasn't pleased. He completely lost his cool with me, berating me in front of colleagues and customers. I couldn't actually believe he was so angry, or understand why. I was still training at his club too, as I had been doing for five or six years. I was just a kid who enjoyed karate and wanted to do it as often as I could. But he couldn't handle that. It was a pretty juvenile reaction from him. I firmly believe that training in different environments is healthy and should be encouraged, but he didn't see it that way. In the middle of a busy shop, I stood there in silence, gobsmacked, as this man roared at me about disloyalty and told me I was no longer welcome to train at his club. The incident left such a sour taste in my mouth that I stopped training in karate entirely shortly afterwards.

★

Being bullied remained a part of my life in secondary school. Outwardly I remained placid and unaffected, but inside it was eating me up. There wasn't a huge amount of physical violence; it was mostly pushing and shoving, and a general sense of constant insecurity. If somebody whacked me in the back of the head, I'd just keep walking. I never fought back. I would just take the punishment and wait until it all passed over. In spite of all the bullying I experienced during my youth, I was never badly hurt until one night when I was eighteen. I was out with some friends, having a few drinks in a bar in Rathmines called The Station. We intended to move on afterwards to Sarah's Nightclub in Rathfarnham. When you're at that age, getting into nightclubs en masse isn't easy, so we agreed to make our way out to Rathfarnham in smaller groups.

As I was walking to the taxi rank in Rathmines with my then-girlfriend, we passed a group of six or seven guys who had pulled a cyclist off his bike, seemingly for no reason, and begun to unload on him. Everyone around just kept their heads down and walked on by, and so did we. But the cyclist was getting a fairly decent kicking, and I started thinking: *I have to do something here, I can't just allow this to happen.* I went back and tried to reason with the guys who were beating him up: 'Come on, lads. He's had enough.'

At that point they turned on me. They held me down and beat me up quite badly. I still remember hearing my girlfriend's screams as they smashed my face into the cold concrete. I was hit by a brick at one point and they even tried to throw me in front of a bus.

Thankfully we got away when my friend Kevin McGinley — who had left the bar after us — came up the road, saw what was happening and bulldozed in to give me some help. We managed to make our way to the police station nearby. I was in a bad way — unrecognizable; I later learned that my orbital socket and my cheekbone had both been broken – but the police just thought I was some scumbag who had been up to no good and they kicked me out of the station. My girlfriend and I got a taxi home.

My parents were going away for the weekend. My mam popped her head around the door the following morning and said, 'I'll see you on Monday.' I just hid my face under the covers and mumbled, 'I'll see you then.' Those guys had done so much damage that I looked like the Elephant Man, and I didn't want her to see it.

The physical wounds mostly healed after a few days, but it was a long time before I was right mentally. Being beaten up in front of a girlfriend is a big fear for a lot of young men. It's very demeaning. It makes you feel completely worthless. I suppose there's that romantic fantasy of beating up the bad guys and walking away with the girl on your arm.

I was really embarrassed in front of her parents when I saw them for the first time after the incident, but they were great about it. When her father saw me he gave me a hug and told me that I had done the right thing. I was mainly glad that nothing had happened to my girlfriend, because that would have destroyed me.

For about a year after that I barely left the house. I went into a depression and was in a constant state of fear. Whenever I did go out, I was always looking over my shoulder in case somebody attacked me from behind. By the time that incident took place I had started to trail away from karate. I had been an All-Ireland champion, but what was that really worth if I was incapable of defending myself? I gradually resolved that if I ever found myself in that kind of situation again, I needed to know how to get myself out of it.

2

Geoff Thompson entered my life at just the right time. I first came across him in *Martial Arts Illustrated* magazine, which I read every month. He was an English doorman who'd recently published the first of what would become a number of books about self-defence and life working on the doors of bars and nightclubs. He had a background in karate, but pure karate wasn't really working for him, so he had to develop a more effective system of defence. I couldn't get enough of what Geoff had to say and I studied his writings meticulously. I attended some of Geoff's seminars, mostly in the UK. He and I then started a correspondence. He was the first person to whom I ever spoke openly about being terrified. That was one of the key principles with him: that it was okay to be afraid. He was an intimidating guy to look at, whereas I thought I was a wimp who just didn't have it in him to stand up to people.

I learned a couple of important things from Geoff when it came to technique and body language, particularly his concept of the 'fence'. This involved putting your palms out in front of you, facing forward, in order to force a potential attacker to keep his distance. Using your hands like that didn't send the same aggressive message as clenching them, but it let the other person know that you were ready to repel an attack. Geoff's theory was that if a person made contact with the fence more than once, then it was time for you to make a move.

However, the primary thing I took away from working with Geoff was an understanding of fear and how to handle it. Fear was the main reason I thought I was unable to fight. In my mind, anybody who felt fear – like me – was a coward. And I assumed that big, strong, tough men like my dad and Geoff Thompson never experienced fear like I did. Geoff taught me how wrong I was. Fear was familiar to him too, but he explained that experiencing fear before a confrontation is the body's way of releasing adrenaline in anticipation of the conflict. Those feelings of weakness in my arms and legs were completely normal, he said. My body was simply preparing itself.

Some friends and I got together and organized our own self-defence classes in the hall at my old secondary school in Rathfarnham. Just a small group of us on some padded mats, with myself as the instructor – my first coaching role, I suppose – based on what I'd been learning from Geoff Thompson, with some karate and fitness stuff thrown in as well. It was a weird concoction of lots of different things, but we generally tried to recreate an altercation on the street – using stuff like the fence, as well as some basic grappling techniques and headlocks I had picked up from Geoff. It was very much novice stuff, but we were enjoying it and, most importantly, I felt I was developing a greater understanding of how to defend myself.

In late 1996, shortly before my twentieth birthday, I was hanging around in town one Friday afternoon with a friend of mine, Robbie Byrne, when we decided to head to Laser video store on George's Street. I loved that shop: they had a great selection of really obscure videos that you didn't find anywhere else. While we were browsing, I came across a video of what appeared to be some sort of crazy martial arts movie. A bunch of guys taking each other on in no-holds-barred fighting inside a cage. *This can't be real*, I thought. But I was intrigued nevertheless. Robbie and I went back to my place that evening with our newly acquired rental copy of *Ultimate Fighting Championship: The Beginning*.

It turned out to be a documentary marking the birth in 1993 of what is now the dominant organization in the sport of mixed martial arts – the UFC. When Robbie and I discovered the video, very few people – especially in Ireland – had heard of the sport. The inaugural UFC event had taken place on 12 November 1993 in front of just over 7,000 people in an arena in Denver, Colorado. Nowadays, over 350 events later, the UFC is a slick production with no expense spared, and the contests are governed by a strict set of rules. But for that inaugural show, there was simply an eight-sided cage in the centre of a dimly lit arena. As long as the fighters didn't bite or eye-gouge, they could do as they wished.

The concept of the event was that eight fighters from a variety of fighting disciplines would compete in a knockout-tournament format. There were no weight classes, and as I watched the video the first thing that struck me was that one of the fighters, a Brazilian guy, was quite a bit smaller than the others. His name was Royce Gracie. He didn't look particularly intimidating or athletic, and with his size disadvantage Robbie and I assumed he'd be eliminated pretty quickly. In a bare-knuckle fight, size meant everything . . . or so we thought.

Robbie and I sat in my living room watching in awe as Royce defeated all three of his opponents – Art Jimmerson, Ken Shamrock and Gerard Gordeau – to be the last man standing. He simply took them down and used his jiu-jitsu technique to force them to submit to chokes. The three fights lasted under five minutes combined. I was blown away by what Royce had done. Absolutely astonished. This little guy had the courage to step into a cage with these monstrous opponents and seconds later he had them begging for mercy.

I barely slept that night. I couldn't get what Royce Gracie had been able to do out of my head. As a small kid who had been bullied by others who were bigger and older, it really resonated with me. It might sound a little bit ridiculous, but I was close to tears. There was a sense of relief too, as if a lightbulb had been switched on inside my head. Royce seemed like a quiet, gentle guy. He came from a background in Brazilian jiu-jitsu, a form of grappling – something I had never heard of before.

I thought, *If Royce Gracie can do that, why can't I?* These were physical moves he was demonstrating, not magic tricks. It was all about technique. Physical strength and aggression didn't really come into it, which was a good thing for me because I had neither at the time. For a long time I had hoped that martial arts could be a vehicle for defending yourself against someone bigger than you, but this was the first time I had actually seen it being done. This was possible. These techniques allowed you to overcome opponents swiftly and effectively, and without having to injure them, which was also a significant part of the attraction.

The following morning, when we met up for our self-defence class in De La Salle, instead of doing push-ups and pad work we were rolling around the floor trying to work out how to choke each other. I had no idea how or where, but I knew I had to find someone to teach me how to do the things I'd seen Royce Gracie do.

There was nobody practising Brazilian jiu-jitsu, or BJJ, in Ireland in 1996, so I had to expand my search. I found out that Geoff Thompson had actually travelled to the USA and done some training with members of the Gracie family – a dynasty that dated back to the origins of BJJ in the early twentieth century. Geoff also demonstrated a few grappling sequences in *MAI* magazine; when first I came across these pieces, I didn't even realize that the methods he was demonstrating came from BJJ. I cut out all his articles and organized them into a file. I kept separate folders for each element – armbars, chokes, escapes and so on. I consumed as much information as I could from other magazines, books and videos. It all went into those folders, which soon became the basis of our classes. Before I showed the techniques to everyone in the training group, I practised them on my mother and my brother. Needless to say, there was a lot of trial and error involved.

The classes eventually moved to the Educate Together school on Loreto Avenue – which was where I'd gone to primary school. Even though I was still just in my early twenties, things got more serious and the classes became quite popular. I was teaching several times a week, a mixture of kick-boxing and grappling, despite the fact that I was still figuring it out myself.

Although the classes were progressing and my confidence was growing as a result, I was still concerned by the fact that I hadn't encountered a proper street fight since the beating I had taken in Rathmines. That was a good thing, of course, as I never went looking for trouble. I had learned a lot more about fighting in the meantime and I definitely felt that I would be better equipped if a similar situation arose again, but I couldn't know that for certain until it happened. I felt I needed to be in a real-life scenario which involved genuine danger.

Here again, Geoff Thompson was my guide. Working on the doors of bars and nightclubs, as Geoff had done, would give me the opportunity to confront my fears directly. I was still carrying the memories of being bullied and beaten up in front of my girlfriend and I didn't know if I would ever be able to simply let go of those demons – I felt I had to defeat them. By getting a job as a doorman, I'd be putting myself into situations where refusing to defend myself wouldn't be an option.

I had just moved out of my parents' place and, coincidentally, the guy I was sharing an apartment with happened to be a doorman, which also helped put the idea in my head. I was nearly twenty-one at the time, but I looked like I was fifteen. I was short, thin and had a boyish, innocent face. The makings of quite an intimidating doorman, right? I'd always looked much younger than I was, but particularly so at that stage. Still, my flatmate knew I had done a lot of martial arts and some self-defence training, and he was able to get me a job.

So here I was, a young man who had never been in a proper fight, trying to maintain order on the doors of some of the busiest bars and nightclubs in Dublin. I worked in various places, but most often in a big pub in Temple Bar called the Turk's Head and a nightclub near O'Connell Bridge called Redz. From the very start I constantly got abuse, night after night. I wasn't on the door watching out for the school principal during a playful game of Royal Rumble any more. This was the real thing.

If I refused someone admission, they'd always put it up to me because I looked so young and unintimidating. But this was my time to face the demons. These were the exact kind of guys I was scared of in school and who had smashed me to pieces in Rathmines. Faced with them while they were angry, aggressive and drunk, shouting into my face, here was my chance to deal with the fight-or-flight syndrome. The Geoff Thompson books I had read really prepared me for that onslaught. Of course, I felt fear and apprehension, but I had learned to accept that as a natural thing.

When the altercations eventually came, what amazed me at first was how easy it was to defeat someone physically. I thought of my favourite childhood superhero, Spider-Man. Before he got bitten he was a complete pushover, but the next day, to his surprise, he was suddenly able to overcome his enemies. That's exactly how it was for me when I started working as a doorman.

While I initially found the psychological side of the challenge very tough, the physical aspect was pretty straightforward. I was sober and, even though I lacked experience, I knew how to fight. The punters were drunk and generally didn't, so when they'd swing at you it was quite easy to subdue them.

The arguments – having someone shouting in your face – were difficult to handle at first, but once it became physical I never had a problem. That ended up giving me confidence for a lot of things in life – negotiating a lease with an intimidating landlord, for example. That's something that would have been daunting for me before. When you have confidence in the physical side of things, you become more confident in the non-physical. You become confident that if it did happen to escalate into a fight, you could handle it. That's how I dealt with the impact bullying and being beaten up had on me. I went face-to-face with that representation of the bullies instead of bottling it up. If they threatened to climb my fence, I made sure they'd never consider doing so again.

I could probably write an entire book based on my memories of my years as a doorman. One night I was working in the basement bar of the Turk's Head while a friend of mine was on the front door upstairs. He refused entry to someone, but the guy had a glass in his hand. He smashed the glass in my friend's face – cutting him badly – and then made a run for it. The first I heard of the situation was over my radio: *Front door! Front door now!*

I ran upstairs and someone pointed me in the direction the guy had run, so I took off after him. Eventually I caught him outside Bad Bob's pub, but as I was closing in on him he turned to me and it suddenly dawned on me how big he was. Fuck! The guy was massive. By now I was thinking: *Oh shit. What have I done?* But I had no choice at that stage.

In my own way, I managed to communicate to the gentleman in question that smashing a glass in somebody's face isn't something that was tolerated at the Turk's Head, and I'm pretty certain that he got the message.

The guy who was on the door outside Bad Bob's was somebody I knew, and in the middle of the whole thing he walked over and went: 'John, how are things?'

'Yeah, pretty good,' I said. 'But I'm a bit busy right now.'

I'm struggling with a guy who's twice my size and this fella comes over for a friendly chat. Who says doormen aren't pleasant and amicable?

When the police arrived, it turned out that they were quite familiar with the big fella – and not because he had been in trouble before. Let's just say that his behaviour didn't exactly befit a guardian of the peace, and that he probably ended up being hauled in for a chat with his boss the following morning.

My nights were taken up by door duty back then, but during the day I was studying at Dublin Institute of Technology (DIT). I had lots of different ideas about what I wanted to do with my life but I had never really settled on anything. I actually started a little landscaping company, doing some fencing and stuff like that. About halfway through that first year after finishing school, my mother suggested that I do a mechanical engineering course. I'm not sure why, because I wasn't particularly leaning towards maths or science at that stage, but I thought it sounded interesting. I ended up really enjoying it and graduated with a 2.1 degree.

Between the certificate and degree courses that were involved, I spent five years at DIT in Bolton Street. I studied hard during the day, trained in the evening and worked late as a doorman. It was exhausting at times but I was quickly becoming obsessed with training, I needed to earn money to live, and my mam insisted that I finish my degree. This was in spite of the fact that with each passing day, I started to accept that nothing really grabbed my attention the way mixed martial arts did. If I'd had my way I would have quit the engineering course and invested all my time in training. But going against my mam's wishes wasn't an option!

Eventually, word started to get around town that there was a guy in Rathfarnham doing this Ultimate Fighting stuff – me. That was when I met Dave Roche, who remains one of my closest friends today. I suppose you could say Dave was a well-known street fighter at the time. He was training in a bare-knuckle boxing club in Ballymun and it was generally accepted that he was unbeatable. Dave came down to join our training group at the school hall on Loreto Avenue and put himself to the test. By now I was learning more about grappling and I was involved in scuffles almost every night in my job as a doorman, so my confidence as a fighter was higher than it had ever been before.

Dave and I had a bit of a battle, but I was eventually able to do my Royce Gracie impression, catching him in an armbar submission. Just as I had been after watching UFC 1, Dave was blown away. That fight was the start of a lasting friendship – we just had to take a few lumps out of each other first. About fifteen years earlier I had been in a school play in the very same hall; now here I was in a scrap with a bare-knuckle boxer. Looking back, it was all a bit mad.

The first time I experienced hands-on contact with a proper Brazilian jiu-jitsu coach was in 1999, with John Machado in London. Machado was a cousin of the Gracie family and one of the most respected figures in BJJ. The chance to train with him was a massive deal because I had basically been teaching myself up until that point. He was a high-level black belt and he had a Brazilian accent too, which made him seem even more authentic. Robbie Byrne and I travelled over for the seminar and we were captivated. When Machado demonstrated some of his techniques, I thought: *Okay, that's almost impossible, I'll never be able to do that.* But when he showed you how it was done, it was as if he had put you under a spell. Your body was doing things you didn't think you were capable of.

On the way back home, all I kept thinking was that if I was going to make progress with jiu-jitsu, I needed to train with John Machado again. So I spent over a year saving every penny I made from teaching classes and working on the doors. In the summer of 2001, just after I had graduated from DIT, Dave Roche and I travelled to Los Angeles and spent three weeks training in Machado's academy. It was an amazing experience. All day, every day, we trained with and learned from elite jiu-jitsu practitioners, including various members of the Gracie clan. At the end of our time there, we didn't want to leave. By now, mixed martial arts had completely taken over my life. If I wasn't doing MMA, I was thinking about it. By the time I returned home from LA, I had already decided what my next step would be. It was time to find a place to open my own gym.

3

My first gym probably looked like a place to keep tins of paint and an old lawnmower, but that's not how I saw it. In my eyes, it was perfect.

It was basically a shed at the back of a house, located down a narrow lane in Phibsboro. It was old, it was cold and it was dusty. But it was mine – a gym I could call my own. Well, at least it was as long as I paid £400 every month to the owner – a nice man from Mayo who was always trying to get me to move into one of the rooms in the house at the front 'for an extra £100 a month'.

Picture a concrete shell, with a sink and a toilet bowl in one corner and twelve flimsy mats on the floor. That was the gym. The walls were thin, so it was always freezing. Part of the roof fell in one rainy evening while we were training. We used to light an old Superser Calor-gas heater, but it never made much of a difference.

Dave Roche and many other people from our training group at Loreto joined me at the place we called The Shed, and I also attracted some new members after placing an ad in *Irish Fighter* magazine. I spent nearly every waking hour there. I had dabbled in a lot of different disciplines; now, with my own gym, I wanted to cater for them all – kick-boxing, wrestling, Brazilian jiu-jitsu, the lot. We trained in small groups, but to this day it's difficult to find anyone involved in the Irish MMA scene who doesn't have some kind of connection to that gym. If they didn't train there themselves, their coach probably did at one point. Our group included Andy Ryan, who went on to form Team Ryano, and Dave Jones, who later set up Next Generation. I suppose you could say the gym was ground zero for Irish MMA.

Initially the gym was called The Real Fight Club. We even had these awful T-shirts made up with the name on the front, which is terribly embarrassing in hindsight. But at the time we thought they were very cool.

I was really enthusiastic about bringing my parents to see the gym. They had started to worry about the direction in which my life was heading, and understandably so. After graduating, I spent a lot of time on martial arts and almost none on finding a job to put my degree to use. I thought they'd be proud and that it would put their minds at ease when they saw that I had opened my own gym.

When they first paid a visit, the reaction wasn't quite what I was hoping for. My dad just shook his head. My mam cried.

'What the hell are you doing with your life?' she asked. 'You spent five years in college getting a degree and now you're going to waste your time by playing around with your friends in this place?'

While their support would have been important to me, I couldn't really complain about their position. At the turn of the century, the UFC was still very small and hardly anyone in Ireland had heard of it. In my parents' eyes, I was chasing a dream that didn't exist. Actually, I'm pretty sure they thought their son was insane.

With the benefit of hindsight, I have a lot of sympathy for my parents regarding that situation. They were just concerned for their child's future. My mother, in particular, was terrified. Her son was pursuing a career that was very unlikely to yield success. Not only that, but it would also involve fighting other men in a cage. Nowadays it's not quite so unusual for a young Irish kid to talk about being a professional MMA fighter, because the path has been laid for them to follow. But that wasn't the case in 2001. I was basically telling my parents that I was going to spend my time grappling with a bunch of guys in a shed, and after that I'd see how things turned out. It wasn't the most reassuring thing for a mother and father to hear.

I did actually apply for a job after I graduated – again, to appease my mam – and I very nearly got it too. It was with Boston Scientific and the role would have required me to move to Boston. I made it to the final stage as one of ten remaining candidates. I recall being in the middle of the last interview when I realized that I had spent the entire time tilting back and forth in my chair, like you'd do in school. In my head I said to myself, *What the hell are you doing? This is a job interview, sit up straight, you clown.*

I can't say for certain if my poor chair etiquette played a part, but I didn't get the job. That wasn't actually the plan, but perhaps subconsciously I behaved like that in the interview as a means of sabotaging my chances. Having finally gotten the degree out of the way and having recently come back from studying under John Machado in LA, there was only one thing I wanted to do with my life.

Making a career in MMA was my aim but I wasn't sure how I was going to do it. Bewildered, my mam and dad spent months and years trying to talk me out of it. But I wasn't for turning. If I had followed up on my engineering degree and found a job in that field, I know I wouldn't have been happy. What brought joy and satisfaction to my life was martial arts. It might all end in failure, I knew that, but at least I was being true to myself by remaining loyal to my passion. If it didn't work out, I could walk away knowing that I'd given it my all.

I was nearly twenty-five when the gym opened but I didn't have a mortgage or a car or a family to support: in other words, no significant financial outgoings. Nevertheless, I was always broke. All the money I earned was spent on training or travelling to England for seminars and fights.

Fighters often still ask me how I got by in those days and the answer is simple: I had something called 'a job'. I receive a lot of messages from people telling me they can't afford the gym fees. The truth is that gym membership is essentially a luxury item. You need to be employed in order to pay for it. That's how life works. The current generation of up-and-coming fighters seem to feel it's necessary to give up their jobs in order to pursue a full-time career in MMA, but I've always felt there's room for both. For the first ten years of my life in MMA, every penny I made was ploughed back in.

By the time I got the gym up and running, I had already competed in a few fights. On visits to the UK for seminars, I'd built up a useful network of contacts. Paying for flights to the UK was already a big enough expense for me so I'd usually ask whoever owned the gym where the seminar was taking place if I could sleep on the mats. I'd throw myself down at night and use my gear bag as a pillow.

The first fight I was offered was on a show in a little hall in Milton Keynes, promoted by a guy called Lee Hasdell. He was a successful fighter himself and promoted the first events in the UK, so he's regarded as the godfather of UK MMA. Lee was running an eight-man grappling tournament, with the winner taking home £1,000, and wanted to put on an MMA fight during an interval after the semi-finals to give the two winners a break before the final. That's where I came in.

I travelled over with Robbie Byrne – at my own expense, as always, because you didn't get paid for fights on the regional circuit back in those days. There was no real distinction between professional and amateur fights, like there is now. A fight was a fight.

Just as I was finishing my warm-up, someone came into the changing room and said there was a bit of a problem. My opponent hadn't shown up. After coming over from Ireland, I was pretty pissed off that it appeared to have been a complete waste of time. But all was not lost. The guy on the PA put out an announcement and asked if there was anyone in attendance interested in fighting. One of the guys who had been eliminated in the first round of the grappling tournament gamely put his hand up, and my fight was back on. It ended quite quickly as I caught him in a triangle choke to win by a first-round submission.

My next opportunity to compete came in September 1999, in the first MMA event ever to take place in Ireland. The venue was the Moyross Community Centre in Limerick, and the organizer was Dermot McGrath, a kick-boxing coach who was another key figure from the early days of Irish MMA. There was a four-man lightweight tournament on the bill and I won that thanks to two armbar submissions. There weren't really any spectators in the hall, just fighters, coaches and teammates. A few of the guys from our training group had travelled down to compete so we booked a minibus for the journey. The vehicle was pelted with stones as we drove off afterwards, although I can't remember exactly why. One of our guys may have beaten somebody from Limerick, or maybe it was just because we were from Dublin.

I didn't fight again until the following summer, when I went back over to the UK and submitted Leighton Hill with a triangle choke inside a minute at a leisure-centre hall in Worcester. The event was headlined by Mark Weir, who went on to fight a few times in the UFC.

After winning those first few fights I had built up a good reputation, and for my next fight, which was against Andy Burrows in Belfast, my face was on the posters which were put up all over the city. That was a first for me and kind of a big deal. For the shoot, I tried to strike a pose that made me look menacing, but failed miserably.

My fighting career may have yielded some good results early on, but my parents' stance still hadn't changed. Each time I returned home after a win, they'd ask: 'Is that it? Are you finished now?' I remember before I travelled to England for one fight, my dad said to me: 'Wouldn't it be an awful shame if you broke your back? What would you do then?' It was another attempt to convince me to give up fighting and get a normal job, but I had passed the point of no return long before then.

I was still studying in DIT when I had my first few fights, and my classmates were a bit freaked out. On Monday mornings they'd be chatting about all the fun they'd had in pubs and nightclubs on the previous Saturday night, then I'd arrive in with a black eye and a shaved head after being away fighting for the weekend. I was often cutting weight too, so I never really went on any college nights out. I mostly fought at featherweight (145lb) and lightweight (155lb), although I could definitely have made bantamweight (135lb) too. Still, I was always watching what I ate and drank. The only time I'd see any of my classmates in town at night was when I was working as a doorman while they were all out having fun.

One of the guys who had been training at The Shed was a chap named Terry. He was from Dublin but had been living in South Africa for years. Terry trained with us for a few months after the gym opened in 2001, but he then returned to South Africa. Shortly after he left Dublin, Terry called me with an offer of a fight. The event was happening in Johannesburg that November and it was being run by the coach at the gym he was training in. I knew nothing about the opponent or the show, but I jumped at the chance. I was probably more interested in the trip itself. While I wouldn't be receiving any money directly, the week-long trip was all expenses paid. It sounded like a once in a lifetime opportunity, particularly for the nature lover in me. A visit to Africa was on my bucket list. They weren't paying for me to bring a corner man, but my friend Derek Clarke decided to follow for a holiday.

When I got to South Africa, I knew almost immediately that I was in over my head. I was actually using my opponent's gym for training. I was in there, alone, and his teammates kept coming over to let me know how much trouble I was in. You couldn't research your opponent on YouTube in those days, so I didn't even know what he looked like until we met at the weigh-in the day before the fight. I weighed about 150lb and he was around 165. His name was Bobby Karagiannidis and he was a South African wrestling champion. I knew I was up against it. It was a pretty big event in a large arena in the Carnival City Casino, where Lennox Lewis had lost his world title to Hasim Rahman just a few months earlier. Until then I had been fighting in small halls, but there would be thousands of people in attendance for this one.

The event was also being broadcast on South African TV. Before my fight, the cameras came into the changing rooms to interview me and the presenter couldn't believe that I had come all the way from Ireland on my own. When he asked me what type of training I had been doing, I tried to crack a joke because I was so nervous. I said: 'I've been spending a lot of time playing the new UFC video game so I think that has prepared me well.' Unfortunately, he didn't really get the joke so we both ended up looking a bit silly.

When the time came to fight, it was like walking out in the MGM Grand. Alone and thousands of miles from home, it was pretty intimidating. My game plan was to take Bobby down and look for a submission, but he was a far better wrestler so he was able to fend off my attempts quite easily. I ended up pulling guard and going for a leg-lock. As I did, he was standing over me and raining down punches on my head. I was taking a fair bit of damage, and I should have let go and adjusted my position, but I was emotionally attached to completing the technique. It's a lesson I've since learned, but my mistake cost me dearly that night. As he was landing punch after punch, I persisted with the leg-lock, searching for the submission, thinking I had him in trouble . . . then all of a sudden I woke up in the changing room. 'Did I win?' I asked. Not quite. I was knocked out in the first round.

Seven years before he became a UFC champion, Forrest Griffin actually fought in the main event that night. Another future UFC fighter who was on that bill was Rory Singer. We all went out together after the show and had a good time. Having been knocked out and concussed, I very stupidly got quite drunk. The hotel I was staying in was in a nature reserve, and I somehow came to the conclusion that it would be a good idea to go streaking around the vicinity at 2 a.m. I found out the following day that I was lucky not to have been some lion's breakfast.

I might not have picked up the result I was hoping for in that fight, but that crazy night turned out to be one of the most important of my life. One of my fellow drinkers was Bobby Karagiannidis's coach – a big American fella named Matt Thornton. Matt and I chatted for a long time. I was fascinated by what he had to say about coaching and we really clicked. He was able to verbalize exactly how I felt about coaching. Matt had a long history with mixed martial arts and was well known in the US, having founded his own MMA academy – Straight Blast Gym – in Oregon.

The following day, Matt was holding a seminar in Johannesburg and I managed to fight through my hangover in time to head along. There, I learned about his 'aliveness' approach, which really struck a chord with me. Consisting of three core principles – movement, energy and timing – the concept was based around recreating the actualities of a fight situation in training instead of your sessions becoming a rehearsal of dead patterns; challenging instead of demonstrating; honing your skills against an uncooperative opponent. Matt's approach created a distinction between live and dead training, and I knew which one I preferred. It may sound like common sense, but the approach was very original at the time.

After I returned home, Matt and I stayed in touch by e-mail. I was eager to work more closely with him, so I invited him to come to Dublin the following summer. Paying for him to come over cost me a fortune, but to say it was a worthwhile investment would be an understatement.

At that stage I had already trained under John Machado, the Gracies and Geoff Thompson, and they were all fantastic in their own ways. But there was something different about Matt that made him stand out. For a start, he was clearly a very intelligent guy. He was also the first proper MMA coach I encountered – a mentor who was adept in all the disciplines, from boxing to Brazilian jiu-jitsu. Matt was a BJJ black belt, so he gave me my first ever grading while he was in Dublin. He determined that my first belt would be purple.

But certainly the most interesting thing about Matt was his 'aliveness' methodology. I wasn't in a position to be able to move my life to the US to work with Matt on a permanent basis, but if he gave me his formula I knew I could put it into practice.

I was full of admiration for Matt, and he obviously saw something in me too. I was officially welcomed into the Straight Blast Gym family, and in 2002 The Shed became SBG Ireland.

Balancing my commitments as a coach and a fighter was always a challenge. The more time I spent on coaching, the less scope I had to train for my own fights. I carried on regardless, beating a

Frenchman called Tamel Hasar by first-round submission (rear naked choke) in Portsmouth in February 2002. That event was the first in Europe to feature a cage instead of a boxing ring. For some reason, a lot of people seem to find MMA in a cage barbaric, yet they don't have the same problem when it's in a ring – in spite of the fact that the cage actually provides a safer environment for the competitors by preventing them from falling through the ropes and sustaining serious injuries.

Even though the rules are the same, there's something very different about competing in a cage instead of a ring. When you hear that door being bolted shut, it can suddenly feel very claustrophobic in there. You're literally caged in. At first, you tend to think: *Shit! This is insane. What the hell am I doing in here?* There are also technical differences: for example it can be much harder to back your opponent up and corner him in an octagonal cage. However, it can also be easier to take him down, as there are no ropes for him to grab on to. I was excited about fighting in a cage, because a part of me felt like Royce Gracie, stepping into the cage to represent Brazilian jiu-jitsu just as he had done at UFC 1 back in 1993.

Just two weeks later, I was back in England to face Leigh Remedios in Salisbury. He managed to beat me by unanimous decision. His next fight, a few months later, was in the UFC.

As I prepared to face Danny Batten in Milton Keynes the following November, I told myself that this would be my last fight. Coaching was taking over and I just didn't have sufficient time to invest in fighting. I simply couldn't balance both commitments any longer. When you're a competitive athlete, you have to be selfish with your own time, but almost all of mine was being spent on coaching. At the end of a session I'd have to take questions from my students instead of focusing on recovering in time for the next session, or doing a little bit of work on my own. My ability to compete was fading away, but more importantly so was the desire. I had never won with strikes before so, in the knowledge that I probably wouldn't fight ever again, I really wanted to get a knockout against Batten. I went right after it and dominated the first round, but I couldn't put him away. By the end of that round, I had completely emptied my gas tank, and he took full advantage, submitting me via keylock towards the end of the second round.

There was no shame in losing to Danny Batten – he was one of the top guys on the UK circuit and later went on to become the Cage Warriors featherweight champion – but I was still really disappointed after that defeat. I felt I was better than him, but I got tired and paid the price.

I felt I couldn't sign off my fighting career on that note. Five months later I was back in Milton Keynes to face another top UK fighter, Robbie Olivier. The fact that coaching was gradually taking over for me was evident at that show. A few fights before my own, I was cornering one of my own students, Adrian Degorski, in his debut. Going into the fight with Robbie, I had to accept that – win or lose – this was definitely the end.

Perhaps I was looking for the fairytale ending to my career, and thankfully I got it. I submitted Robbie with an armbar in the first round. Now I could retire on a winning note.

Robbie Olivier ended up having a really good career in the UK. He beat several guys who were later signed by the UFC – Brad Pickett, for example – so it was a bit surprising that he never got a shot in the UFC himself. Having beaten Robbie, there was definitely a part of me that wondered how far I might have gone if I'd carried on competing, and I certainly got a kick out of it when I saw how successful he turned out to be. But it was still just a very small part of me that felt that way. Teaching was my passion. I knew from early on that fighting didn't inspire me the same way coaching did. I look at the competitive nature of my own fighters down through the years and I recognize that that was never me. I didn't have anything close to the passion for competition that they possess. For many years I still packed the gumshield when travelling with my fighters, just in case there was a pull-out and they needed someone to step in on the show. And I continued to compete occasionally in Brazilian jiu-jitsu tournaments. In 2005 I won a gold medal as a purple belt at the European Championships in Lisbon. That was a massive moment for me, and Matt Thornton rewarded me with a promotion to brown-belt status. But the MMA game was getting a lot more serious, and quickly. Any remnants of a desire to compete in MMA soon disappeared entirely.

I've always been a teacher and a mentor. By the time I was awarded my black belt in karate at the age of twelve, I was already helping out with teaching beginners, including some who were in their twenties and thirties. I wasn't the boss, but I enjoyed being delegated a little bit of responsibility to assist the instructor. It was the same in other areas of life too. I taught my mother how to use a computer well. When I was in college, I regularly helped study partners with problems or questions they were struggling with.

Whenever I fought, in order to motivate myself I needed to do something that I always tell my fighters not to do, and that is to become emotionally invested in a contest. My friend Robbie Byrne would often have to make up some crazy stuff before a fight to get me interested: 'John, I heard this guy saying terrible things about your sister earlier on. Make him pay for it.' I'd then charge out from my corner and tear into my opponent. It didn't matter that what Robbie was saying wasn't true, it succeeded in getting me wound up.

Looking back, I can see that fighting – like working on the doors of bars and nightclubs – was also a way for me to get rid of the lingering demons I had from being bullied and scared to defend myself at school. But I didn't care about belts or money. I wasn't earning anything from it anyway. It actually cost me money to fight. And, unlike the majority of aspiring MMA athletes, I definitely didn't see myself one day making it to the UFC. At least not as a fighter.

Kieran McGeeney, who captained Armagh to the All-Ireland Senior Football Championship in 2002, is now a coach at SBG Ireland. He often says that you need to have a darkness inside you to compete at a high level in any sport. If you can't tap into that dark side, you'll quickly come unstuck. I was an example of a fighter who didn't have access to the dark side. I can recall being in control during fights and part of me would feel like telling my opponent what he needed to do to get out of a position or something: 'No, move your hand here.' Coaching and teaching always came more naturally to me than competing and winning.

4

With my own fighting career a thing of the past, I was able to focus entirely on coaching. The challenge was to make SBG Ireland as successful as we could possibly be, and to put together a fight team to represent the gym accordingly. And we weren't going to be able to achieve that from a shed down a back alley in Phibsboro.

After a couple of years, The Shed's membership was steadily increasing and those four thin concrete walls were struggling to hold us all. If SBG was to grow, we needed more space.

In 2003 we relocated to Greenmount Avenue in Harold's Cross. The place we found was like a palace in comparison to The Shed. It was much larger and brighter, and it even had a shower. With such luxuries, we really felt like we were moving up in the world. The unit had been a Thai boxing gym before we moved in, so it was fit for purpose. Upgrading to a facility like that was very exciting, and the fact that I could afford to do so was a good indication that things were heading in the right direction.

Still, there was more than a hint of sadness about leaving The Shed behind.

Sure, it was smelly, damp, cold and not at all suitable for elite athletes, which was what we were aspiring to be, but I had built up an enormous feeling of attachment to the place and the other guys felt the same. No matter what happened from here on in, regardless of the direction in which the journey was about to go, The Shed was where it all started. Because of that, it will always have a special place in my heart.

Having brought my own fighting career to an end, I was able to focus completely on putting together a competitive fight team and making sure that they were coached well. A few of the guys were making an impact on the UK scene. Mick Leonard was one of

SBG's top fighters at the time; Andy Ryan also had some good wins; and even though he didn't compete very often, Dave Roche absolutely ran through his opponents whenever he fought.

Probably the most impressive athlete we had at the time, however, was Adrian Degorski. He was Polish, part of the large migration into Ireland from eastern Europe at the turn of the century, and he arrived with an extensive boxing background. Grappling never came easily to Adrian, but his striking was outstanding and he was a phenomenal athlete. Adrian had been a member of Poland's national amateur boxing team and had a record of something like 50–1. He fought with a broken foot in the only bout he lost, which seemed less surprising as I got to know him a bit better, because the guy was as tough as a coffin nail. He had quite a short temper, too. I got him a job on the door of a pub and he knocked out the first guy who gave him hassle with one punch. I tried to explain to Adrian that he couldn't hit everyone who caused a problem, but I'm pretty sure he thought I was joking.

Another member who joined SBG at The Shed was an eighteen-year old street kid from Ballymun who came down one evening with Dave Roche.

'John, this is Owen Roddy,' Dave said to me. 'He can't afford the fees for now but if you allow him to train here he'll clean the mats every night.'

'I clean the mats myself, Dave,' I responded. 'It only takes me thirty seconds.' But I'm a bit of a sucker in those situations. Dave kept pushing me and Owen seemed like a really nice kid, too. He was both polite and enthusiastic – two essential characteristics for me – so I gave him a chance. And I'm glad I did. Owen would eventually prove to be worth his weight in gold to SBG.

For those of us who had been there from the beginning, 2003 was an exciting time for the sport, with promotions like Cage Warriors and Cage Rage having launched in the UK the previous year. The circuit was still very small. The promoters were shuffling a small deck of cards. If you were competing at an event, you'd keep a close eye on the other fights too because the likelihood was that you were studying a future opponent.

More often than not we were heading across the Irish Sea for fights, but there were occasionally events in Ireland too. The biggest regular show on the island was Cage Wars – the promotion which had used a cage in Europe for the first time in 2002. It was organized by Paddy Mooney and Tom Lamont, two promoters who put on some really good events at the King's Hall in Belfast featuring fighters like Jess Liaudin and Samy Schiavo, who went on to appear in the UFC.

However, as my fight team expanded, there still weren't enough events taking place to satisfy their appetite for competition. How did I find a solution to that? By doing what I had always done before: I decided to do something about it myself. I had no previous experience as a promoter, of course, but I thought: *How hard can it be? Let's get a ring, put it in a hall, have a bunch of guys fight each other and charge people to watch it all.*

The venue was the Ringside Club, which is the small hall next to the National Boxing Stadium in Dublin. It held around 300 people, and while it wasn't easy to shift all the tickets – social media hadn't arrived yet so we couldn't rely on Facebook and Twitter to put the word out – we still managed to sell out our two or three events a year. The show was also where most of Ireland's future stars of the UFC got their first taste of competitive action. At €15 a ticket, I always felt the spectators got value for money. They were fun nights.

I called the promotion Ring of Truth, because the fights took place in a boxing ring and, as I saw it, this was truth in combat: two guys who weighed the same, blending a variety of fighting styles to see who was truly the better fighter. Later, when I could afford to hire a cage from the UK, it became Cage of Truth. It was the first regular show in the Republic of Ireland and it was also where many fans were first exposed to MMA, so it played an important role in the gradual growth of the sport.

The first event happened on 1 October 2004. It featured fighters from gyms around the country who had travelled to compete. Many of them – like John Donnelly, Francis Heagney, Micky Young and Greg Loughran – were laying the foundations for relatively successful careers.

As productions, the first shows couldn't have been more basic. We put a ring in the middle of the Ringside Club and opened the doors to the punters. We didn't have proper lighting and there certainly weren't any TV cameras present, although there is a bit of dodgy footage available on YouTube if you fancy checking out how primitive it all was. It was proper spit-and-sawdust stuff. As both the promoter and a coach, it was sometimes tricky to make sure the show was running smoothly while cornering my fighters, but it was always enjoyable. As for the medical checks, a guy from St John Ambulance would basically ask: 'Are ya all right? Grand, in ya go.' That was all there was to it. That side of things would eventually become much more scrupulous, and rightly so, but back then we didn't really know any better.

The shows didn't generate a profit, but I never accumulated any debt from them either. The aim was to give my guys fights, not to earn money, so it was mission accomplished. The main difficulty we faced was that fighters often pulled out at short notice, so you'd spend the final days beforehand e-mailing gyms in the UK and France to see if anyone was available to step in. On one occasion we had ten bouts on the card, and six of them involved fighters who were travelling down in a convoy of cars from Northern Ireland. At 7 p.m. on the night of the show, with the doors open, the venue packed and the first fight about to start, there was still no sign of the guys from up north. In a state of panic, I phoned one of them and learned that after driving around Dublin for a while, unable to find the venue, they had just decided to head home. With only four fights left on the card and three hundred people having paid for a night of entertainment, I had to scramble around to fill the void. I was looking for anyone in the hall with a bit of martial arts experience to help me out. I ended up putting two guys into the ring to do a judo demonstration, as well as a little kid to show off some karate techniques. It was an absolute disaster, but we got through it without too many complaints.

MMA was never illegal in Ireland – and at that point the vast majority of Irish people weren't even aware that it existed – but we weren't sure how the authorities would react. Thankfully, we never ran into any difficulty on that front. I think that was partly down to how we advertised the shows. Even when we started using a cage, the posters referred to a martial arts event and not a cage-fighting show. Rightly or wrongly, the two seem to have very different connotations.

Another show that was being planned in Dublin around that time went down the opposite route. It was due to be held at the Red Cow Hotel and, as a one-off, I had actually agreed to fight on it. I was quite excited about this one because it was going to be me, in my Brazilian jiu-jitsu gi, against Jim Rock, a well-known Irish professional boxer. I pictured myself playing the part of Royce Gracie at UFC 1.

Unfortunately, it never got off the ground. A week out from the show, despite the fact that hundreds of tickets had been sold, it was shut down by South Dublin County Council. The promoters had put posters up that advertised 'cage fights', including a massive one at the Red Cow roundabout. I guess it attracted some unwanted attention from the authorities and they pulled the plug.

One afternoon in 2005, at the gym in Harold's Cross, we were paid a visit by this Lithuanian guy. A year later, when Sacha Baron Cohen's film *Borat* came out, we started referring to the Lithuanian by the same name: they were like the same person. The accent and the garish suits were almost identical.

'Borat' ran a popular promotion called Rings, which had staged nearly a hundred events around the world since 1995. He wanted to bring the show to Ireland and asked if some of SBG's fighters would be interested in competing. The event was scheduled for 12 March 2005 at the Point Depot – later rechristened the O_2 Arena and now known as the 3Arena. It would be the biggest MMA show ever seen in Ireland, so we were obviously on board. There were some really good fighters brought in from abroad to compete on the show, including Gegard Mousasi, who later became a Strikeforce champion and is a top contender in the UFC even now.

Matt Thornton travelled over from the US to be there and it felt like a big night for the gym. After building up a reputation as the top team in Ireland, with fighters who were capable of mixing it with the best in the UK, this was an opportunity to make a statement on an international stage. I was really keen to impress Matt, too, and was conscious of his presence as I took the guys through their warm-ups and guided them from the corner during their fights.

But it was a bad night for SBG. Some of my guys were slaughtered, and the show itself was a bit of a catastrophe. Occasionally, even at the very highest level, you get those nights when the fights don't deliver, the crowd are restless and it's a soundtrack of jeers instead of cheers. Rings was one of those. The low point of the night came with the main event. Rodney Moore from Northern Ireland was due to fight a guy called Jimmy Curran, who was a noted kick-boxer from Dublin, although he didn't really have any MMA experience. Jimmy had sold a lot of tickets for the show, so in many ways he was the star attraction.

Rodney walked out first and went to his corner but when Jimmy's name was announced, he didn't appear. There was an awkward silence, before 'Borat' — who was also the announcer — gave it another go: 'Let's try that again. From Dublin, Ireland, Jimmy Curran!' But there was still no sign of him. The crowd weren't happy and bottles of beer started to rain down on top of those of us near the ring, so we all ran for cover.

When we got backstage, we found out that Jimmy had changed his mind about fighting and had climbed out the window before he was due to walk out to the ring. Unfortunately Jimmy soon had other, more serious problems to deal with. Three weeks later, in an unrelated incident, he was shot dead in a Dublin pub.

I was completely despondent for days after the Rings event. Not only had it been disappointing for SBG, it was a shambolic night for

Irish MMA as a whole. I was upset, embarrassed and disillusioned. It was one of those nights when whatever could go wrong did go wrong. I took a lot of abuse from Irish MMA fans on internet forums as a result – 'John Kavanagh embarrassed Ireland on the world stage' – but I was even more concerned by what it might mean for the sport in the country overall. MMA was already struggling to get off the ground in terms of popularity and this was hardly going to help its cause. For many people at the Point Depot that night, it was their first taste of the sport. If they never wanted to experience it again they couldn't have been blamed. It was that bad.

The aftermath was challenging, but in tough times you must persevere. It was a difficult period, but I never once considered throwing in the towel. Soon we were all back in the gym preparing for the next batch of fights. If there's a perception that the growth of MMA in Ireland followed a constant upward curve, I can assure you that certainly wasn't the case. There were almost as many downs as ups, particularly early on, and that was one of several setbacks. However, if you're on the road to success, you cannot reach that destination without encountering some failures along the way. The people who matter, they don't care whether you've won or lost. You lose on a Saturday night and start afresh on Sunday morning. That's why I've never gotten carried away with celebrating when we win, just like I don't get too down in the dumps after defeats. Winning and losing are two sides of the same coin. Win or learn is the SBG mantra, not win or lose.

One of the many benefits of being a part of Straight Blast Gym has been meeting and getting to know other members of the SBG family worldwide, some of whom have become close friends. Karl Tanswell in Manchester, for example. Karl is an outstanding coach and a great man to have on your side. Travelling the world for the sport we love, we've shared some great experiences.

Ireland will always be my home but there's a big place in my heart for Iceland too. I first went there in 2005 following a request from Matt Thornton to travel over to do some seminars and coaching at a gym called Mjölnir in Reykjavik. Matt had been going there once a year, but in 2005 he asked me to stand in for him. More than anything I saw it as a holiday in an interesting part of the world; I certainly didn't think it would turn out to be the first of many trips to Iceland. It was also quite an honour that Matt felt he could place his trust in me to that extent.

Mjölnir was full of enthusiastic athletes, but two guys immediately stood out. One was Arni Isaksson, a pretty intense character who was always looking to test himself. His nickname, 'The Ice Viking', was appropriate. The other was a sixteen-year-old kid called Gunnar Nelson. I had been told about Gunni before I left Dublin. He had very high-level karate and, while grappling was still new to him, he was taking to it like a duck to water.

When I arrived, Gunni asked me for a private lesson, and his potential was very evident when we rolled. Still, just to remind him who the coach was, I held him down for a while and tickled him at the end of the lesson.

My first encounter with Arni wasn't quite as good natured. Wearing just a pair of Thai shorts and sweating from head to toe after a training session, he walked up to me with a crazed look in his eye and said, in his broken English: 'You do stand-up?'

I thought he was looking to fight me, so I just responded: 'Not with you, I don't.'

But what he was actually asking was if I coached stand-up fighting as well as ground fighting. After that initial hiccup, Arni and I really hit it off. Just twenty-one years old, he was a good kick-boxer who was eager to make an impact in MMA. When I returned to Dublin, Arni came with me to train at SBG.

The initial plan was for him to stay at my apartment in Ranelagh for a couple of weeks, before finding a place of his own. Three months later he was still living with me. Every day I scanned newspapers and websites, looking for a room for him to rent somewhere in Dublin. I'd send him off with the addresses, but every time he came back with bad news.

'Didn't get it.'

What's going on here? I wondered. Arni was a nice guy, and it seemed strange that nobody would rent him a room. The next time Arni went out to look at a place, I went along too. And then I realized why nobody wanted to rent to him.

When we arrived at the house, a young woman answered the door and Arni just barked: 'I want room!' He had a black eye – as he usually did – and wore his hood up. Slightly terrified by this angry foreigner with a busted-up eye who had arrived at her front door, the girl just said 'It's gone' and slammed the door.

Confused, Arni turned to me and said: 'This happen every time.'

Arni made his MMA debut in Dublin later in 2005, and it marked the beginning of a good professional career that would yield big wins against guys like Greg Loughran and Dennis Siver, as well as a Cage Warriors welterweight title shot.

Another of the promising youngsters in the gym at Harold's Cross was a very exciting seventeen-year-old named Tom Egan. Tom was really slick on his feet, he had a lot of charisma and was a superb athlete. As far as SBG's younger generation was concerned, he was the main man in the gym at the time. There was also my very first female fighter, Aisling Daly. When she first showed up at the gym I was apprehensive about a teenage girl training with a load of guys, and she seemed like a quiet, nerdy person who wouldn't be cut out for that environment. I had to give Aisling the same treatment as any of the lads, so I put her through hell in order to see if she had what it took to fight. Every time I did, she kept coming back for more.

As the gym continued to expand, we were welcoming a wide array of new members through the doors, from young kids to retired adults. With the summer of 2006 approaching, I was in a position to upgrade the home of SBG Ireland once again. After agreeing a lease on a really nice unit in Tallaght, I notified the landlord at the Harold's Cross facility that we'd be vacating the building.

However, three weeks before we were due to relocate, it all fell apart. The owner of the place in Tallaght called and said he'd had a change of heart, despite the fact that we had shaken hands on the deal months earlier. According to him, the planning permission to house a mixed martial arts gym in his building was too complicated, so he was backing out. By now it was too late to salvage the Harold's Cross lease, so I was left completely in limbo.

The four months we spent looking for a new premises were extremely tough. In the meantime I had to run classes on a part-time basis from a school hall in Crumlin. I was painfully aware that the longer the wait for a new gym rumbled on, the more detrimental it would be for the future of SBG Ireland. How could we be taken seriously as an international fight team if we were training only a few times a week on mats that were supposed to be for children to use during PE class?

Operating on a part-time basis took a toll on my income, and as a consequence I resumed working on the doors of bars and nightclubs several nights a week. A couple of years earlier, when the gym was growing and I was able to drift away from door work, I had told myself that if I ever ended up having to rely on that job again, it was probably a sign that it was time to give up on the dream of making a successful career in martial arts. I was starting to feel the pressure to get what my parents would call 'a real job'. At one stage I locked myself in the bathroom at home, curled up on the floor and just cried for a couple of hours. It all stemmed from the fear that I might have wasted years of my life going down a dead-end when I could have been taking advantage of my education.

Then, as the summer ended, we finally found a new home. It was in an industrial estate in Rathcoole, about fifteen kilometres from Dublin city centre. The location was by no means ideal: it required at least two bus journeys to get there from the centre of town. But it was a nice building for a gym, and we hadn't lost a single member during the fallow period. The dream was still alive.

5

One afternoon late in 2006, a scrawny eighteen-year-old lad with a shaved head walked into the gym in Rathcoole. He had been at school with Tom Egan. Tom introduced us.

'This is a friend of mine, Conor McGregor. He's been boxing for a few years but he'd like to train with us here as he's looking to take up MMA.'

I can't remember exactly what Conor said to me during our first exchange, but I do know that he referred to himself as a future UFC champion. It was immediately obvious that if it wasn't going to work out for this guy, it wouldn't be due to a lack of confidence.

Conor was very eager to make an impression in his first sparring session at SBG. As a result, he dropped Owen Roddy with a big body-shot. That wasn't the way we did things in sparring at SBG, but I decided to let it slide. I understood his enthusiasm as it was his first session and Owen was doing really well at the time, having already fought professionally on several occasions. Conor wanted to make a statement against one of our top fighters. I also knew that Owen would get his own back before long.

What happened next, though, was definitely unacceptable. I was sitting in my office when I heard someone outside say, 'That fella is after dropping Ais.' I knew straight away it was Conor, because Aisling Daly had stepped in with him after Owen. I came out of the office and saw Ais keeled over in the ring. She was in tears. Conor had hurt her with a body-shot.

Okay, I thought, *I let you away with that once, but you've got another thing coming if you think you can come in here and bully people.*

'Right, Conor, I'm next,' I said. After strapping on a pair of gloves and stepping into the ring, I took Conor down and beat him up until he received the message loud and clear: *These people are your teammates, not your opponents.*

When we finished, Conor looked at me and said: 'Yeah, I deserved that.'

He was a scrapper when he walked into the gym at first. An old-school scrapper, plain and simple. Crumlin Boxing Club, where Conor had been training, is a fight gym. When you walk in there, what you see in front of you is fights, fights and more fights. SBG, on the other hand, is about learning.

After I'd delivered my little message, Conor and I hit it off. He was back again the next day and he settled in quickly. He still sometimes let his competitive side get the better of him, but it was difficult to be angry with Conor because he was always funny and entertaining. At one stage we were doing a winner-stays-on wrestling drill, in which the person who's taken down first is eliminated and a new person comes in. But when Conor was taken down, he'd just keep on fighting.

'Conor,' I said, 'did you see when your back hit the mat? That was the end of the round.'

In every training session he was exceptionally intense and competitive. There were always a lot of questions afterwards, too. I'd be at home watching TV late in the evening and the text messages would come through: 'That escape you demonstrated tonight, can we go through that again tomorrow?' He had an obsessive mind when it came to learning. I don't think he ever switched off.

The following week we were going through the same wrestling drill again and Conor managed to slam me down. Before I could get back to my feet, he stood over me and said: 'Did you see when your back hit the mat? That was the end of the round.' It wasn't the first time he'd made me laugh and it certainly wouldn't be the last. It was the same with his teammates. His personality kept us all amused and he had a bit of charm about him too. His teammates knew he was cocky, but he never expressed that brashness at their expense. The other fighters in the gym afforded him respect and he repaid them in kind. Conor loved being part of the team.

From the start, looking at Conor, I found myself thinking: *That's a world champion*. Between his personality and his athleticism, it was evident that the raw materials were there. Fighters can sharpen their skills to an elite level with the right amount of investment in their training, but developing that golden touch necessary to rise above the crowd and become a champion? I've yet to see someone who has managed to do so: it's something you need to have inside you from the start. Conor had it.

It was clear that there was enormous potential there, and his striking was exceptional, but there were huge cracks in his ground-game that would need to be filled in. And that wouldn't be an overnight job.

Another concern was that he seemed to have a lot of distractions away from the gym. Dublin isn't a massive town, and I soon discovered that Conor was hanging around with the kind of people who were best avoided by anyone wanting to become a successful professional athlete. Conor would be in the gym for hours every day for weeks at a time – and then he'd suddenly be gone, and you wouldn't see him for a few weeks. He was especially good at disappearing when it was time to pay his membership fees.

But as soon as Conor was back in the gym, he gave you his undivided attention. He and Tom would often train together at home too. Tom helped Conor with his Brazilian jiu-jitsu and Conor passed on some of his boxing expertise in return. When Conor first came to SBG he was still boxing as well, and I had no issue with him doing both. However, I'm not sure if his boxing coaches felt the same way. Eventually, Conor made a choice between the two. His future was in MMA.

During our time in Rathcoole I was working with some very promising young fighters who were in the early stages of their development, so I look back on those days with fond memories. But it was also a period of significant personal achievement for me.

In 2007 I went to Turkey to compete in the World Grappling Championships, which were being staged under the jurisdiction of

FILA, the international governing body for wrestling. There was an abundance of elite competitors there from around the world, and when I looked at some of the names I began to worry that I'd be exposed in such prestigious company. But I guess I shouldn't have been concerned.

I made it all the way to the final, where I was beaten via footlock by Ricky Lundell, who has since coached top UFC fighters like Jon Jones and Frank Mir. Having reached the last hurdle, I was extremely disappointed not to have won, but it was a major milestone for me and one that I can appreciate even more with the benefit of hindsight. Standing on the podium to receive my silver medal, with the Irish tricolour ascending behind me and the national anthem being played, was a very proud moment. The vast majority of the flags being raised at the tournament were for the USA, so it was satisfying to see Ireland in amongst them.

It was also in Rathcoole where I reached the top of the Brazilian jiu-jitsu ladder. A BJJ black belt is extremely difficult to attain. I'm a lover of all martial arts, but if someone tells you they're a black belt in karate, it can mean two very different things. It could be an eight-year-old girl performing dance-type sequences, like I was doing when I started out. Or it can be Lyoto Machida, who's been using karate to brutally knock people out for years in MMA. The point is that if someone tells you they're a black belt in karate, it's impossible to know if they can actually fight or not until you see them in action. However, if someone has a black belt in BJJ, it's safe to assume that they're a pretty tough dude.

In order to become the first Irish person to achieve black-belt status in Brazilian jiu-jitsu, after so many years of training, I had to overcome one final massive hurdle. Matt Thornton came to the gym in Rathcoole to grade me in the last challenge. It is called an 'iron man' and it requires you to spar with every person in the gym to submission. There were seventy people in the gym that night.

It was a huge task and it took absolutely everything out of me, both physically and emotionally. When it finally came to an end and Matt wrapped the black belt around my waist, I was struggling to hold back the tears. I was completely overwhelmed. The first time I'd encountered BJJ was on my TV screen at home when I watched Royce Gracie at UFC 1. I had no idea what he was doing or how he did it, but I knew I wanted to learn. Just over ten years later, here I was being acknowledged as an elite practitioner of that very art. Being awarded a BJJ black belt had long been an objective of mine, but most of the time it seemed more like a pipe dream. Nobody in my country had ever reached that level, but I suppose I've never been deterred by things like that.

The funny thing about Brazilian jiu-jitsu is that reaching the top tier doesn't mean you've completed the journey. Far from it. BJJ is so complex that you can't perfect every single aspect of it. You never reach the finish line. So while there was great satisfaction in receiving my black belt, I soon reverted to the mindset I had always approached the game with: *Okay, there's still a lot to learn here so let's get back on the mats and resume that process.*

While that was a landmark moment for me, it was also significant for BJJ and MMA in Ireland as a whole. The country now had its first black belt and there were many others, such as Andy Ryan, making progress up the ladder. It was another indication that the Irish MMA scene was heading in the right direction.

By 2007, SBG Ireland was known as a team to be reckoned with. Owen Roddy, Aisling Daly and Tom Egan were all winning regularly. So too was Gunnar Nelson. Gunni first came to Dublin to train in 2006, a year after we had initially met in Iceland. The improvements he had made in that short period of time were remarkable. Gunni had a lot of support from his family, particularly his father Halli, and they were always willing to get behind his pursuit of success in MMA, whether that required travelling to Ireland, the US or anywhere else for training. While Gunni was in Dublin he stayed in my apartment. He was obsessive about improving. Sometimes there would be a knock on the door of my bedroom at 1 a.m. It would be Gunni with a question about technique that had been keeping him awake.

'Gunni, go to sleep. We can talk about this tomorrow,' I'd sleepily respond.

He fought five times in 2007, picking up four first-round wins after a draw in his debut. It was clear, even at the age of nineteen, that there were big things on the horizon for Gunni. One of his greatest assets was his relaxed mindset. Whether he was watching TV or about to walk out for a fight, Gunni always seemed as though he didn't have a care in the world. He managed to stay completely calm every time, which is quite rare. After a victory, there wouldn't be any wild celebrations. His only concern would be where to go to eat. Then he'd immediately turn his attention to the next fight.

Gunni's rate of progress was almost unprecedented. As well as MMA, he was having a lot of success in Brazilian jiu-jitsu tournaments. Just three years after meeting him I awarded him his brown belt. This was a very proud moment for me – we'd grown close when he stayed with me during his trips to Dublin, almost like brothers. And four years after beginning his BJJ journey, he was awarded a BJJ black belt. The only other person who could rival that achievement at the time was legendary former UFC champion BJ Penn.

Conor McGregor also joined the fight team as an amateur in 2007, before making his professional debut the following March. He cut through his first couple of opponents like a hot knife through butter because the quality of his striking was just so advanced at domestic level. After his first win, I did have to call Conor into my office the following Monday morning. He got a little bit carried away with the celebrations and fired his gumshield into the crowd. It hit a guy in the face and he wasn't too happy. I could understand Conor's elation, given that it was his very first fight, but I wanted him to know that he needed to keep himself under control. 'Don't ever celebrate like that again,' I said. 'That's not what this gym is about.'

For Conor's third professional fight, I decided to raise the bar. At Cage of Truth 3 on 28 June 2008, he'd face Artemij Sitenkov from Lithuania. This opponent was older and more experienced, and although he wouldn't be able to trouble Conor if the fight stayed standing, Sitenkov had an extensive background in the Russian martial art of Sambo, which has its roots in various forms of wrestling and involves lots of leg- and arm-locks. In other words, I knew the fight would be over for Conor if it went to the ground. But perhaps there was a side of me that felt this cocky boxer needed to be submitted in order to appreciate the importance of that aspect of the game. And maybe that side of me also felt that he needed to be taught a lesson, because Conor's mind still seemed to be focused more on partying than on training. When fighters turn up at my gym, they'll get everything they need from me. But I won't drag them to the gym. That's something each individual needs to be accountable for.

The plan for Conor in the fight was to land his strikes and back away, but Sitenkov wasted no time in shooting for a takedown, so that blueprint went straight out the window. Conor actually defended the takedown attempt well. Sitenkov opted to pull guard: dropping to his back, with his legs wrapped around Conor. Conor sought to posture up and land strikes, but then he made a costly error. In an attempt to pass guard – effectively, to breach Sitenkov's defences – he allowed Sitenkov to transition and lock on to his leg in search of a kneebar submission.

I just sat there thinking: *What on earth are you doing? You don't even know how to pass guard yet!* The excitement of having so many of his friends and family there among the few hundred spectators in the crowd had obviously got into Conor's head, and he pursued an ambitious move a little too enthusiastically in search of the finish. He didn't yet possess the grappling pedigree to carry it out. As Sitenkov aimed to extend his leg and execute the finish, Conor tried to fight him off with punches on the ground. But eventually Sitenkov got what he wanted and Conor tapped out.

That night was the first time I met Conor's parents. They'd turned up to see him fight and it was all over in sixty-nine seconds. Parents and other loved ones are often worried about fighters getting badly hurt, but that's never the primary concern for the fighters themselves. Their main issue is that they don't want to be embarrassed in front of people they know. That's what young men in the changing room have told me countless times: 'Whatever happens, I just don't want to look silly.'

To be in a bloody brawl and being smashed to pieces, there's probably a small part of them that enjoys that. But to be quickly knocked out or submitted is every young fighter's worst nightmare, and that's exactly what happened to Conor against Artemij Sitenkov.

That wasn't the only problem which arose from that fight. As the promoter of the Cage of Truth events, I used to give the local fighters tickets to sell on to friends and family. They'd pass the proceeds on to me, minus a commission. Conor had taken 25 tickets at €20 each, so we're talking €500 worth of tickets.

At the end of the night, when the other fighters on the show were handing in the money from their ticket sales, Conor said he didn't have his with him.

'Sorry, John. I forgot to bring it with me,' he said. 'I'll bring it into the gym next week.'

That wasn't unusual for Conor. He rarely paid fees at the gym, but I was always lenient with him, perhaps in the knowledge that it might ultimately pay off. But the truth was that he didn't have the money. As he sold the tickets in the build-up to the fight, he was spending the proceeds on the premise that he'd just replace it later on. In the end he'd spent it all and there wasn't a cent left.

That week went by and there was no sign of Conor. A week then became a month. Eventually, I gave up on calling him.

Another month or so had passed by the time I finally received a phone call from the McGregor household, but it wasn't Conor on the other end of the line. It was his mother. Although I had been briefly introduced to her at the Sitenkov fight, we had never really had a conversation. When she called and told me who she was, I thought to myself: *Oh yeah, that little shit who took my money and ran away. What could his mother possibly be calling me for?*

'I was wondering if you could come up and see Conor,' she said. 'He hasn't been training at all lately and he has lost his way a little bit. We're a bit worried about him.'

To be honest, I didn't really want to know at first. Why would I? Conor was in my debt. I owed him nothing. My gym was by no means thriving financially at that stage, so I wasn't exactly in a position to be nonchalant about €500.

'Sorry,' I said, 'what did you say your own name is again?'

'Margaret.'

Ah. That sort of hit me because my own mother's name is also Margaret. A small thing, but it resonated with me. It immediately helped me to see that this was just a concerned mother who was pleading with me to help her son. Fifteen years earlier, if I had been going through something difficult and my mother had asked somebody to get involved, would I have wanted that person to ignore her? It was clear from speaking to Margaret that something was wrong. She didn't sound good as she told me that Conor was going through a rough patch.

'I don't think anybody other than you can help him,' she said.

It didn't surprise me to learn that Conor had veered off course during those weeks he'd been away from the gym. In the short time that I had known him, I was well aware that he had a tendency to drift.

I agreed to call up to the family home in Lucan to have a chat with Conor. All the family were there: Conor's parents and his two sisters. They all looked worried, concerned for their son, their brother.

They told me a bit more: that he seemed to be in a state of depression and was refusing to leave his bedroom. He didn't want to train. He didn't want to do anything – other than tell people to fuck off and leave him alone.

Conor didn't know I was downstairs with his family. He wasn't expecting me at all. I went up and knocked on his bedroom door.

'Wha'?' a voice grumbled from inside.

When I opened the door, he looked like he had seen a ghost. He certainly didn't resemble the healthy young athlete I had gotten to know.

I sat down on the bed and we started talking. I told Conor that I knew he was mixing with people he shouldn't have been mixing with and getting up to things he shouldn't have been getting up to. I told him that it clearly wasn't doing him any good. I asked him to tell me if I was wasting my time. Should I leave the house and never come back again? Or, do you want to start off with a clean slate?

This was a Friday night, so I told him if he came to the gym on Monday we could forget about the tickets and start from scratch. But first, I needed to hear that acceptance of responsibility: *Yes, I've fucked up, but I'm willing to do whatever it takes to make it better.* If that hadn't been there, I would have walked straight out the door. I didn't want to do that. In spite of the incident with the tickets, I liked Conor and knew he had the ability to go places in MMA. His family had gone to great lengths to have me come over and speak to him. I was willing to give Conor a clean slate, but from Monday onwards it was never to get to this stage again.

'Whatever you need, I'll provide,' I said. 'But you don't take a step back or fall off this path. You've got to give me everything back, one hundred per cent.'

Conor took it all on board, looked me in the eye and said: 'You're right. Let's do it.'

He accepted that he was pursuing an ominous lifestyle, hanging around with the wrong people and heading down a dangerous road. Throwing his life away, basically. There were tears – from both of us – but we made a commitment to each other there and then. The following Monday, Conor returned to the gym.

If Conor hadn't come back, he was on such a slippery slope that it's difficult to guess what might have become of him. Fighting was his passion. Without that, where was he likely to go? I'm happy that Conor's mother picked up the phone and called me that evening. I'm also glad that her parents decided to name her Margaret! That personal connection was a factor in me getting involved, though I had a soft spot for Conor anyway. He was sort of like a little brother, even back then.

I get phone calls from concerned parents fairly regularly. I remember one kid's mother ringing me to say that her son was refusing to do his homework. She put the boy on the phone to me and I told him he wouldn't be allowed to train at the gym unless his homework was done. As I was speaking to him, I began to realize that I didn't recognize his voice. His name wasn't familiar either. When his mother took the phone again, I asked her if he was a member at Straight Blast Gym.

'No,' she said. 'But I knew he'd listen to you and that you'd put him straight.'

Fair enough.

Not so long ago, the punishment for kids was to ground them or take away their PlayStation. Now it seems they're being told that they can't go to SBG unless they behave themselves!

Conor still needed a bit of supervising after that. If he stayed out until 1 a.m., I was aware of it and I let him know. So he knew not to push his luck. But the bottom line was that he kept showing up to the gym. He stayed on track. I still wasn't convinced that he would react differently to another defeat, but only time would tell. Giving Conor a clean slate after the Sitenkov saga cost me a few hundred, but it would soon prove itself to be a very worthwhile investment.

6

Keeping an eye on Conor McGregor was by no means the only challenge I faced in 2008. After nearly two years in Rathcoole, we had settled in well at the new gym. In spite of its peripheral location, membership was steadily increasing, particularly among the younger age groups.

Then, quite suddenly, I was hit with an unexpected setback that would push me closer than I've ever been to throwing in the towel.

While going through the post in my office one morning, I came across a letter from the owner of the building. It was short and to the point. The businesses on either side of us in the industrial estate weren't happy about kids running in and out of the gym. They were concerned about a child being hit by a van or a forklift. In hindsight they were absolutely correct: an accident could very easily have happened. But at the time, focused on the implications for the gym, I didn't really see it that way.

I was given one week to vacate the premises. I stared at the letter in disbelief. Finding the place in Rathcoole had been an enormous chore, yet less than two years later we were back in the same position: looking for a new home.

I really wasn't sure if I had the mental energy to go through it all again. My dad helped me look for new premises, but the search was a bit half-hearted. Thankfully, we managed to convince the owner of the building to give us a few weeks' grace, so we were able to keep going while looking for a new premises, but I felt like I was only postponing the inevitable. It seemed as though I was approaching a crossroads in my life.

My parents, while still not fully on board with the whole MMA thing, had seen how much effort I had invested in it, and they were supportive during what was a difficult time, but ultimately they were still in favour of me putting my engineering degree to use. I was starting to come around to their way of thinking. I'd never expected MMA to make me rich, but I had believed it was possible to make ends meet while doing something I loved. Seven years after opening my first gym, it appeared that I was back at square one. Sure, we had come a long way, and there were now some very promising fighters in the team, but the reality of my situation was that I was a thirty-one-year-old with an engineering degree, but with no clear prospects and not a cent in my bank account. When I evaluated the pros and cons of continuing to pursue a career as an MMA coach, the cons heavily outweighed the pros. For the first time in my life, I opened the jobs section of the newspaper and assessed my options.

Fed up and lacking motivation, I was quite close to giving up altogether when I was tipped off about a potential premises on the Long Mile Road. I needed a lifeline and perhaps this was it. I had no idea if the place was even going to be suitable, but it was the first positive development in the three months since we had left Rathcoole, so I clung to the hope that something good might come of it. I went to take a look at it and brought my dad with me.

'This place is a dump,' he said. And that was before he had even spotted the tree that was growing down at the back of the building. A tree! Indoors! How is that even possible? Apparently the place was an old woollen mill that hadn't been occupied for many years. It was absolutely filthy. But it was an available space, and immediately my optimism returned. My dad couldn't see how it was going to work, and I sought to reassure him: 'It's not so bad. A bit of cleaning, a lick of paint and a lumberjack will sort this out.'

'For Jesus' sake, John! There's fungus growing out of the walls.'

One thing the place definitely did have going for it was that it was much closer to the city centre. But that would also come at a cost. I was already €25,000 in the red, having taken out a loan for Rathcoole. Relocating to Long Mile required an additional top-up of €15,000. For that, the bank needed someone to act as guarantor. My parents obviously had a little bit of faith in me because they stepped up to the plate when I needed them, putting their house at stake in the process.

With a €40,000 loan to pay off, I signed a lease to move Ireland's top MMA team into an old mill so damp that it had an indoor tree. It might not sound like anything to get excited about, but after a weekend clear-out I was ready to give one last push to get SBG Ireland back on track. Over the course of a couple of days, almost every one of our sixty members chipped in as we set about making the place look like a gym. No matter where the gym has moved to over the years, the people involved have all stayed with me, as well as helping to get each new version set up. I'm eternally grateful for their incredible loyalty.

My parents, sister and brother also made a massive contribution to the painting and cleaning. By the time we got someone to remove the tree, the place actually looked pretty good: like a gym where we could build success.

Quite soon after we set up camp on the Long Mile Road, a major opportunity presented itself. For the first time ever, the UFC announced that it would be hosting a show in the Republic of Ireland. Taking place in Dublin on 17 January 2009, the event would feature legends like Dan Henderson, Rich Franklin, Maurício Rua and Mark Coleman.

This was a massive development for MMA in Ireland. The UFC had been to Belfast eighteen months earlier, but that was viewed by most as another UK event. For the UFC to acknowledge its growing fan base in the rest of Ireland was significant. Since its first event back in 1993, the UFC had developed into the world's largest organization in mixed martial arts. It was where every fighter aspired to be. MMA was still very much a niche sport in Ireland, but the UFC had decided to come nevertheless. This was a huge opportunity for SBG Ireland.

I knew the UFC would be looking for a local fighter to compete on the card. In my mind, there wasn't a shadow of a doubt about Tom Egan being the right man for the job. At twenty years of age and having fought – and won – just four times, Tom was still quite inexperienced. He had only competed in small local shows so far, and the step up to the UFC would be enormous. It would be a big risk, but I was adamant that it was a risk worth taking. If the UFC were looking for a fighter to represent Irish MMA, nobody had a better chance of doing the job successfully than Tom.

When it was announced that UFC 93 would be taking place at the O₂ Arena, I managed to get contact details for Joe Silva, the UFC's matchmaker. For weeks I bombarded him with e-mails, explaining why Tom Egan was the fighter he needed to represent Ireland.

He eventually responded: 'You want to put a guy with just four fights in the UFC?'

'You're going to give a debut to an Irish fighter for this card,' I replied. 'Trust me, I've been around the Irish scene longer than any-body and I can assure you that Tom Egan is the best fighter in the country.'

Although his grappling was yet to mature fully, Tom was as well-rounded as any fighter in Ireland at the time, and his striking was particularly impressive. He was young, he was charismatic and he could hold himself well in front of a TV camera. I just thought it all made sense for the UFC.

Joe was in touch again a few days later to say that the UFC were offering Tom Egan a four-fight contract, starting with a bout at UFC 93. That was the good news. The bad news was that Tom's opponent was dynamite. John Hathaway was an unbeaten welter-weight from England, and although he too would be making his UFC debut, Hathaway was significantly more experienced, having bulldozed through the UK scene to accumulate a record of 10–0. More significantly, however, he was a monstrous grappler.

Tom and I had been hoping for a match-up with Dan Hardy, who had made his UFC debut just a few months earlier. Hardy, like Tom, was mostly a striker. Hathaway, on the other hand, would provide a really tricky test for Tom at such an early stage in his development as a mixed martial artist. Nevertheless, we embraced the challenge and prepared to put on a show. Tom was going in as the token Irish guy, but we were determined to prove that he deserved his shot.

Having the UFC in Dublin was an amazing experience. For the first time ever, MMA was making the news in Ireland. The organization gave it a huge promotional push and the tickets – just under 10,000 of them – sold out within a fortnight. As Tom was about to become the first fighter from the Republic of Ireland to compete in the famed UFC octagon, he had a fairly hectic schedule of media commitments in the build-up to the event. But none of that was a problem as far as we were concerned. This was what we had been striving towards, so we made sure to enjoy it all. Seeing Tom at press conferences and photoshoots with some of the biggest names in the sport was pretty surreal. There was a massive buzz around Dublin throughout the week, with the likes of UFC president Dana White being in town. This was our first taste of the big time. It was also a massive deal to have UFC TV crews turning up at our little gym on the Long Mile Road. That was fun, and it was also very welcome from a commercial point of view. Conor McGregor was having the time of his life, running around all week taking selfies with the UFC legends who were in Dublin.

When fight night finally arrived and we made that first walk to the octagon, the noise the Irish fans generated was absolutely deafening. I had actually helped Matt Thornton with cornering duties when Rory Singer fought for the UFC in Belfast in 2007, but this was one of my own fighters so it was a much bigger occasion for me. The UFC was the reason I fell in love with this sport in the first place. Just over twelve years earlier, I was in awe as I watched these guys battling it out inside that octagon for the first time. Now a fighter I had coached was about to become one of them. Thinking about that aspect of it was quite overwhelming, so I tried to put it to the back of my mind.

Standing cageside behind Tom as Bruce Buffer introduced him to the crowd – 'From DUB-LINNN, IRELAND . . .' – I had to resist the urge to pinch myself. For years I had been watching Bruce roar the names of fighters from the USA, Brazil and other parts of the world, but now it was the turn of an Irishman. An Irishman who was part of a team that had been based out of a tiny shed in Phibsboro just six years earlier.

As for the fight itself, there's no point in sugar coating it. Hathaway was able to secure a takedown, dominate in top position and force a stoppage due to strikes with twenty-four seconds remaining in the first round. Stylistically, it was one of the most difficult match-ups Tom could possibly have been given. With a little bit of good fortune, perhaps things could have been different. He just wasn't prepared for a guy of that kind of grappling calibre yet. There was absolutely no shame in losing to John Hathaway, who went on to do extremely well in the UFC and has since been unlucky to see his progress hampered by injuries.

In spite of the defeat, nobody was feeling despondent afterwards. We didn't get the win, but we learned a hell of a lot. Having experienced coaching one of my fighters in the UFC, I realized that, while we weren't quite at that level just yet, we were certainly within touching distance. Up until that point, the established fighters in the UFC seemed like they were up on a pedestal, looking down on small teams like us. What UFC 93 taught me was that it wouldn't be long before we caught up. We didn't need to rip up the blueprint and start again from scratch. I had been wondering if we needed to train in America in order to go to the next level, but now I believed that if we continued to do what we had been doing all along, we'd soon reach the top.

I had been giving the other teams far too much kudos. In the warm-up rooms throughout the week, rolling with some of the guys from the other camps and watching them on the pads, I realized that there was nothing extraordinary about them. Okay, we were a little bit behind, but that was purely because they had been doing it longer. There was absolutely nothing daunting about what they were doing.

I also felt that the family vibe we had among ourselves was something other teams didn't have. Our team was basically a bunch of crazy kids in their late teens and early twenties. They were all like siblings and that was something special. Some of our most promising fighters were guys who had joined the gym quite recently – the likes of Cathal Pendred, Chris Fields, Paddy Holohan and Artem Lobov. The SBG fight team was really beginning to blossom and many observers were telling me that I was dealing with a golden generation of young fighters. When we competed with other gyms, my fighters were mowing down their opponents. I suppose that made me realize that maybe we were doing things a little differently, and for the better. It was an 'iron sharpens iron' scenario in the gym, with everybody on the team pushing each other on. All my fighters were pulling in the same direction, and that kept the standards high. The way I saw it, we were in the lab all week preparing, and Saturday-night shows were where we ran the experiments. More often than not, the results were encouraging.

In the days after UFC 93 I kept telling myself: *Some day we're going to be major players in the UFC, and that day isn't very far away.*

Tom Egan's contract had been for four fights, but the UFC released him after that defeat. Was that a harsh call? You could argue it both ways, but I wasn't surprised. Four-fight deals are standard entry-level contracts for fighters joining the UFC, but that's for the benefit of the organization, not the fighter. They don't actually guarantee you four fights. If you turn out to be a superstar, the UFC have got you tied down; but if you don't perform, they can cut you loose without offering a second bite at the cherry. Unfortunately, Tom wouldn't get another chance, but he had blazed a trail for his teammates to follow.

UFC 93 merely added to my desire to achieve success. I was much stronger at the end of that week than I was at the beginning. Now that we knew how to get to the UFC, the next step was to ensure that the next person through the door had what was required to stay there.

7

I've had some success in many areas as a coach, but one thing I could never quite do in those years was to convince Conor McGregor to embrace the art of Brazilian jiu-jitsu. Conor had a laissez-faire attitude when it came to grappling. He really only trained in it when I forced him to. What's the point of grappling when you can just knock people out instead? That was Conor's outlook.

After the weaknesses in that area of his game were exposed in his defeat to Artemij Sitenkov, I hoped that he might be inspired to change his approach. But he remained defiant. Conor was adamant that he'd never find himself in that situation again. I tried my best to stress the importance of all aspects of mixed martial arts to him, but he was certain that all he needed to reach the top was the power and precision in his left hand. When he bounced back from the Sitenkov setback with a couple of first-round TKO wins, that belief was only further enhanced.

With his record standing at 4–1, Conor was offered a Cage Warriors fight on Saturday, 27 November 2010. It was to be a lightweight fight at Neptune Stadium in Cork against an undefeated guy named Joseph Duffy, who was coming off a stint on *The Ultimate Fighter*, the UFC's reality TV series. Duffy was accomplished in all areas of the game and more experienced than Conor too, having been competing in a wide range of martial arts from a young age, so we knew it would be a sizeable challenge. In a large cage for one of the top promotions in Europe and in front of proper TV cameras, this was Conor's biggest fight so far.

Duffy was supposed to fight Tom Egan in a welterweight bout not too long before Cage Warriors 39. It was on a small show in Donegal. As we do for every professional bout, we weighed in twenty-four hours before the fight. When Tom turned up on the afternoon of the fight, the promoter claimed there were same-day weigh-ins. He wanted Tom to lose a kilogram, but there was no way I was sending one of my fighters into a sauna to cut weight just a few hours before taking head shots in a fight. So that fight never happened; but having seen Duffy there that day, I knew he was a big guy and that he'd have a size advantage when he faced Conor. While Duffy was coming down from welterweight, Conor was moving up from featherweight.

Conor clipped him with a big shot after just twenty seconds, which opened up a significant cut above Duffy's eye. Duffy then managed to counter Conor's combination with a single-leg takedown. Sixteen seconds after Conor's back hit the mat, the fight was over. As had been the case against Sitenkov, Conor didn't have the grappling skills to handle himself when the fight was taken to the ground, and Duffy very comfortably secured a submission with an arm-triangle choke. The fight had lasted a total of thirty-eight seconds.

When we headed back up the road to Dublin after the fight and Conor and I went our separate ways, it was difficult to escape the feeling that I was probably never going to see him again. Given how he had reacted to his only other defeat, I expected him to go missing again – and this time I wasn't going to chase after him.

When I arrived at the gym on Monday morning to find Conor on the mats, I was massively surprised. Just thirty-six hours after being beaten, he was back in the gym and ready to right the wrongs. We had a chat and Conor admitted that although he was hugely disappointed with the result, he was by no means disconsolate.

'Fuck it, shit happens. I know where I went wrong and I know that you can show me how to fix it. Let's do it,' he insisted.

This time, Conor's only response was to get back up and persevere. From that day onwards, I never had to worry about Conor's commitment to grappling. Within a few months, he had begun to appreciate everything that's good about BJJ, wrestling and other forms of grappling. Then there was no stopping him. He couldn't get enough of it.

Joseph Duffy had succeeded where I had failed. He was

responsible for Conor's acceptance that grappling wasn't an optional part of MMA. I'll always be grateful to Joe for that. In my mind, that Monday was Conor McGregor's first day as a professional MMA fighter. Conor had been a member of the SBG team for four years at that stage, but that was the first time that I really knew he was in it for the long haul. It felt like a turning point. He still exuded the same remarkable levels of confidence, but at the same time he accepted that there was plenty of work to be done if he wanted to be the best. Recognizing where he needed to improve was a clear indication of how much he had matured since he first came to the gym. Better late than never.

Nowadays, if somebody comes to SBG from a striking background and says they don't like grappling, I have to pull them to one side and tell them that's not going to work. It's okay if grappling isn't your favourite part of mixed martial arts, but you can't simply ignore it. Otherwise the sport of MMA just isn't for you. You can't pick and choose the parts of the game that you want to focus on if you have aspirations to go far. I won't allow someone to say: 'I hate grappling.' I make them amend that to: 'Although grappling is not my favourite aspect of MMA right now, I'm excited about learning and improving it.' I believe we become what we continuously say we are, so the words we use are important.

Conor proved his commitment by taking a fight for the following February – eleven weeks after his defeat to Duffy. The bout was at featherweight, which meant he needed to keep his weight low over Christmas – not an easy task. Conor's decision was another strong sign that his attitude had completely changed as a result of what had happened in Cork. He worked on all areas of his game in preparation for the next fight, which was against Hugh Brady in Derry. Now he was finally ready to respect every facet of martial arts en route to achieving his goals. Having said that, again it was his hands that did the damage. After dropping Brady with a right uppercut, Conor followed up with ground-and-pound to get the stoppage after two minutes and thirty-one seconds of the first round.

Conor fought four times in as many months in the first half of 2011. All four fights ended in victories by KO or TKO, three of them in the first round. One of those contests lasted just sixteen seconds – a pretty drawn-out affair compared to the next one, which was a four-second knockout. Due to the fact that Conor was using his striking to clock up those wins, it might have appeared that he was still just a boxer who was a novice on the ground. But between the four walls at SBG on the Long Mile Road, he was working tirelessly every day on his grappling, which was improving rapidly.

That run of wins earned Conor a five-fight contract from Cage Warriors. After the disappointment of his first fight for the promotion, he had an opportunity to make amends in September 2011. We were off to Amman in Jordan for Cage Warriors Fight Night 2 to face Niklas Bäckström, an undefeated fighter from Sweden who had built up a big reputation. Aisling Daly and Cathal Pendred were also on the card.

Four days before fight night, we landed in Amman. When I stepped off the plane there was a message on my phone advising us of a change in circumstances. Bäckström was out. Apparently he had fallen and broke his arm while running to catch a train to the airport. Instead there was an option of a lightweight fight against a Norwegian guy, Aaron Jahnsen, who was willing to step in at late notice. 'No problem whatsoever,' was our response. It was a taste of what was to come for Conor, because he'd soon become accustomed to having his opponents withdraw from fights.

I've always told my fighters to never get too hung up on who they're fighting because you're never guaranteed anything until you're facing each other across the cage on fight night. Sometimes, after two or three changes of opponent, a frustrated fighter has come into my office to say they don't want to take the fight any more because there's been too much messing around. I could never understand that outlook. Your opponent will always be a human being who weighs about the same as you, with a head, two arms and two legs. I recall the build-up to one of my own fights when the promoter kept ringing me to let me know about one change of opponent after another. In the end I just asked him to stop calling me.

'I'll be there on the night,' I said. 'As long as there's an opponent in there with me, that's all I need to know.'

That's an attitude I've passed down to my fighters, because late pull-outs are a part of the game that you just have to get used to. Our philosophy is that there is no opponent because we can only control our own actions, so let's just get on with it. If an opponent is particularly adept in one area, of course you can ensure that you're ready for that. But spending time obsessing over it is likely to be detrimental to your own preparations.

The main benefit that Conor took from the late change of opponent was that he was already almost on weight by the time we arrived in Jordan. Having been preparing for a 145lb bout, he was now competing at 155lb instead. Things weren't so straightforward for his opponent, who had eighteen pounds to cut due to the late call-up. Conor got quite a kick out of the fact that he was relaxing in the sunshine on the morning of the weigh-ins, while Aaron Jahnsen ran laps of the pool while wearing a sauna suit in order to shed the weight.

'Look at your man,' Conor laughed. 'Will I ask him to run over there and get me a nice glass of iced water with a little umbrella in it?'

But we certainly weren't taking Jahnsen lightly. He was a big, intimidating, tough-as-nails Nordic guy who made Conor look quite small. And on fight night, he got the crowd on his side by holding a Jordanian flag aloft as he walked to the cage.

This was undoubtedly the biggest occasion of Conor's career so far. The fight was taking place in front of a couple of thousand people in a brand-new arena on the other side of the world, and it was being televised live back in Ireland on Setanta Sports. There was pressure on him to deliver too, given that his last Cage Warriors fight ended in defeat. But the pressure was no issue – it barely registered. As an ambitious young fighter, this was exactly the type of environment Conor wanted to be in.

Aaron Jahnsen's grappling was his greatest strength, but I had no concerns about Conor's ability to handle it. I had seen how hard he had worked since losing to Joseph Duffy and I knew how much he had changed. In the Duffy fight, he was leaping in with big shots and there was a sense of panic when he was taken down. He just wasn't comfortable. The fight with Jahnsen was in stark contrast. Conor was in no hurry. Relaxed and composed, he was enjoying being in there. Savouring the experience.

Jahnsen did everything you'd want from a guy fighting Conor McGregor. He threw some good right high-kicks, which are often dangerous for a southpaw boxer like Conor, but they made no impact. He also had a good clinch game and made some powerful takedown attempts, but all of that was nullified with ease. Jahnsen was a tough opponent with a significant size advantage, but Conor made it look straightforward with a first-round TKO.

That performance showed how much Conor had matured in the space of less than a year, and offered an early glimpse of the fighter he would gradually develop into. He was much more patient when firing off his strikes, whereas previously he had almost seemed to be in a hurry. The improvements in his grappling were also on display. He looked relaxed in successfully defending against a big takedown attempt after just thirty seconds. Conor stayed on his feet as Jahnsen drove him back against the cage. They clinched and Conor handled it comfortably, without any sense of panic which may have been there in a similar scenario before. He put into practice what he'd been doing in the gym so there was no need to be concerned. He knew what to do. His opponent was tough, but Conor made it look straightforward. After taking some big punches, Jahnsen covered up as Conor unloaded and the stoppage came after three minutes and twenty-nine seconds of the first round.

Conor was becoming a more refined MMA fighter, displaying a wide range of skills. He was no longer relying solely on that left hand. There was no magic potion or secret recipe. The giant strides he was making were down to hard work and nothing else. Conor was doing the right things in the right way in the gym, and he was being rewarded for it in the cage.

★

As an MMA coach, training your fighters to compete isn't your only duty. Far from it. There's a lot of responsibility on your shoulders in the role. One of your many jobs is to act as a babysitter, which I've had to do several times over the years. One of those occasions was in Jordan for Cage Warriors Fight Night 2.

Conor McGregor had never fought outside of Ireland before, and Cathal Pendred (who drew his fight against Danny Mitchell) had never competed further afield than Britain, so the whole experience was a big deal for them. After being flown halfway across the world to a plush hotel, the lads wanted to make sure they made the most of the hospitality. (Aisling Daly – who needed a mere twenty seconds to submit Angela Hayes – had already fought twice in the US, and was a bit less giddy about the whole thing.) As soon as the weigh-ins were out of the way, Conor and Cathal kept the restaurant staff on their toes with their room-service requests. They then spent the day after the fight sampling the contents of the cocktail menu by the pool.

By the time we went to check out of the hotel the following morning, the two lads had run up a fairly hefty bill for their extravagance. By now, still knowing nothing of this, I was waiting outside the hotel in a car, along with Aisling and Philip Mulpeter, another excellent SBG fighter who was there to lend a hand with cornering duties. When Conor and Cathal got into the car that would take us to the airport, they both looked quite sheepish and were surprisingly quiet. We must have been only a couple of minutes into our journey when the driver's phone rang. After a brief conversation with the caller in Arabic, the driver hung up the phone, stopped the car, turned to us and said: 'Hotel. Big bill. Food. Beer. Many beer. Money to pay. It's you?'

That's when Conor and Cathal explained themselves.

'We thought all the food and drink was on the house so me and Cathal were necking pina coladas like there was no tomorrow,' Conor said.

They realized they were mistaken when they went to hand back their room keys. The pair of them managed to slip away from the reception discreetly without settling the bill, but the hotel wasn't going to let them away with it that easily.

'Right,' I said. 'We're going back to the hotel and you can sort this out.'

The lads begged me to let it slide. They had spent so much that it was going to cost them almost everything they had earned from their fights, which was around €1,000 each. But that was their problem. I told the driver to turn the car around and return to the hotel. Conor and Cathal paid their bill and barely said a word to me as they sulked all the way home to Ireland.

8

As recently as 2012, the most talked about fighter in our gym was not Conor McGregor. It was Gunnar Nelson. In fact, there was no non-UFC fighter in all of Europe who was generating as much excitement as Gunni.

In February of that year he extended his unbeaten professional record to ten fights with another first-round submission – the sixth of his career. It seemed like only a matter of time before the UFC would be in touch, and the call came in July. They offered Gunni a contract, beginning with a welterweight bout against German fighter Pascal Krauss in Nottingham on 29 September.

It was Gunni's ability as a fighter that earned him the UFC call-up, yet people also seemed to be intrigued by his demeanour. Regardless of the situation, he's always calm. His emotions never appear to change. Whether he's teaching a kids' class or in a bloody battle in the octagon, Gunni's manner is always the same. He's one of the biggest celebrities in Iceland but fame means nothing to him. As a European fighter with a certain enigmatic quality about him, I think his personality reminded a lot of people of the legendary heavyweight Fedor Emelianenko when he first came to prominence. He was a breath of fresh air.

Gunni's progress was truly remarkable, particularly when it came to grappling. Having taken up Brazilian jiu-jitsu in 2005, he became a black belt just four years later. By the time he was signed for his UFC debut, the days of me taking Gunni down and tickling him had long since passed. If anything, the roles had been reversed.

When Gunni made the move to the UFC, there weren't many guys with the ability to simply execute a takedown, pass guard, mount and then submit. Gunni was doing that easily and often. In theory it's a straightforward concept and Gunni certainly made it look uncomplicated, but it was seldom seen from other fighters. It was almost like a throwback to the days of Royce Gracie.

Before he had even fought in the UFC, I was completely confident – as I still am now – that Gunni was eventually going to become a UFC champion. But some observers had their doubts about his ability to make a seamless step up in competition. The regional scene in Europe and the UFC are completely different levels, they said. Others were convinced that Gunni would be exposed in the welterweight division; that he's too small and should actually be a lightweight. That theory was further enhanced when there was some reshuffling with Gunni's opponent for his UFC debut after Pascal Krauss was forced to pull out. Then his replacement, Rich Attonito, withdrew too. Ten days before the fight, the experienced DaMarques Johnson – who had already fought nine times in the UFC – stepped in. Originally scheduled to be a 170lb fight, the late notice saw it amended to 175lb. However, Johnson ended up tipping the scales at 183lb on weigh-in day. Amid the calls for Gunni to compete at lightweight, we were now set for a UFC debut at middleweight. To those on the outside looking in, the odds were stacked against Gunni. But there was never any doubt in my mind that he was about to surprise everyone.

This was my first time back in the UFC since Tom Egan's defeat in Dublin three and a half years earlier, so you might assume that there was pressure and nervousness. However, I was totally relaxed throughout the build-up. This time I knew we were there on merit and not due to circumstances. Gunni had earned his place among the elite of MMA by virtue of his performances. This was where he belonged. The only thing I was actually nervous about was meeting Jeremy Horn, who was in DaMarques Johnson's corner. Having fought well over a hundred times, Jeremy is an MMA legend and also one of the very few guys who I'd ask for a photo.

When the time came for Gunni to enter the UFC's octagon, it was business as usual. He put on a beautiful performance, doing exactly to DaMarques Johnson what he had been doing to guys on the European circuit all along. He was able to get a takedown quite early in the fight, and after that it was only a matter of time. Gunni took Johnson's back, locked in a rear naked choke, and it was all over after three minutes thirty-four of the first round.

It seemed like an occasion to celebrate: Gunni's first UFC win, and mine too. Pop a few bottles of champagne at an after-party, perhaps? Instead, we celebrated Gunnar Nelson style.

'Should we get a steak and head back to the hotel?'

And that's exactly what we did, but not before I got my photo with Jeremy Horn.

Gunni's victory capped a very satisfying September for the team. Three weeks beforehand, Chris Fields had put in a brilliant display to win the Cage Warriors middleweight title against the Ukrainian fighter Pavel Kusch. At the time, winning a Cage Warriors title meant you were basically the European champion in your division, so it was a big deal. But that wasn't SBG's first Cage Warriors crown. In fact, that had arrived just a few months earlier.

After his impressive defeat of Aaron Jahnsen in Jordan, Conor McGregor's next outing was at Cage Warriors 45 in London on 18 February 2012. His opponent was an English fighter, Steve O'Keefe, who was a very capable grappler, so it was another opportunity for Conor to showcase his improvements in that area.

As we waited to be summoned from the changing room at the HMV Forum in Kentish Town, Conor was watching the fight before his own on one of the backstage TV monitors. The guy who won had done so via some vicious elbows to his opponent's head. Conor turned to me and said: 'That looked good. I'm going to do that in my fight. Watch.'

Conor defeated Steve O'Keefe in just ninety-three seconds. The manner of victory? Elbows to the head.

I'd eventually get used to Conor's ability to accurately predict the outcome of his fights. He got pretty good at it.

When he signed his five-fight contract with Cage Warriors in 2011, Conor set himself a target of winning the promotion's feather-weight belt, which had just been vacated by Danny Batten – the same Danny Batten who beat me ten years earlier. Following the win against O'Keefe, Conor was rewarded with a shot at the title. Cage Warriors announced their first ever show in Ireland – Cage Warriors 47 – which was to take place at The Helix arena on the Dublin City University campus on 2 June 2012. With my fighters in title contention in several Cage Warriors divisions, the event had a strong Straight Blast Gym influence. Half of the bouts on the main card featured SBG fighters – Cathal Pendred was paired with UFC and Pride veteran David Bielkheden, Aisling Daly was to face a pioneer of women's MMA in Rosi Sexton, while Englishman Dave Hill stood in the way of Conor's bid to clinch the vacant Cage Warriors featherweight title.

From early in the evening, there was definitely a sense that something special was brewing. The Helix isn't a massive arena – it can barely hold 1,000 people – but it sounded like half of Dublin had managed to squeeze in there. The noise was incredible when I made the first walk to the cage with Cathal Pendred. An enthralling back-and-forth battle ended with Cathal deservedly being awarded a victory which sent a message out to the welterweight division that he was a guy capable of going all the way to the top.

There was no time to reflect on Cathal's win because I was straight back out again for the next fight. Aisling Daly's bout against Rosi Sexton was a brilliant contest which could have gone either way, but Rosi managed to pip Ais narrowly on the scorecards. Nevertheless, Ais could still hold her head up high after a very encouraging display against an experienced opponent who has fought for the biggest promotions in the business.

Then came our opportunity to bring a Cage Warriors belt back to SBG Ireland for the first time. It was a big fight for Cage Warriors and they had promoted it accordingly. That gave Conor scope to show that he was as entertaining in interviews as he was in the octagon. Still, I didn't truly realize the extent to which Conor had captured the imagination of the MMA world until he began his walk to the cage that night at The Helix. The reception for Cathal and Aisling had been loud, but it went to another level when Conor appeared. People were going crazy. I was genuinely shocked by it. *This is something very different*, I thought. It's a cliché, but there was an electricity in the air as Conor entered the cage. Dave Hill is an excellent fighter; solid and well rounded. His grappling is his main strength. He was Conor's toughest opponent yet. But having seen how well Conor had trained, I was absolutely certain that he was going to be victorious. The atmosphere only strengthened that belief. It seemed that Dave Hill wasn't just fighting Conor; he was taking on the entire arena.

As the referee, Neil Hall, brought the fighters together for their pre-fight instructions, Conor was busy having his own conversation with Hill, letting him know in his own inimitable way that he wasn't going to enjoy the next few minutes, while chants of 'There's only one Conor McGregor' filled the arena. Inspired by seeing how well his teammates had performed earlier in the night, Conor was very pumped up and determined to put on a show.

What followed was another complete performance by him. It took Dave Hill only four seconds to shoot for his first takedown. The manner in which Conor responded was a perfect illustration of how his grappling had developed. Instead of simply looking to sprawl, he actually pursued a guillotine-choke finish. Realizing that the submission wasn't there, he played guard, then easily got back to his feet when Hill sought to pass the guard. From there, Conor dominated in both the striking and grappling exchanges and it soon became apparent that this fight was all about how long Dave Hill could hang in there. He was extremely durable and took a lot of punishment, but Conor was never in any danger. Conor was taken out of the first round for only the third time in his career, but it was just a matter of time before he sealed the win. It came with fifty seconds of the second round remaining: he took his opponent's back and secured a rear naked choke for his first ever submission win. Grappling dominance against a grappler who had never been submitted: not bad for a guy who was supposedly no more than a boxer with a good left hand. I'd consider myself to be primarily a BJJ guy, so I was a very proud and satisfied coach.

That night was when the Conor McGregor phenomenon was born. He celebrated by jumping out of the cage and running into the crowd, who absolutely mobbed him. In all my years of involvement in this sport, I had never seen people connect with a fighter like that. Conor's popularity among MMA fans had been building gradually, but this was more than just support. This was a movement – albeit on a small scale in the overall scheme of things, because MMA was still on the periphery of the Irish sporting landscape. People recognized that the confidence Conor had wasn't forced or manufactured. It was authentic and he backed up his pre-fight promises when the time came to perform. He also displayed an ability to use that confidence as a means of getting a head start on his opponents during the build-up. Mind games, mental warfare – call it whatever you want, but for Conor, the battle begins long before he stands across the cage from his opponent. I do my utmost to impart my own knowledge and experience to all my fighters, but that's one element of Conor's approach for which I can claim no credit whatsoever. That unique personality is all Conor McGregor. Back in the changing room after the win over Dave Hill, it dawned on me for the first time that Conor was not just going to be a successful fighter. He was going to be a superstar.

I met up with Conor's parents later that night. They were relieved as much as they were proud. Conor had been working as a plumber, but quit the job in order to train full-time as an MMA fighter. Cage Warriors might have been a top promotion in Europe, but it's still not a lucrative place for a fighter to ply his trade. Unless you're in the UFC, being an MMA fighter is generally a loss-making business. Still, that night was reassuring for Conor's parents. No Irish fighter had ever earned enough in MMA to make a career of it, but observing the adulation their son received, they finally started to believe that Conor was on course to be the one to buck the trend.

The morning after the night before, I looked back on that Cage Warriors event as SBG Ireland's best night yet. Cage Warriors was the number one European show at the time, so winning a title – not to mention Cathal's big victory and Aisling's excellent performance – was a validation of everything we were doing. A lot of people involved with the biggest gyms in the UK and on the continent, gyms I had always admired and looked up to, were mentioning on social media and in interviews about how they believed SBG Ireland was now the top team in Europe. That gave me an enormous feeling of pride. Whenever we attended events after that night, I could sense the increase in respect from the other teams towards us. Coaches I had a lot of time for were now approaching me, asking for advice and feedback. For me as a coach and for SBG as a team to receive that level of recognition from our peers who shared the same objectives really meant a lot to me.

In the aftermath of nights like that one at Cage Warriors 47, I always took a moment to remember the highs and lows of the journey – but mostly the lows, because without them my appetite would never have grown big enough to strive for the highs. I looked back at the tough nights of working on the doors, the struggles to find places to train after we left Harold's Cross and Rathcoole, the disagreements with my parents . . . and I smiled, knowing that it was all worth it. Sometimes I won, sometimes I lost, but every time I learned.

It was a really positive time in the gym. The belief in what we were doing was growing all the time because the guys' hard work was manifesting itself in the form of positive results.

My fighters had been cutting their teeth on the domestic stage in Ireland, winning fights and making progress. When they made the considerable step up to European level, the results stayed the same. For us, Cage Warriors was like a mini-UFC in Europe. It provided a perfect introduction for when the time eventually came to move on to the big show. The way the events were run, from the medical exams down to the media schedules, was a small-scale replica of how things were done at the UFC. Sometimes you see new teams coming into the UFC and they're completely overwhelmed by the size of it all. But that transition would prove to be pretty seamless for us.

After Conor's victory against Dave Hill, there was a lot of speculation over his next move. Many believed that a contract offer from the UFC was imminent, but there had been no contact from them, so we focused on a defence of Conor's Cage Warriors title. A bout against American challenger Jim Alers was fixed for 1 September 2012. Alers came from a grappling background so – yet again – it was claimed that he was an opponent who could cause problems for Conor in that area. But I didn't see Alers as a step up in competition. In fact, in terms of skill, I didn't rate him as highly as Dave Hill. Alers had a record of 8–1, but it wasn't as impressive as those numbers suggested. Outside of the UFC, it's much easier to build up a good record on the US circuit than it is in Europe. Many of the professional fighters over there are the equivalent of good amateur fighters in Ireland and the UK. Getting your first few wins as a professional in the US isn't very difficult at all. In my view, one of the reasons a fight with Alers got people talking had nothing to do with the strengths and styles of the fighters. It was that until then, Conor had been fighting white Europeans. Alers was a black American, and perhaps for Irish MMA fans there was almost something exotic about the match-up.

Unfortunately, Conor and Jim Alers never got the chance to lock horns. Two weeks out from the fight, Conor was hurt in a sparring session. He and Artem Lobov often used to train together behind closed doors. When the gym was empty one Sunday evening, they locked themselves in, strapped on their gloves and went toe-to-toe. Their sparring sessions weren't for the faint-hearted. Conor and Artem are the best of friends but neither of them took a step back when it was time to trade blows. I wasn't a fan of that method of training and I had told them so on many occasions. Whenever I did, they'd look at me blankly.

'This is how you train, coach,' they'd say. 'You have to train the same way you fight.'

Despite my attempts to moderate their private sparring sessions, the guys continued to do things their own way. I knew it would take something drastic to alter their outlook – and that's what happened just a fortnight out from Conor's scheduled fight with Jim Alers. As they went through round after round of heavy sparring, Artem cracked Conor with a shot on his upper jaw. They finished out the session but Conor knew something wasn't right. He was in pain and there was even a dent visible in his cheekbone, just in front of his ear. After having it examined at the hospital the next day, Conor discovered that he had fractured his zygomatic arch, and to repair it would require surgery which would keep him out of action for at least six weeks. He still wanted to fight, but that was never an option. It was the first – and, as of the time of writing, the only – time that Conor has been forced to withdraw from a bout.

Having to do so was a massive blow, but something good came from the setback: the incident convinced Conor and Artem that trying to take each other's heads off in training wasn't the wisest course of action. In any combat sports gym, there are going to be elevated levels of sparring every once in a while. You're talking mostly about alpha males in their twenties and thirties, so sometimes things get a bit out of control.

I'm strongly opposed to teammates competing against each other in training, whereas I know in some gyms that it's almost encouraged. In a lot of those gyms it's about whittling down the numbers, so that they're left with five or six guys who are able to beat up everybody else.

Take the 'Doghouse' sparring sessions they do at Floyd Mayweather's gym, for example. That involves two guys in a full-on fight in the gym until one of them quits. I've watched some footage of that and it almost made me sick. It's irresponsible and moronic. The environment Mayweather has created is undoubtedly going to produce one or two amazing guys, because you obviously need an incredible amount of physical and mental toughness to get through something like that. However, the number of people who are risking significant head trauma from that kind of a set-up would keep me awake at night. The TV cameras should follow those guys to find out about their stories, because I can guarantee that they don't have happy endings. I want every experience at my gym to be positive. That's not going to happen if you're knocked out by a teammate at the end of a continuous thirty-minute round.

There have been many occasions over the years when I've sat down with fighters in my office and said: 'You've got to start taking it easy. You prepare for fights in this gym. You don't win them here. The gym is a place for improvement.'

At first they're confused. Their philosophy is the harder you spar, the more prepared you are when the time comes to fight. In reality, though, if a fighter is holding nothing back in sparring for six to eight weeks, the likelihood is that they won't even make it as far as the fight. Communicating that message to them is important to me, because it's a mistake I made many times myself.

During my fighting career, there wasn't really a distinction between a sparring session and a fight. You approached both in the very same manner. You gave it all you had and that's how things were done in every gym. For a long time, that's also how I ran things as a coach. But I'm an evidence-based guy and the evidence told me that even when fighters managed to make it through a full training camp while sparring like that, their bodies had been beaten up before the time came to compete for real, so they weren't operating at their best. If they weren't injured, they were completely worn out.

It seemed to me that there had to be a better way of doing things. I bounced some ideas off Matt Thornton, the founder of Straight Blast Gym in the US, and decided to introduce the very simple concept of lowering the contact but keeping the training as realistic as possible. You want to recreate a fight scenario as closely as you can, but you do so without the same level of impact. Throw your big shots but pull them before they connect.

We call this 'flow sparring'. It requires experience and intelligence on the part of both athletes involved. If you're standing over someone who's on their back and you're throwing these big shots, the other person can't simply ignore the strikes just because they're not really being hit. They might be tempted to work for a leg-lock while you're throwing your shots, but they have to respect the fact that you're in control and those shots wouldn't allow them to set up that leg-lock in a fight situation. Otherwise you'll end up with the guy who's in control being unfairly submitted because their sparring partner refuses to acknowledge the strikes. You'll have two guys claiming 'I got you first!' and it complicates the entire process. Next time, the guy might actually decide to land his shots properly.

For sparring sessions, I like to replicate every aspect of a fight without the damage. Therefore, if fighters can master the concept of flow sparring, they don't need to wear any additional protection. They can spar using four-ounce gloves, which they'll be wearing in a fight. I even encourage them to wear the same shorts. Every detail is important.

I can recall wearing a T-shirt during every training session while I prepared for one of my very first fights. When it was time to fight and I suddenly had no T-shirt on, it actually threw me off. It didn't feel familiar because that's not how I had prepared. So if my fighters are sparring without tops on and they're complaining that it's too slippy and awkward, I just remind them that it's exactly how it'll be on fight night. Add in a little blood and it becomes even trickier. Karl Tanswell at SBG in Manchester sometimes even uses theatrical blood in sparring sessions to get his guys used to that. If there's blood flowing during a fight, they're already accustomed to it. It's about creating an environment in the gym that resembles a fight in every respect, with the exception of force and power.

It took me a couple of years to introduce this way of thinking as the norm in the gym, but it's now widely accepted as the most productive method of training. Ironically, Conor and Artem have probably become its two biggest advocates. We refer to it as 'updating the software without damaging the hardware'. My fighters can still train hard but there's no need to take unnecessary damage while they do so.

We saw significant results from this change in approach very quickly. In the last few years, I can't imagine that any other team can rival our track record for the lowest number of pull-outs from fights at all levels, from the UFC down to the domestic circuit. I'm not suggesting that we're the only team who train this way, but it's not something I see in a lot of other gyms.

Conor McGregor's fight against Jim Alers was rescheduled to take place at Cage Warriors 51, at The Helix on New Year's Eve. For a change of scenery and to freshen things up, we decided to move our training camp to Iceland. However, with about five weeks to go, the fight fell through again. This time it was Alers who had pulled out. Conscious of the fact that it had now been six months since Conor last competed, I spoke to the organization to see if an alternative bout could be arranged. I was aware that Cage Warriors were trying to put a lightweight title fight on the same card. The belt was vacant and a Slovakian fighter, Ivan Buchinger, had been handed a shot. But his original opponent had backed out. With both Conor and Buchinger in need of opponents, I suggested a match-up between the pair of them for the lightweight title. The proposal was given the green light and Conor was pleased. Now, fighting at 155lb instead of 145lb, he could enjoy a much bigger Christmas dinner the week before the fight. It was also a chance for him to become the first fighter to be the champion of two unified weight classes in Cage Warriors simultaneously.

I've always been confident before Conor's fights, but I was particularly so in this case. For the first time, I felt he wasn't going to be facing a guy whose sole intention was to take him down. Having looked at Buchinger's previous fights, I expected this to be a kick-boxing match. Without having to be too concerned about the threat of a takedown, that would give Conor the freedom to truly express just how spectacularly diverse his striking skills are. In his other fights, Conor's opponents always tried to grapple with him, so things often became scrappy. But this was a fight I was certain would stay on the feet and, from a spectator's perspective, that excited me.

It was another memorable night at The Helix, just as it had been the previous June for Cage Warriors 47, as we rang in 2013 by adding another Cage Warriors title to the SBG mantelpiece. Conor put on an exhibition of striking, an absolute masterclass, as he knocked out Buchinger with a stunning slip-counter-left-hook after three minutes forty of the first round.

As Conor walked back to the changing room after the fight with a Cage Warriors belt draped over each of his shoulders, I felt certain that the next time he entered the cage it would be for his UFC debut.

9

I was in Iceland helping Gunnar Nelson to prepare for his second UFC bout when I received a couple of interesting phone calls.

It was 3 February 2013. Gunni was scheduled to face Jorge Santiago in London a fortnight later, so we were in the final stages of his training camp.

The first call that morning was from the gym back in Dublin, informing me that Conor McGregor hadn't shown up to coach his striking class the night before. That didn't come as a huge surprise to me.

On the surface, everything was going great for Conor. He held two Cage Warriors belts. The video of his KO of Buchinger had gone viral and everybody seemed to want a piece of him. Some of the biggest names in the sport, including UFC commentator Joe Rogan, had reached out to Conor via social media on New Year's Day to let him know how impressed they were.

'I just caught your fight, Conor,' Rogan tweeted. 'Congratulations, you looked sensational! Hope to see you in the UFC someday. Best of luck!'

We were inundated with interview requests from MMA media. Even the mainstream press in Ireland, which hadn't yet really embraced MMA, were finally beginning to show some interest in the guy from Dublin who was being hailed as a potential UFC star of the future.

Conor was eager for his chance to prove himself in the UFC. It was the only place where his career as a full-time fighter could be financially viable. His teammate Gunni Nelson was preparing for another outing on the biggest stage in the world, having earned $16,000 for his UFC debut a few months earlier – over six times what Conor had been paid for his last fight. All the while, Conor was broke, and relying on Dee, his girlfriend, to get him from A to

B in her old Peugeot, which needed to be push-started. As the weeks passed by without a call from the UFC, Conor was losing hope. Dismayed and disillusioned, he started to wonder if there was any point in going on. It didn't help that his coach was in Iceland. Conor was beginning to drift.

The second call I received that day put paid to any thoughts Conor might be having of throwing in the towel. I was eating dinner at a restaurant in Reykjavik when my phone rang. It was Halli Nelson, Gunni's father. While I was helping his son prepare for his next UFC fight, Halli was helping me with management duties related to Conor. Double-jobbing as Conor's coach and manager was becoming increasingly difficult, now that Conor was in such demand.

'I've been speaking to Sean Shelby about Conor,' Halli said.

I liked the sound of that. Sean Shelby was the UFC matchmaker. 'They're offering him a place on their card in Sweden on 6 April. It's for $8,000 plus an additional $8,000 to win. Are you happy to accept that?'

'Hang on, Halli,' I said. 'Are you telling me the UFC are offering Conor a fight?'

'Yes. So, are you interested?'

'Of course we're interested! It's the UFC. We're in, no doubt about it. It doesn't matter how much money they're offering.'

I was so keen to tell Conor the news that I hung up on Halli without asking for any other details, such as who the opponent was going to be. I dashed out of the restaurant, into the snow, and dialled Conor's number.

No answer. I tried again. And again. And again. It then dawned on me that Conor was probably avoiding me. He would have been expecting a bollocking for not showing up to coach his class. But I kept calling and finally Conor answered.

'Look, John, I'm sorry I didn't take the class last night but –'

'Conor, just shut up and listen! How would you like to fight for the UFC in April?'

'Are you serious? Fucking hell, let's do it!'

★

The timing of Conor's UFC call-up couldn't have been any better. If he had drifted any longer, he might have ended up passing the point of no return. Instead, Conor immediately began the preparations for his UFC debut.

SBG Ireland received a couple of significant boosts during his training camp. Gunni Nelson picked up another UFC win before Cathal Pendred dethroned Gael Grimaud to become the Cage Warriors welterweight champion. In the space of nine months, SBG had won all four Cage Warriors titles from featherweight to middleweight.

It was only when news of Conor's UFC contract broke in the media that I learned his opponent would be Marcus Brimage. He was an American guy who had already gone 3–0 in the UFC, so on paper it was a tough task for Conor. But fights aren't contested on paper. I didn't know anything about Brimage and I didn't look into him in any great detail either. What I did know was that when Conor faced him in the octagon, the world was going to be blown away. With his range of skills, Conor was going to bring something completely different to the table. Even though Conor hadn't yet made his UFC debut, I already felt that there was nobody there capable of troubling him outside of the top five guys. And since this guy was still on the preliminary card in his fourth UFC fight, I had no concerns about him at all. In my view, most of the guys on UFC prelims were a level below the likes of Ivan Buchinger and Dave Hill anyway, so this wasn't a step up for Conor, despite how it was being billed by fans and the media. All I had ever wanted was for him to get one shot on this stage to show the world what he was capable of. Now that the opportunity had finally arrived, there was almost a sense of relief. We felt we had already completed the toughest part of the journey – getting to the UFC.

Following Conor's Cage Warriors exploits, both in the cage and in interviews, there was a lot of excitement among the MMA community as the fight approached. It peaked during an interview with well-known reporter Ariel Helwani live on his show, *The MMA Hour*. Conor had never been exposed to such a large audience, particularly in North America, so it was going to be intriguing to see how it all unfolded. His charisma and sense of humour had already made him popular with fans in Ireland and the UK, but would that also translate across the Atlantic?

I watched the interview and what I saw was Conor just being Conor – no act, no gimmick, what you see is what you get – so I wasn't anticipating the incredible reaction that followed. The internet exploded. I really didn't expect people to be so captivated by him. They thought he was hilarious and were intrigued by his confidence. I already knew he had the ability to fight his way to the top, but as I observed how people were so taken by his personality, I thought: *This isn't going to do any harm at all.* From there, the media couldn't get enough of him.

Conor was also keen to point out that this wasn't just about him: 'When I get to the UFC, I'm going to kick the door down for my teammates to follow. We're going to take over.'

Conor may have been the one garnering all the attention, but helping his friends in the gym to realize their dreams was just as important to him as his own success.

Conor's UFC debut was set to take place on Saturday, 6 April 2013, at the 16,000-capacity Ericsson Globe Arena in Stockholm. Conor and I left Dublin on the Tuesday morning before the fight. His clash with Marcus Brimage was buried deep down in the prelims of the thirteen-bout fight card, but it was being billed as 'The People's Main Event'. I met Conor at his family home in Lucan, where I had organized a little surprise for him. We had spent most of his training camp in Iceland – a place where Conor and other SBG fighters could prepare away from the distractions of family and friends – and in the evenings we watched episodes of the Irish crime drama series *Love/Hate*. Before we headed for the airport that morning, I managed to arrange for Peter Coonan, who plays the role of Franno in the show, to pay Conor a visit. Peter came in to wish Conor all the best. Conor obviously wasn't expecting it, and it gave him a nice little boost before we left.

We were actually cutting it tight if we wanted to make the flight – Conor was running behind schedule, as usual – so we quickly hopped into Dee's Peugeot and she eventually managed to get it started. As we were pulling away from the house, Conor asked Dee to stop at the post office in Lucan.

'I need to go in and collect my dole,' he said. Conor was getting €188 per week in unemployment benefit.

'Conor, I can loan you the money,' I said. 'We haven't got time.'

But Conor insisted on stopping. For weeks leading up to the fight, he had been all over Irish TV, radio, websites and newspapers, as they reported on the much-hyped young Dubliner who was aiming to become the first Irishman to win in the UFC. Yet here he was, queuing up in his local post office en route to his UFC debut, waiting to collect the €188 that he couldn't afford to be without. While I was panicking in the car, certain that we were going to miss the flight, the other people in the queue were asking Conor for photos and autographs. Thankfully, we just made it to the airport on time.

When we arrived in Stockholm I was surprised to bump into a familiar face. Back in 2003, just after Matt Thornton welcomed me into the Straight Blast Gym family, I had to travel to Oregon in order to attain my SBG instructor's certificate. Part of that process involved a fight in the gym, in which my opponent was a guy called Chris Connelly. We had a good scrap but I never saw Chris again . . . until I was passing through the lobby of the hotel in Stockholm. I knew Chris had previously coached Marcus Brimage in Alabama, but Brimage had since moved to American Top Team in Florida, so it never occurred to me that Chris might be in his corner for the fight. It was good to see him after such a long time. Given that we were about to be on opposite sides once again, we had a quick chat and agreed to put friendship aside until after the fight, when we'd have a proper catch-up over a beer. We left it at that, but there were still some awkward moments around the hotel as the week went on. That's the nature of MMA: while the sport has grown significantly in recent years, it's still quite a small community. I've become well accustomed to ensuring that competitive rivalries don't get in the way of friendships.

When I woke up on Wednesday morning, Conor told me he was in a lot of pain from a wisdom tooth. It had kept him awake for most of the night. The combination of that and the tough weight-cut down to 145lb meant that he wasn't exactly feeling on top of the world. All the while, he was putting on a brave face as he dealt with his various media commitments. By late afternoon the pain in his tooth was really bothering him, and I was concerned that it was only going to deteriorate further if we ignored it. An injury is something a fighter can often push on through, but a toothache is the sort of pain that can drive you crazy. We went off in search of a dentist.

The guy we found assured us that it was nothing to worry about. There was a bit of an infection in the tooth, so he'd remove it. Conor would be back to normal in seven days.

Seven days? With Conor's fight now just seventy-two hours away, that wasn't going to work for us. We explained the situation to the dentist, who suggested cleaning the tooth in order to reduce the infection. It wasn't going to be a long-term solution, but it managed to provide enough relief for Conor to get through the next few days.

It's at the weigh-ins when Conor really begins to go into animal mode. In Conor's mind, at this stage, he's about to compete against somebody for his next meal. Add in the fact that he's already feeling abrasive from the weight-cut and it usually makes for a tense stare-down. More often than not, someone needs to step in to prevent things from boiling over. Overseeing his first weigh-ins since joining the organization, UFC executive Garry Cook was thrown in at the deep end with this one. Conor towered above Brimage and they butted heads before being separated. The crowd loved it. Backstage afterwards, Brimage and Chris Connelly smiled in our direction as they remarked that the incident would serve to 'hype the fight up'. But Conor wasn't playing games.

'Get the fuck away from me,' he said. 'I'm going to destroy you.'

Reinforcements arrived from SBG for fight night, as Owen

Roddy and Artem Lobov flew over from Dublin to join me in Conor's corner. With the exception of some of Conor's family and friends, I wasn't expecting there to be many Irish supporters in the crowd. But when we walked out, Conor was greeted by a massive roar. I looked around the arena and there was green everywhere. To see that so many people had gone to such effort and expense to be there for Conor's UFC debut was quite overwhelming.

Although there had been a significant increase in mainstream media coverage of Conor in Ireland, we hadn't attracted any sponsors for the fight. Most fighters in the UFC walk out for their fights with sponsored hats, T-shirts and shorts, as well as a banner displaying all the brands they're endorsing. Conor made that first walk with just his own shorts and the Irish tricolour. But struggling to find sponsorship would very soon be a thing of the past.

Marcus Brimage was game for the battle and came forward without fear. But as the occupants of the UFC's featherweight division were about to discover, trading punches with Conor McGregor is a strategy that will never end well. Just over a minute after the contest began, Conor was celebrating his first win in the UFC while Brimage was on the canvas, wondering what had just happened.

In his post-fight interview in the octagon with UFC commentator Kenny Florian, Conor had the audience eating out of his hand. Given the manner in which he put Brimage away, I was confident that Conor would be in with a good shout of being awarded the 'Knockout of the Night' bonus worth $60,000 – a significant financial boost considering that his pay for the fight was $16,000. As the interview was drawing to a close, I mouthed to Conor: 'Ask for the money.' UFC president Dana White was in attendance, and I thought he might be persuaded by a cheeky young Irish newcomer asking for the bonus. Conor grabbed the microphone and shouted: 'Dana: 60 Gs, baby!'

Conor had put on a beautiful display of striking and evasive footwork. People hadn't seen striking like it before. Most guys in the UFC come from a grappling background and then they add the striking to that, so it's very basic and rough around the edges. But with his wide variety of crisp shots, his angles and his movement, Conor was already light years ahead. I knew he only needed one chance to show that, and he had grabbed it with both hands.

When we got back to the changing room after the fight I looked at my phone and was blown away by the reaction to the result. A small number of people were already talking about Conor as a potential opponent for UFC featherweight champion José Aldo. The majority of fans laughed at that thought. It was far too soon to be even mentioning Conor in the same sentence as Aldo, they said. But nobody on the SBG team was laughing. Conor was heading for the summit, and if Aldo was the man occupying top spot, then that's who we were aiming for.

Conor was brought straight into a private room at the arena to meet Dana White, who asked him for a photo. Dana couldn't contain his excitement at having a new star in the UFC. He recognized that Conor was something special. Irish fans had been tormenting Dana for a long time on social media about bringing Conor to the UFC. Now he understood why.

'Welcome to the UFC!' Dana laughed. 'There's been a lot of hype. I guess the hype is real . . . People are going crazy on Twitter, man. People are going fucking crazy. Ireland's going nuts! We're pumped!'

In the post-event press conference, Dana couldn't praise Conor highly enough: 'I'm blown away. First of all, it's his first fight ever in the UFC. He walked out tonight and got into the octagon like it was his hundredth fight in the UFC. From the minute the bell started, he was nice and relaxed . . . and even after he gets the knockout, it's like he's been here before and done it a hundred times. The kid is totally relaxed. He's a beast. I'm impressed.'

Conor's win really felt like the conclusion of an emotional roller-coaster ride. Five years earlier I'd been sitting beside him on his bed in his parents' house as he was in tears due to his life's apparent lack of direction. Yet here he was now, the talk of the UFC, with the president of the organization falling at his feet. It was hard to take it all in, so I had to escape and find a quiet room where I could have a few minutes to myself. I lay down on the floor and let the wave of emotion sweep over me. I just needed a chance to allow it all to sink in. Taking that little bit of time to myself has become a ritual that I follow after every big fight.

'To be honest, I don't know what's going on here,' Conor said later. 'I'm just after hearing sixty thousand dollars and I'm thinking of what I'm going to spend it on. I'm going to buy myself a car, anyway, and maybe some nice custom-made suits.'

On the way to the fight in Sweden, Conor had collected the dole. On the flight home, there was a cheque for $76,000 in his pocket. I sat back, closed my eyes and smiled. Now that the public had been introduced to Conor McGregor, things were never going to be the same again.

10

I suppose it's quite ironic that while it was the quietness of karate classes that first drew me into martial arts, much of my involvement nowadays is focused on the showbiz environment of the Ultimate Fighting Championship. Large arenas, raucous crowds, loud music, flashing lights – a UFC event is the exact opposite of that calm, soothing dojo setting that I first experienced as a four-year-old. In spite of that, I've never found it difficult to focus on the task at hand. Sure, when I'm walking out for a fight behind Conor McGregor and the fans go crazy, we're enveloped by a massive cacophony of noise. It's like being punched in the gut at first. But when I'm cageside and it's time for work, I can honestly say I've never been aware of the presence of a crowd – whether it's thousands of people at a big arena in the US or a couple of hundred at a Dublin GAA hall. All I see and hear is what's happening in the cage. Despite the noise from the fans, I've somehow always been able to project my voice without having to shout. My fighters have often told me that no matter how big the crowd is, they can hear me above everything else. It almost seems intimate. It's me, my fighter and the problem in front of us. It's as if we're simply having a discussion about how to solve it.

Coaching fighters on small local shows for so many years certainly allowed me to get the hang of that routine by the time we were ready for the UFC. When the cage door closes, it's the same proposition every time: my fighter against an opposing fighter. Everything else – venue, attendance, atmosphere, consequences of the result – is irrelevant. That's something we often speak about at SBG Ireland. Whether that cage is in the gym on a quiet weekday or a massive arena in Boston or Las Vegas on a Saturday night, what difference does it make? It can have an emotional or mental impact, but only as much as you allow it to. As long as you want it to be, the fight takes place in the same environment you've been training in for the previous six to eight weeks. I understand entirely why many people might read that and think it's not that straightforward, and for 99 per cent of people it's probably not. But the fighters who learn how to approach a fight in the same manner as a Tuesday-afternoon sparring session are the ones who are the most successful.

My first real experience of such a frenzied crowd was for Conor McGregor's second UFC fight. Between his final Cage Warriors bout and his UFC debut, Conor's following in Ireland had increased drastically. But that was nothing compared to how quickly things took off after the win against Marcus Brimage. He was described as an overnight sensation, which wasn't quite correct because the recognition was a result of years and years of hard work. But from then on it was difficult for him to walk down the street in Dublin without being mobbed for photos and autographs. Every TV show, radio station, newspaper and website wanted an interview. Conor was regularly appearing on the back pages of the papers, and even on the *Late Late Show*. These were all unprecedented landmarks for an MMA fighter in Ireland. Conor was breaking new ground for the sport in his own country. Having always been on the periphery, MMA was beginning to join soccer, rugby and Gaelic games at the forefront of the Irish sporting landscape.

It was high time to delegate Conor's commercial and media commitments to somebody else, because that aspect of his career now required far more time, experience and business nous than Halli Nelson and I had between us. It was starting to take me a couple of hours each morning to sift through the interview requests in my inbox to find important e mails relating to the day-to-day running of the gym. Conor subsequently handed his management responsibilities over to Audie Attar and the team at Paradigm. They took care of everything away from the gym, allowing Conor to maximize his profitability while he and I concentrated on the day job – winning fights.

After the defeat of Brimage, the UFC were keen to bring Conor across the Atlantic, and where better to kick things off than in the Irish capital of the USA? His next assignment would be against Andy Ogle in Boston on 17 August 2013. Given how impressively Conor performed in his debut, there were a lot of calls for him to be given a highly ranked opponent next. But Ogle was also quite new to the UFC, having amassed a 1–1 record in the octagon. He was, realistically, a bottom-tier featherweight. Perhaps that suited the UFC at the time. It was still early days for Conor, so they were probably keen to ensure that they didn't unnecessarily accelerate his progress. On top of that, a demolition of an Englishman would surely go down well with the large Irish crowd that was inevitably going to be at the event in Boston.

Six weeks before the fight, Ogle pulled out and in came Max Holloway. The change didn't mean anything for us. Holloway wasn't a big name either; as far as we were concerned, he was just another guy to take out en route to the title. But in hindsight the switch was a good thing. Holloway would go on to win eight fights in a row after facing Conor, and in my opinion he became the second-best featherweight in the UFC, so it was a bigger fight for Conor than it appeared to be at the time.

For his part, Conor was already of the opinion that it was a bit of a waste of time facing anyone other than the champion. He already believed he was at that level, so these fights in the meantime were merely a formality.

Regardless of the opponent, the fight was going to be a big occasion because it was to be Conor's first time competing in the USA. As is generally the case in the entertainment industry – which the UFC is very much a part of – cracking the American market is an essential part of the journey to success.

Conor required a work visa to compete in the USA, but it was late in the day – about four weeks out from the fight – before the process to apply for one actually began, and obtaining a US work visa can be difficult enough at the best of times. For reasons I didn't understand, the UFC advised us that the quickest way to resolve it was to fly to Canada, spend a couple of days in Ottawa while doing some paperwork, then fly from there to Las Vegas to complete more paperwork. Apparently entering the USA via Canada would speed up the process. With the fight less than a month away, interrupting our training camp to fly all the way to North America – before heading home to Ireland and then back across to Boston again a couple of weeks later – wasn't ideal, but it had to be done.

Not long after we landed in Ottawa, Conor's tooth started acting up again. It appeared that the cabin pressure on aeroplanes was aggravating the issue. He was in a lot of discomfort. Just as we had done in Stockholm, Conor and I took off through Ottawa in search of a dentist. I'll never forget the guy we ended up paying a visit to. He reminded me of Dr Nick from *The Simpsons* and he ran this very tacky place called 'No More Pain' – which we later christened 'More Pain', because the guy wasn't able to do much for Conor's tooth. In fact, he was more interested in getting photos with Conor and calling his friends to let them know that a UFC star was in his surgery. That really took us by surprise, because we had been under the impression that Conor's newfound fame was mostly confined to Ireland. Yet here we were in Canada and some dentist was acting as if Al Pacino had just walked in: 'Oh my God! You're the actual Conor McGregor!'

As for the tooth, I made sure that Conor underwent surgery to have it removed after the Holloway fight. We'd had enough of roaming the streets of random cities to find dentists at that stage.

From Ottawa we moved on to Las Vegas to complete some more paperwork. It was the first of many trips to Vegas for Conor and it gave him a chance to spend time building up his relationship with UFC bosses like Dana White and Lorenzo Fertitta. Conor and I stayed at the Palace Station Casino. It's a very basic hotel and a far cry from the suites at the Red Rock which Conor would eventually become accustomed to. Then we headed back to Dublin to complete the training camp, before flying back out to Boston a couple of weeks later.

It was great to get to Boston. As well as being a home away from home for the Irish, it also allowed us to catch up with Tom Egan.

Tom had moved over there a few years earlier, so we hadn't been in touch for a while. Since his loss at UFC 93, he had continued to fight at a good level, though he hadn't been able to put together a streak of wins that would capture the UFC's attention again. He was beginning to develop into a promising coach, too. Seeing him again was fantastic. He was also able to help us out with somewhere to train during the final few days before the fight. We worked out at Peter Welch's boxing gym, which was also where we had Conor's media day. That was really interesting because it was the first time the US media had had direct access to Conor. He delivered the goods and they lapped it up. The main event in Boston was Chael Sonnen versus Maurício Rua, but the vast majority of the media coverage was being reserved for Conor. His clash with Max Holloway was still only on the preliminary card, but there was no mistaking which fight the fans were most looking forward to.

On the Wednesday before the event, Conor and I were walking down the street in Boston when I sensed a change in his demeanour. He stopped talking mid-sentence and his back went up like a dog anticipating a fight. That's when I noticed a group of four guys walking towards us. I didn't recognize any of them, but they were all staring intently at Conor. I was starting to feel on edge, thinking to myself: *Okay, what on earth is going to happen here?*

When we reached them, they gave us a wide berth and passed on either side. Both groups then just continued on their way.

'Little rat!' said Conor, as he looked back in their direction.

'What the hell was that all about?' I asked.

'That's that fucker. He was talking shit.'

The name Conor mentioned meant nothing to me, but he explained to me that he was a UFC featherweight who was also fighting on the Boston card, and apparently he had spoken negatively about Conor in an interview or on social media.

'He disrespected me,' Conor added. 'I don't like that. I don't like that at all.'

Even though he was only one fight into his UFC career, many fighters had already been calling Conor out in the media. Perhaps they were envious of the publicity he was receiving. Guys who had been in the UFC for years were now seemingly being ignored, while Conor, this cocky newcomer, was suddenly the centre of attention. Some of them expressed their frustration by trash-talking Conor. When they did, Conor marked it down. Every single time. If you're a UFC fighter who has ever had something negative to say about Conor, rest assured that he has taken note.

That doesn't just apply to fighters. I remember Conor once recorded a 'Good luck on your wedding day' sort of video message for a friend of a friend of a friend of Owen Roddy. Later that day, I was chatting to Owen in my office when Conor burst through the door.

'Don't send that video!' he shouted at Owen. 'I just realized why I recognize that guy's name. He's a snake.' Seemingly the guy who was getting married had given Cathal Pendred a hard time on Twitter a couple of years earlier.

I've always liked that about Conor. He gets the lion's share of the praise, attention and recognition, but if somebody speaks negatively about anyone at SBG, Conor takes it on board. He looks out for his teammates with an elephant's memory. Even if I mention to him who Paddy Holohan is fighting next, Conor will say something like: 'I've watched his last few fights, here's what we need to watch out for . . .'

He'll often pull his teammates aside in the gym and give them his assessment. Conor is a great guy to have on your side, a really good teammate.

At the TD Garden in Boston for Conor's second UFC fight, I could tell that some of the other fighters in the locker room were sizing Conor up. Diego Brandão was one of them. He'd have to wait for his opportunity.

This fight was the first time that a huge convoy of Conor's fans made the journey to the US. When I think of the lengths people go to just to be there to lend their support, it's pretty overwhelming. The Irish fans are incredible. With each fight, their presence grows larger. They certainly know how to enjoy themselves, too. Sometimes they're criticized for going overboard with the craic, but I've only very rarely encountered guys being irritatingly drunk. The atmosphere is overwhelmingly positive and the support is brilliant. People are spending their life savings in order to be there. That gives me a boost and it gives my fighters a boost.

When it was time for Conor to walk out to the octagon, we had no idea what the UFC had planned. Ordinarily, you're brought as far as the curtain that separates the backstage area from the arena. Then you emerge from behind it when given your cue. But this time, after leaving the changing room, we were stopped in the security area in the corridor. His apparel was now sponsored by Dethrone Royalty sportswear, but Conor still had the tricolour draped over his shoulders. Conor waited to be prompted forward, while Tom Egan and I stood behind him. There seemed to be a lot of UFC crew running around, then a bunch of cameras appeared in front of us. It still didn't dawn on me at the time, but the UFC were giving Conor an extended walk-out and the lights-out treatment that's usually set aside solely for the fighters in the main event of the night. Another unprecedented move.

When Conor appeared, the noise from the crowd was deafening. It seemed like every person in the arena was waving an Irish flag. I tried to play it cool by acting as if it was no big deal, but my stomach was performing somersaults.

Conor had only fought in the UFC once before. Even the biggest stars and legends of the sport rarely received a reception like this. We'd soon discover what it was like to experience being involved in an actual UFC main event, but this was a perfect introduction.

I have no idea what was going through Max Holloway's mind as he witnessed Conor's entrance and realized that, despite being an American fighter in America, he was effectively on enemy territory. It must have been an intimidating prospect for the twenty-one-year-old Hawaiian, the second-youngest fighter on the UFC roster at the time. I do believe from early on in the fight that he looked like a guy who was just trying to get to the finish line. He never seemed to be chasing the win. And I say that as a big fan of Max Holloway. Max is usually really aggressive, coming forward with a very high output of strikes. Against Conor, he allowed himself to remain on the back foot from the very beginning. He was extremely elusive, intelligent defensively and made himself difficult to hit. But he never once threatened to win the fight. If you watch that fight and compare it to his others, the difference in his approach is very evident. Conor is at his best when he can encourage his opponents to come at him because he's a great counter-fighter. I'm not sure if you'd say Holloway was smart or afraid, but it seemed like his only priority in there was to survive. It's hard to put away a guy like that.

Conor was totally comfortable as he out-struck Holloway for the first round and a half, before taking him down and continuing his dominance on the ground. At the end of the second round, when Conor stood back up to walk to the corner, I thought I noticed his left knee buckling. He sort of wobbled as he returned to his feet. However, he didn't mention anything during the break so I didn't ask. Instead I just encouraged him to continue where he had left off.

'You look beautiful,' I said. I wish I hadn't, because it was picked up by the TV mic, and people have shouted that phrase at me randomly ever since. I'd like to think they're complimenting me, but unfortunately they're just poking fun.

Early in the third and final round, Conor once again opted to show off his takedowns and grappling ability as he remained in control all the way to the end. But he didn't look himself. His mobility seemed to be impaired and I could only assume that an injury was to blame. As the fight ended, with Conor comfortable in top position in Holloway's guard, he looked right at me and smiled.

'What?' I asked.

'My knee is gone.'

I stood up to walk into the octagon. As I entered, Joe Rogan was going in to do his post-fight interview. In the interview, Conor explained to Joe that he felt a pop in the knee when he was trying to pass Holloway's guard. Afterwards, Rogan turned to me and said: 'That sounds like it's his ACL.'

An anterior cruciate ligament injury is one of the most serious a fighter can suffer, but I was probably in denial because I just brushed it off: 'Nah, I'm sure it's nothing to worry about.'

Deep down, though, I had a strong feeling that it wasn't going to be good news, and in the changing room afterwards, I grew very concerned. An ACL tear generally kept fighters out of action for at least a year. Such a long layoff would be a crushing blow to Conor's progress. I asked Stitch Duran, who was working as a cut man that night for the UFC, if he wouldn't mind strapping an ice pack to Conor's knee.

'You know what, if anybody else asked me to do something like that I'd tell them to get out of here, but anything for my favourite Irish boys,' he said. The doctor then came in and performed some preliminary tests but it was impossible for him to tell exactly what the problem was. Conor would require an MRI scan to reveal the full extent of the damage.

I was scheduled to fly home the following day, so while I was heading east to Dublin, Conor was going west to meet a specialist in Los Angeles. He was confident.

'I think it's only a minor injury,' he said. 'Three or four weeks out and I'll be back in time to fight in Manchester at the end of October.'

I didn't share his optimism. When I arrived home, I had resigned myself to the fact that it was probably going to be a long time before I made that walk to the octagon with Conor again.

11

The history books will recall that August 2013 was when Conor McGregor recorded his second win in the UFC, but it was also the month in which I found my dream gym. The premises on the Long Mile Road had served us well but it felt like it was time for an upgrade. Conor's success was starting to have a positive impact on our membership and I was confident that the numbers would continue to increase. The opportunity to train in the same gym as Conor McGregor was an attractive proposition.

It was a sign that things were going in the right direction that I could now consider relocating the gym on my own terms, instead of being forced out as I had been on previous occasions. While I wasn't actively looking to move with any great sense of urgency, I was keeping my eyes peeled for suitable places. That's when I came across a vacant unit on the Naas Road, a five-minute drive from where we were based and just around the corner from my apartment. It was spacious – almost 10,000 square feet – and bright; the perfect place for a gym. Of course, it was completely empty when I first saw it, but I already had the entire thing planned out in my mind. It was everything I ever wanted from a gym.

The problem was that I really didn't think I could afford it. If I relocated SBG Ireland to the Naas Road, my monthly financial outgoings would multiply by seven – and I was still paying that €40,000 loan back to the bank. After viewing the building one afternoon, I went home and resigned myself to the likelihood that it was beyond my reach. But I couldn't get the place out of my head. I wanted it so badly that I went back out that evening, walked up to the unit, stood outside for a while and just stared at it. I did the same the following night. And the night after that. Yeah, I stalked a building. A couple of weeks later, my dad came with me to take a look at it.

'It's a great place, John,' he said. 'But you can't afford it and you'll never fill it. It's massive. Just forget about it and keep an eye out for somewhere else. You'd be crazy to take the risk.'

But I refused to be diverted. I had become a little bit obsessed with moving the gym to this unit. It sounds cheesy but I had a vision for how the gym would look in there and I couldn't shake it off. It was exactly how I had always pictured my ideal gym. Even though the interest in SBG was growing, I still only had just over a hundred members. But that fact wasn't enough to deter me. All logic seemed to suggest otherwise, but I really believed the move could be successful. I was convinced there would be a goldfish-bowl effect – that we'd fill whatever space we were in. As soon as I returned from Boston after Conor's win against Max Holloway, I began the paperwork for SBG Ireland's next move.

It was early on the Friday after Conor overcame Holloway that I received a call from Audie Attar, Conor's manager. He seemed to be in a bit of a panic.

'John, Conor has gone missing,' Audie said. 'He's taken my car and isn't answering my calls. He's been gone for a few hours now.'

'Hang on, Audie,' I replied. 'What's the problem? Why did he disappear like that?'

'He found out earlier that he's torn his ACL. He's going to be out for a long time.'

Conor had been for an MRI scan in Los Angeles on the Wednesday. On Thursday night he received the results of the scan . . . via Twitter. Dana White had given an interview to Fox Sports, who then revealed to the world – including Conor – the news that he had ruptured his anterior cruciate ligament. Nobody at the UFC had thought to notify Conor, myself or his management about such an important development. Instead, Conor found out that he probably wouldn't fight again for a year via social media, just like everybody else. This was a potentially career-threatening injury that would require reconstructive surgery. I was furious that Conor learned the bad news from the internet. He wasn't happy either, which is why he'd lost his temper and taken off in Audie's car.

An ACL tear, while it's a relatively common injury, can be very tough to recover from. It's a long road back. After years of hard work, Conor's career was finally beginning to take off. Now it had ground to an unexpected halt. If his initial thoughts were overwhelmingly negative, it was understandable.

I called Conor and he answered. He was angry at first, so I allowed him to get that out of his system. Then I sought to calm him down before discussing the reality of the situation. He was injured. He needed surgery. Then he'd face six months of rehabilitation. There was no getting away from that. No alternatives. That's what he was faced with. Conor had two choices: he could feel sorry for himself, throw in the towel and forget about his goals, or he could embrace the challenge that came with the injury and vow to come out stronger at the end of it all.

'Conor, champions conquer all adversity. That's what separates them from the challengers,' I told him. 'There's been adversity in the past, there's adversity right now and there'll be even more adversity in the future. But you've overcome it before and you're going to overcome it again. Why? Because you're on the road to becoming a UFC champion and this is just a minor obstacle along the way. This time next year we're going to be laughing about all of this.'

In a scenario like this, appealing to Conor's competitive side is the best way to get through to him. So that's what I decided to do. We made it a competition. He might not have been able to fight for a while, but that didn't mean he couldn't compete in other ways.

'You're going to shock people with how fast you recover from this. And if they thought you were good before, they're going to be blown away by what you show them when you come back. You'll recover from this injury quicker than GSP did.'

Stuff like that really struck a chord with Conor. The chance to take on an MMA legend grabbed his attention. Former UFC welterweight champion Georges St-Pierre sustained the very same injury in 2011 and was lauded for returning just 322 days after surgery to beat Carlos Condit. Conor latched on to that.

'Yeah, fuck it. I'm going to break records with this. People have seen nothing yet.'

That was the beginning of his journey to recovery. On 7 September, Conor was operated on in Los Angeles by the renowned Dr Neal ElAttrache, who had previously worked on some of the top stars in US sports, such as Tom Brady and Kobe Bryant. The UFC ensured that Conor was given the very best treatment. He spent the next five months in LA, going through a rigorous programme of rehabilitation under the guidance of Heather Milligan, an outstanding physical therapist who would play a vital role in Conor's recovery.

That was the longest we've ever been apart, but we talked on the phone every day. I knew LA was the right place for him to be during his rehabilitation. He had access to world-class medical treatment there every day, and the little bit of sunshine that Dublin unfortunately can't provide helped to keep his mindset positive. He even made a few celebrity friends while he was there, with Arnold Schwarzenegger – Heather Milligan's boyfriend – paying him a visit during a rehab session.

There were ups and downs along the way, which is to be expected when a professional athlete is confined to the sidelines with an injury like that for such a long period of time. There were a few occasions when Conor would call and tell me he was finished; that he didn't want to do it any more. But I knew he just needed some encouragement and those thoughts were soon forgotten about. As his coach in that situation, that's all I could do: play my part in keeping Conor in the right frame of mind. He missed the day-to-day routine of being in the gym and training alongside his friends. While Conor was restricted to simple things like calf-raises and an exercise bike, his teammates were sparring and preparing for fights. I often sent him video clips of the guys sparring in the gym to ensure that he never began to feel detached from the team. Despite the bad days, Conor's updates were mostly positive. 'Another good day of work here,' he'd say. 'Making progress every day. I am a machine.'

I never had any doubts about Conor's ability to ace the

rehabilitation process from a physical point of view, but the key to making a success of it was how he handled it psychologically. Conor kept his mind active. He didn't sit around feeling sorry for himself, eating ice cream and watching TV. He used the opportunity to learn. Even though he couldn't spar, I used to send questions to him by text message about how he'd respond if he were to be caught in a certain position during his fight. That kept his mind sharp and in the game.

I would challenge any medical professional to take on Conor McGregor in a quiz about the anatomy of the knee. During his rehab, he studied it intensely. Conor became obsessed with knowing every detail of how the knee works in order to have a clearer understanding of his rehab. There's not a thing he doesn't know about it now. He also examined in detail the recoveries of other professional athletes from similar injuries.

Heather Milligan taught him a lot about the movement of the human body, and that had a significant influence on Conor's approach to training and how to get the best out of himself physically. It also encouraged him to embrace the concept of light sparring even more. Heather told Conor that his muscles were too tight, so he became fixated with making sure that he was always loose and supple. He learned the importance of massage, and came to understand that lifting heavy weights really isn't necessary for building strength. It was all about focusing on soft training.

Conor competed for a long time before he saw any financial rewards, so when he reached the UFC, maximizing his earning potential was one of his priorities. Thanks mainly to the 'KO of the Night' bonus he was awarded after beating Marcus Brimage, he had gotten off to a pretty good start on that front. However, the injury layoff provided him with a good opportunity to ensure that he was ready to take things to another level. When he wasn't in the gym or receiving treatment, Conor devoted plenty of time to learning about how the UFC is run as a business and the role of a fighter in the media. He recognized the importance of promoting himself effectively, particularly given that the injury could very easily have pushed him away from the spotlight. The majority of fighters are only in the news when they've got a fight on the horizon, but Conor had different ideas. In spite of the injury, significant commercial offers were starting to come in from companies who were keen to be associated with him. That only served to encourage Conor to sharpen his business acumen. He didn't fight for almost a year, but Conor managed to become an even bigger star in the interim. During Conor's time on the sidelines, people were constantly asking me how his recovery was going. Even the elderly woman behind the counter in my local shop would ask: 'How's his knee? Is he going to be okay?'

He couldn't train or fight for a long time, but Conor improved in absolutely every area during his recovery. As he inched closer to full fitness each day, his mind gradually became bulletproof. In hindsight, the break was a blessing in disguise, in that it gave Conor a chance to take a step back and clearly assess the opportunities that were in front of him, which meant that he was prepared to make the most of them when they came along. His handling of the injury was a perfect example of the 'win or learn' philosophy I've encouraged at SBG. For 99 per cent of people it would have been a negative experience, but Conor turned it into a positive one. Instead of losing during his time out, he learned.

In December 2013 I finally got the keys to the unit on the Naas Road. The process of securing the lease had dragged on for months, so it was a relief to have it signed and sealed. During some complications with solicitors, for the first time I played the Conor McGregor card. They'd quiz me about my plans for the building and I'd just say: 'You know Conor McGregor? Well, this is where he'll be training.' After that, things were a lot smoother.

Again, I couldn't have relocated the gym without the incredible contribution of the members. So many of them sacrificed their weekends to help with the move. Jimmy Donnelly, in particular, invested countless hours in getting the new premises kitted out. Their assistance was hugely important in keeping the costs down, because I was already feeling the pressure financially.

We scheduled the grand opening for Saturday, 11 January 2014. When the work on the new gym was completed, it had a reception area, a coffee dock, an MMA shop, a competition-sized octagon, a boxing ring, changing rooms, consultation and physiotherapy rooms, offices, and separate areas for grappling and striking. I was delighted with how it looked. Of course, I'm biased, but my initial feeling was that it would be difficult to find a better facility anywhere in the world. Now I just needed to pay for it.

Conor came back from the States for the opening, which certainly helped to drum up some publicity. I wanted him to stay in LA to continue his recovery, but he insisted on being there for such an important occasion for SBG Ireland. It was a mark of his quality as a man, because this was at a critical stage in his rehab. I was anticipating that about a hundred people might show up on the day, but with all my top professional fighters present, 1,500 people came through the doors. Even looking back now, I still can't believe we had attracted such a big crowd. It wasn't so long ago that we couldn't even draw that many people to the guys' fights, let alone the opening of a gym. The place was absolutely packed, with people of all ages. The day was yet another indication of how rapidly MMA was growing in Ireland.

On opening weekend alone, our membership numbers doubled. That meant that I had already covered the increased expenses that came with the move. I was very relieved because there really was no Plan B if things went tits-up. The team's profile was still exploding, but there was no guarantee of that continuing. What if Conor's comeback failed? I knew the bubble could very easily burst. But that first weekend removed so much of the financial burden from my shoulders. I was confident then that we would continue to bring in new members, because the word quickly got around that this was a world-class facility that catered for all levels. It was early days yet, but it felt like the gamble was about to pay off. Later that year I received a letter from the bank confirming that my loan was finally cleared. It was one of the most satisfying moments of my life. I'll never forget it. I still can't help but smile now when I think of it.

*

Following the move to the Naas Road, the increasing membership numbers allowed me to make some adjustments to how the gym operated. We introduced a consultation process and foundation programmes for beginners. This was geared towards anyone who was curious about taking up martial arts but also a bit intimidated by it. It was important to let people know that if they joined SBG, they could learn from scratch at their own pace. They weren't going to be thrown in for a sparring session with Conor McGregor on their first day.

It's quite a small percentage of SBG members who actually train to compete. Many people come to us because they want to lose weight or improve their general health and lifestyle. Hearing their success stories is just as satisfying for me as any big UFC win for one of my fighters. To see somebody who has turned their life around as a result of joining SBG means the world to me. More often than not, they've never even set foot in a cage or entered a competition.

This approach also made the gym a friendly place for kids. We call them the 'Growing Gorillas'. Given my own history of being bullied and unable to defend myself as a child, that had been a priority for me for a long time. I regularly meet parents who are worried about their child being bullied. Owen Roddy is fantastic in that regard. He has 'mat chats' with the kids in his classes and explains to them how best to handle those situations, encouraging them to get a teacher involved and let their parents know what's going on. But he also teaches them how to respond if they're being physically attacked in the schoolyard. Bullies are like predatory animals. They can sense when somebody is, or is not, going to be an easy target. We aim to make sure that our kids stand tall and exude confidence. If there's a rumour around their school that they're training in the same gym as Conor McGregor, all of a sudden they're not such an easy target. So the bullies move on to something else. Nobody wants to jump on a guy walking down the street with a gym bag over his shoulder.

As the gym began to flourish, one concern I had was that it was

Dub grapples for total glory

THE buzz word in martial arts these days is Total Fighting.

And tomorrow John Kavanagh, a 22 year old Dubliner, becomes the first Irish fighter to compete in this no-holds barred sport when he steps on the mat at a special tournament in Milton Keynes.

Kavanagh, with a background in kenpo karate, has also trained in judo, wrestling and boxing and runs three clubs in Dublin.

"Total fighting was brought to England by a man called Lee Hasdell, who had trained in Japan, and saw the sport in the USA, says Robert Byrne, a clubmate of Kavanagh's.

BANNED

"Over there it was banned initially before people realised the skills involved."

"In Britain, the rules are strict and it's ranked only 10th on a list of dangerous sports behind soccer and rugby."

Total fighting takes from all the martial arts, but to the untrained eye looks most like Olympic wrestling.

Fighters spend a lot of time grappling on the floor, a skill unknown to kick boxers or karate fighters.

"There are two sets of rules - ring rules for the professional sport and vale tude which is amateur," says Byrne.

"This is what we do - fighting on mats, and wearing special gloves as well as shin, instep and knee pads,"

LINDIE NAUGHTON

says Byrne. Under vale tude rules, fights consist of one four minute bout.

In the pro game, the fights are longer. The sport is a breakaway from the traditional fighting arts, with the emphasis more on the sport than on self-defence.

"John describes himself as a martial athlete. He trains every day, both in the gym and on the mat," adds Byrne.

If he wins in Milton Keynes, Kavanagh plans a number of "knowledge sharing seminars" around the country.

LEARN

"That's the way we see it - we're willing to learn from other systems and we're not saying one is better than another," concludes Byrne.

"All we ask of them is that they come along and see what we have to offer. If they don't like it, that's fine, but hopefully, we'll all have learned something."

☐ NO HOLDS BARRED: John Kavanagh who competes in the Total Fighting tournament at Milton Keynes tomorrow.

1. (*top left*) The karate kid: in the garden at home in Dublin.

2. (*top right*) This photo was taken shortly after I'd become the All-Ireland kenpo karate champion, aged fifteen.

3. (*left*) MMA was nowhere near the mainstream when I made my fighting debut in England, but I got a bit of press coverage back home.

4. (*top*) With Conor McGregor, Clive Staunton, Cathal Pendred, Alan Duffy, Artem Lobov, James 'Sexual' Heelan, Aisling Daly and Paddy Holohan on the night of Cage Contender 8 in March 2011, in Dublin. Conor knocked out Mike Wood in sixteen seconds that night, and Cathal successfully defended his welterweight title. (*Tommy Lakes*)

5. (*bottom*) In what became a bit of a Straight Blast Gym tradition after a good night's work, Cathal, Artem, Owen Roddy, Conor, myself, Ais, Chris Fields and Paddy posed for a celebratory shot in the octagon after Conor became Cage Warriors featherweight champ – his first title – in June 2012. The noise and electricity in the Helix that night were like nothing I had ever experienced. (*Dolly Clew*)

6. (*top*) Overseeing a grappling session at SBG, 2012. (*Tommy Lakes*)

7. (*bottom*) With Cathal Pendred and Chris Fields, cornering for Artem Lobov during his Cage Warriors fight in Amman, Jordan, in September 2012. (*Tommy Lakes*)

8. (*above*) With Conor in Philip Mulpeter's corner at Cage Warriors 56 in London, July 2013. Even as his fame and success have exploded, Conor has remained a brilliant teammate to his fellow SBG fighters. (*Dolly Clew*)

9. (*below*) Walking the floor of the MGM Grand Garden with Conor and Artem before Conor's Las Vegas debut, against Dustin Poirier at UFC 178 in September 2014. (*Orlagh Hunter*)

10. (*top*) Before the weigh-in for the Poirier fight, I turned to Dana White and said, 'Are we in Las Vegas or Dublin here?' The Irish support for Conor was massive, and Poirier was rattled. (*Tommy Lakes*)

11. (*bottom*) With Conor, his partner Dee Devlin and my partner Orlagh Hunter at the Red Rock hotel just before heading to the MGM Grand for the fight.

12. (*above*) Sipping whiskey
with Gunnar Nelson and
Conor at the party in Dublin
to celebrate my engagement
to Orlagh. (*Orlagh Hunter*)

13. (*right*) Rolling with Conor
in the buildup to UFC 189.
We'd been preparing for a title
fight against José Aldo, who
fights mostly on his feet, and
Conor was carrying a knee
injury, so we'd gone relatively
easy on the grappling drills.
When Aldo pulled out and
Chad Mendes – a top wrestler
– stepped in, I was a bit
nervous. But Conor just said,
'They're all the same.'
(*Orlagh Hunter*)

14. (*above*) With Orlagh on a night off in Vegas before the Mendes fight.

15. (*below*) Celebrating with a bloodied but victorious Conor after he knocked out Mendes, to take the interim UFC featherweight title. (*PA*)

16. (*top*) After the noise and adrenalin of a big fight night in Vegas, I like to find a quiet spot, lie down on the floor and let everything sink in. After Conor took thirteen seconds to knock out José Aldo, becoming the undisputed featherweight champ, I reflected on what a long and unlikely journey it had been. (*Orlagh Hunter*)

17. (*bottom*) At the Aviva Stadium in Dublin for a Six Nations rugby match, February 2016. Apart from being my fiancée, Orlagh is a valued colleague at SBG – but we enjoy doing things that have nothing to do with MMA.

becoming increasingly difficult to retain the feeling that SBG was like a little family. Sadly, it took a dreadful tragedy to remind us all of the importance of sticking together.

Kamil Rutkowski was a key figure at Straight Blast Gym. He had come to Ireland from Poland and joined SBG shortly after we moved to the Long Mile Road. You couldn't have met a happier, friendlier, more helpful person than Kamil, and there wasn't a more popular guy at the gym. He very quickly developed into an outstanding Brazilian jiu-jitsu practitioner, and by the time we relocated to the Naas Road he was a brilliant coach and one of my most trusted friends.

A few months after we were up and running on the Naas Road, in April 2014, Kamil and I were the last two people left in the gym one evening. As we were preparing to close up and go home, Kamil came into my office and asked if we could have a chat. He had seemed slightly out of sorts for a few days, so this didn't surprise me. I could see that there was something on his mind.

When he sat down and spoke, Kamil didn't seem like himself at all. He was acting very strangely. He appeared angry and agitated. I had never seen him like that before. He rambled on for a while about some minor issues in the gym. It was all a bit bizarre. None of what he was saying made any sense. Then he claimed that some people at the gym – including myself – had been talking about him behind his back. There was no substance to that whatsoever, because there wasn't a more liked and respected guy at SBG than Kamil. The conversation actually became quite tense, and I was worried that he was going to lunge over the desk at me, but I insisted to him that none of what he was saying was true and that he had nothing to worry about.

I was very concerned about Kamil when I got home that night. Our talk was just so out of character for him. I got in touch with a few of the other coaches and they agreed that his recent behaviour was cause for concern. We decided that we would contact Professor Dan Healy, a neurologist at Beaumont Hospital who is SBG's team doctor, to speak to Kamil about his situation. Looking back, there had been a few signs that Kamil was struggling. On Facebook he had been posting a lot of pictures of himself alone, as well as other little things that didn't reflect his usual bubbly personality. He had cut himself off from people in the gym who considered him a close friend. While it was hard to detect at the time, he was clearly suffering from depression.

The morning after our conversation, Kamil came into the gym and taught his class at 6.30 a.m., as usual. He collected some fees, did a few other bits and pieces and then left in his car. By early afternoon we began to worry, as he had been gone for several hours and that was extremely uncommon. I called him but his phone was turned off. He wasn't at home either. As dinnertime approached there was still no sign of Kamil, so we phoned the police.

That night, at around 9 p.m., I was on the mats coaching a class when the word came through to the gym that Kamil had been found. But it wasn't good news. A couple who were out for a walk in the Dublin mountains discovered him hanging from a tree. He was thirty-five.

It's hard to describe your feelings at a time like that. It's not sadness. It's not anger. It's just emptiness. Nothing. For a while I just stood there, speechless. Then Kieran McGeeney pulled me away to one side. That's when it hit me and a wave of emotion engulfed me. That night, my sister Ann and I stayed behind at the gym to give ourselves time to let the reality of what had happened sink in. But mostly we shared stories that reminded us of what a brilliant person Kamil was. Ann ran the reception at the gym, and Kamil always kept an eye out for her. She said he was like her guard dog. Kamil was a vital member of SBG and his passing left a massive hole.

A couple of nights later we had a send-off for Kamil in the gym. Everybody came down. Some said a few words of remembrance. It was an emotional occasion, particularly for Kamil's brother. We invited him down and I presented him with a BJJ black belt on Kamil's behalf. We all raised some money to send Kamil's body back to his family in Poland. It also paid for the funeral. It was nice to be able to do that, because it took some of the pressure off his family at a very difficult time.

We found afterwards that Kamil had been suffering from severe pain due to a back injury. The medication he had been prescribed for it didn't mix well with the effects of depression, and that seems to have pushed Kamil beyond breaking point.

To be completely honest, I knew absolutely nothing about depression. I'd had some tough times myself over the years, but never anything to that extent. Kamil's death taught me that depression is a serious issue that shouldn't be ignored or dismissed. It could happen to anybody. It was a lesson to us all at SBG and it encouraged others to open up if they had concerns over their mental health. As a result, the gym became a place where people felt comfortable speaking about those issues. They realized that it's okay not to feel okay, but the first step should be to let those closest to you know. Don't isolate yourself and keep it all bottled up. It raised our awareness of an important topic. Afterwards, others came forward too. Aisling Daly was one of them. She admitted to suffering from depression, something I had never been aware of. Ais has since spoken publicly about it, and doing so helped her deal with it.

Conor McGregor was also affected by Kamil's death. He wrote on Facebook:

> We all go through pain in life so please speak to each other and pay attention to another person's feelings. Offer help and guidance. We are all one. Suicide is a problem that hits us all in life, please pay attention, your words are powerful to you and those around you. Use them to encourage. We all feel the same emotions as each other, good and bad, just at different times in our life. Awareness is everything. Our relationships with each other are worth more than anything else. They deserve all our time and focus. I feel sick to my stomach here. His life was the gym, his life was jiu-jitsu. I wish I just paid attention to him instead of talking about and worrying about my own meaningless shit. It all means nothing in the end. Absolutely nothing. What the fuck is money anyway when it drives people to unthinkable things?

SBG subsequently became involved with Pieta House, a charity which helps people who are suicidal or self-harming, and we now take part in their Darkness Into Light event each year. We also have posters around the gym, reminding people to remain aware of depression and the fact that it can be a consequence of concussion.

What happened to Kamil was horrendous, but nothing can be done about the past. What you can do is learn from it and do as much as you can to make sure that it doesn't happen again. It's important to extract some good from even the very worst situations, and Kamil's death caused the team to become closer. The change of location and the increase in membership numbers had possibly resulted in a slight disconnect, but this brought us back together again. By the beginning of 2016, SBG Ireland had 700 members, yet it's still a family – albeit an enormous one. There's a support system there, so you know that if you're having a rough time, you'll have three or four people watching out for you.

Kamil's passing was the greatest loss SBG ever suffered, but it also gave us the most valuable lesson we ever learned.

12

Conor McGregor's career in the UFC may have been on hold as a result of the ACL injury, but several of his teammates at SBG were getting closer to their own dreams of fighting for MMA's premier organization. In 2013 Paddy Holohan, Cathal Pendred and Chris Fields all competed on *The Ultimate Fighter* – a reality TV show geared towards unearthing new fighters for the UFC.

Cathal, in particular, saw it as one last shot at earning a UFC contract. In my view, he should never have had to rely on *The Ultimate Fighter* to get into the UFC. He had already proved that he was worthy of a place on the roster by beating several of the best welterweights in Europe en route to becoming the Cage Warriors champion. I lost count of how many times I contacted the UFC about giving Cathal a shot, but the answer was the same every time: He needs to start finishing his opponents in order to be considered.

That was Cathal's problem. While he was winning his fights comprehensively, he was mostly doing so via decision instead of knockout or submission. Even though his record was good, that aspect of it went against him because the UFC ideally like to see exciting stoppages.

Cathal joined SBG late in 2008, not long after we had moved to the Long Mile Road. He was a novice at the time because he had only recently taken up mixed martial arts, never having trained in the sport before. He was actually a pretty promising rugby player, winning a Leinster Schools Senior Cup medal with Belvedere College alongside guys like Cian Healy and Ian Keatley, who went on to play for Ireland.

Because he was only starting out, Cathal needed a lot of work, but he certainly had the right attitude. He was incredibly keen to learn and improve. Aware of the fact that his opponents generally had a head start on him when it came to skill and technique, Cathal knew that he needed to level the playing field by working harder than them and wanting it more. And nobody wanted it more than Cathal. Just a few weeks after joining the gym, he took a fight. He was a learn-on-the-job type of guy. He threw himself in at the deep end and defied his lack of an extensive background in MMA by displaying remarkable resolve to grind out results. After every win, Cathal told me the same thing.

'I want to fight someone better next time. Get me the best opponent you can find. I want to be fighting the top guys in the world in the UFC as soon as possible.'

It quickly became evident that Cathal was a pretty special guy. I used to call him the Billy Goat. You could leave him on a mountainside for a few weeks, eating nothing but grass, but he'd still be thriving when you came back. He had the kind of mindset that meant he always got by, regardless of the circumstances. Toughness is probably a prerequisite when you earn a living by fighting men in a cage, but Cathal brought new meaning to the word. He was absolutely bulletproof. Before he fought Danny Mitchell in Jordan, he did eight hours in the sauna – without a break – to make weight. I've seen guys break and end up in tears after eight minutes in a sauna, let alone hours. That's Cathal Pendred. Whatever had to be done to succeed, Cathal did it. In terms of his mentality, he's absolutely unique. I doubt I'll ever coach somebody like him again.

During one of his earliest fights, I came into the cage at the end of the first round and Cathal was on his hands and knees, searching for something on the mat.

'Cathal,' I said, 'what the hell are you doing? Get over here and sit down!'

'Sorry, coach,' he responded. 'I'm just looking for my teeth.'

Cathal had picked up many big wins before he competed on *The Ultimate Fighter* in 2013, but the fight that stands out for me when I look at his career was the one against David Bielkheden at Cage Warriors 47 in June 2012. It was probably overshadowed by the fact that Conor won the featherweight title later in the evening, but

Cathal's bout with Bielkheden was absolutely incredible – one of the best MMA fights ever to take place on Irish soil.

When you looked at the respective credentials of the two guys, the fight probably shouldn't even have been allowed to happen. It seemed like a total mismatch on first inspection. Bielkheden was a Brazilian jiu-jitsu black belt who had been fighting professionally for over ten years. He had already competed for the biggest organizations in the world. Cathal was fourteen when Bielkheden made his MMA debut. When Bielkheden moved to the UFC, Cathal had yet to walk through the doors of SBG. Weighing all of that up, this was a fight in which Cathal shouldn't have stood a chance. But that's what Cathal had been told on countless occasions before. He may have been a newcomer to MMA, but as soon as he started, Cathal never stopped. He was constantly in the gym. Although he didn't have the years and years of training behind him that his opponents had, Cathal's heart and determination were attributes they could never match.

Within the first minute of the fight, Cathal almost knocked Bielkheden out with an uppercut. That set the tone for a memorable performance from Cathal. He dominated the first two rounds and showed a gritty resilience in the third and final round to withstand a desperate comeback from Bielkheden. The win was undoubtedly his biggest yet and it was a statement that he was capable of going all the way. When we decided to accept the fight against Bielkheden, we knew that this would determine whether Cathal had what it took to compete with fighters at the highest level, or if he was destined to be confined to the regional circuit. He delivered an emphatic response to that question. After that, there was never any doubt in my mind about what Cathal could achieve. If his work ethic had already paved the way for him to defeat guys who had been fighting at the highest level since before he had ever even thrown a punch, there was going to be no stopping him from realizing his dreams now.

One of the striking things about the win against David Bielkheden was that it took place at the Helix arena on the Dublin City

University campus – where Cathal had been doing his exams just a couple of weeks earlier. In the build-up to the fight, he'd come into the gym very early in the morning to train, dash off for the day to do exams and then come back in the evening and train until the gym closed. Cathal later graduated with a degree in Analytical Science. Whenever any of the guys in the gym would complain about finding the time to train, I'd just point at Cathal and tell them to stop moaning.

Within a year, Cathal was the Cage Warriors champion and had cleared out the entire welterweight division. He was itching for a chance to fight in the UFC, but the call just didn't look like it was going to come. That's when an opportunity arose with another big organization in the US called World Series of Fighting. They were offering Cathal $10,000 to fight and another $10,000 to win. That was life-changing money for him, and approximately ten times what he was earning with Cage Warriors. However, the problem was that a clause in his Cage Warriors contract allowed him to leave for the UFC but for no other organization. Reluctant to lose one of their biggest stars, Cage Warriors wouldn't budge on the contract. It was a frustrating situation because Cathal, who was about to turn twenty-six, was at a stage where he needed to start earning money from fighting. He had graduated with a degree and there was pressure on him to use it – similar to the situation I was in all those years ago. There was a chance here for him to finally make a good living from the sport he had been pouring his heart and soul into for the past few years, but a line in a contract was preventing him from taking it.

Chris Fields got married in July 2013. Cathal and I got talking at the wedding. He was really upset about the World Series of Fighting situation. I brought him outside to the car park for a chat and he burst into tears of rage and frustration. He told me that maybe it was time to call it a day; that perhaps this was a sign that he should retire from fighting. At times, he had been so strapped for money that he had stayed at my apartment, or on the floor of his brother's bedroom. He was often just living out of his car. But there was no way I was going to allow him to walk away now that he was within touching distance of his objective. The UFC had announced a season of *The Ultimate Fighter* for middleweights and light-heavyweights. Although Cathal was a welterweight, I was absolutely confident that he could be successful fighting at fifteen pounds heavier.

'The tryouts are in Las Vegas,' he said. 'I can't afford to go all the way over there.'

I insisted on lending Cathal the money because I knew that he'd repay me — not just financially, but also with the satisfaction of finally seeing him in the UFC. It was the bones of €1,000 so he was reluctant to accept it, but I wasn't taking no for an answer.

'Cathal, there's no risk for me here whatsoever,' I said. 'You've overcome much bigger challenges than this already. I know you'll make the most of this opportunity.'

After Conor McGregor came back to Dublin for the opening of the new gym in January 2014, he was able to do most of the remainder of his rehab in Ireland. Within a couple of months of being back at home, it was as if he had never been injured at all. He was bigger, stronger and faster, and his movement was just so much more fluent. Not that I had any doubts about it, but it was obvious that he had been working phenomenally hard while he was in the US. Conor was desperate to get a fight booked, and when the UFC revealed some significant news regarding Ireland in March, he had a date to aim towards for his comeback. The organization would be returning to Dublin for a show on 19 July — their first Irish event since Tom Egan competed at UFC 93 five and a half years earlier. Even though he still hadn't been medically cleared to compete again, we knew the UFC weren't going to come to Ireland without putting Conor on the card.

It wasn't until the end of April that further details of the show were finally announced. Conor was headlining the card. He was set to face an American fighter named Cole Miller, a contest the fans were seemingly excited about because the two of them had been trading insults in interviews and social media.

When we were told that Conor was going to be the star attraction at UFC Fight Night 46, there was a mixture of shock and relief. After he picked up the injury, part of me was concerned that Conor's progress in the UFC might be undone and that he would have to go back to the end of the queue. There's probably a perception that before he went under the knife, the UFC put an arm around Conor's shoulder and told him not to worry, that he'd be catapulted straight into a main event in his home town as soon as he returned. But that certainly wasn't the case. No such assurances were given. For all we knew, he'd be returning on a preliminary card on a small event somewhere abroad. But this was something very special. Headlining a UFC event in the town where he grew up – the stuff dreams are made of. That's why Conor's media activity while he was injured was so important. If he had retreated into anonymity, there's no way he would have been given such a high-profile slot. In spite of the layoff, he regularly made the headlines with his interviews and continued the process of making himself a superstar. Having been injured in a fight on the prelims, now he would be returning in a main event. An absolutely remarkable achievement in itself.

That wasn't the only good news for SBG. Gunnar Nelson was booked to fight in the co-main event on the night, and there were a couple of debutants too. Paddy Holohan was handed the chance to kick things off by competing in the opening bout on the card. And finally there was a long-awaited call-up for Cathal Pendred. Both guys had obviously made a good enough impression during their appearances on *The Ultimate Fighter* to earn UFC contracts, although Chris Fields wasn't quite so fortunate. Cathal had been in limbo since filming for his season of *The Ultimate Fighter* had wrapped in October 2013. His contract prohibited him from competing anywhere else until the show aired the following spring, so Cathal had to wait around five months until he finally learned that the UFC was going to give him a shot in Dublin. It was a tough time but the outcome of the fight made it all worthwhile.

It was shaping up to be a massive night for the team, with four fighters competing on a UFC card in Dublin. One of the first things

Conor said when he signed with the UFC was that he was going to break down the door for his teammates to follow. It was starting to look like he had been true to his word. When the UFC last came to town we were begging for the 'token Irish guy' spot on the card. This time it was them approaching us to carry the show, with SBG featuring in four different bouts – including the top two on the bill. We were there on merit. The circumstances couldn't have been any better for Conor's return to the octagon. As his popularity continued to grow, so too did the profile of mixed martial arts in Ireland. UFC Fight Night 46 was going to be one big celebration of that.

Conor had been on the sidelines for a long time, but I had no concerns over his readiness to return. I had been watching him closely in training, observing how his rehabilitation had left him in better shape than he had ever been before. Some fans and sections of the media doubted if he could be the same fighter again, and they were right – because he was even better than the guy they had seen previously. When I saw those questions being asked I just smiled and thought to myself: *Just wait and see. You have no idea what you're about to witness.*

The gap between Conor's surgery and his return to action was going to be 315 days – seven days shorter than Georges St-Pierre's hiatus.

The build-up to the event was a lot of fun. There seemed to be press and TV crews in the gym nearly every day, looking for access to Conor, Gunni, Cathal and Paddy. Irish journalists and reporters who had never reported on MMA before were suddenly looking for a piece of the action. Ireland was gripped by UFC fever. There was no escaping it. The tickets sold out in minutes, which ultimately became a bit of a headache. I was receiving messages from people I hadn't spoken to in years: 'Two will do fine, John. I don't need any more than that. Thanks.'

Six weeks before the event, we received the by-now almost mandatory call informing us that Conor's opponent had pulled out.

Those calls didn't come as a surprise any more. Cole Miller had picked up an injury, so Conor was instead going to face Diego Brandão – who was billed as a Brazilian jiu-jitsu black belt and a ferocious striker. Some people said Cole Miller was going to be the guy to finally expose Conor McGregor. Then they said that it was going to be Brandão.

As usual, the change made no difference to us. Conor was going to be there on 19 July 2014. Whoever the UFC put in front of him, I was convinced that person would be disposed of convincingly.

In the days leading up to the fight, Brandão seemed really up for it. Conor had already started to divide opinion in the MMA world. The people who admired him got behind him fervently. Those on the opposite side of the fence couldn't stand the sight or sound of him. They wanted to see him beaten and they weren't shy in letting his opponents know. Brandão was receiving social media messages asking him to 'Put some manners on McGregor' and 'Shut that Irish guy up' – that sort of thing. But perhaps he was feeling the pressure of that because when he squared up to Conor at the open workouts in front of the fans in Dublin a few days before the fight, he looked extremely worked-up. Tense. He was like a dog on a leash, but I knew he had more bark than bite.

'He's emotionally invested in the contest already,' Conor said to me afterwards. 'This isn't going to end well for him.'

That theme continued at the weigh-ins. Normally how it works is that the UFC line all the fighters up backstage in pairs, so opponents are standing alongside each other while they wait to go out and step on the scales in front of the fans. I don't really know why they do that. It's a bit ridiculous, because sometimes they have to wait there for up to thirty minutes. But I knew Conor wouldn't just stand beside Brandão like some obedient schoolboy, so I brought him up to the front, away from the others. That's what I've since done for every weigh-in, and UFC officials don't ask him to line up with everybody else any more. They know it's safer if Conor and his opponent keep their distance.

Still, Conor and Brandão didn't take their eyes off one another as they both paced back and forth like a couple of ravenous predators sizing each other up in the jungle. Next, Brandão took his T-shirt off and started flexing his muscles. Then Conor did the same, before picking up his Irish flag. Brandão responded by grabbing his Brazilian flag. It was all a bit juvenile, but entertaining at the same time. And I could tell Conor was in control. In these situations, I always know there's method to his madness. Just before it was our turn to head to the stage, they started to exchange words and that's when Brandão said something that I felt was really bizarre.

'When we have the rematch in Brazil, we'll see how much of a tough guy you are then.'

What the hell? They haven't even fought yet and this guy is already talking about a rematch? That, to me, suggested that he had already accepted defeat. I really couldn't get my head around it. Conor laughed.

'A fuckin' rematch? I'm going to destroy you so badly that you'll never even want to see me again, let alone have a rematch.'

It was weird to see how rattled Brandão was psychologically. When I'd seen him earlier in the week he'd been in impressive shape physically, so he had obviously trained extremely hard for the fight, despite the relatively short notice. *This guy is definitely ready for this*, I'd thought. But his mind clearly wasn't prepared. He was all over the place emotionally and that became more evident as the week went on.

It reminded me of something my mam always says to me: 'Why don't you tell Conor to be nicer to his opponents? Maybe then they won't train so hard and that'll be better for him. It's like he's always poking them with a stick.'

But that's exactly what Conor has in mind. He wants to beat the best version of his opponent in order to leave no doubt, uncertainty or excuses. Brandão was an example of a guy who seemed to have done everything right on the physical side, but that wasn't going to count for much when he was an emotional wreck.

It's become traditional for UFC president Dana White to bring the fighters together for a sort of pep talk after the weigh-ins. As they entered the room, the verbal sparring between Conor and Brandão was still going on. Brandão was shouting incessantly like a maniac. He had completely lost it. He then picked up a bottle of water and flung it at Conor. It narrowly missed his head but nearly caused a riot. Afterwards, when they were leaving, Brandão was almost having to be restrained and Conor was just enjoying it all. I felt sorry for Brandão at that stage. Fear leads to anger and hatred, and he was in a bad place mentally. It didn't bode well for what would face him twenty-four hours later.

UFC Fight Night 46 at the O$_2$ Arena in Dublin on Saturday, 19 July 2014, was the greatest night of my professional life. Nothing has topped it since, and I can guarantee you that nothing ever will.

Several factors combined to make that night absolutely perfect. My dream gym had just opened and was thriving; I had four fighters competing on the card; it was in my home town; and the occasion itself was just unbelievable. What an atmosphere. But perhaps most importantly, my parents were there to watch it. I was able to get them cageside seats so they had a great vantage point for all the action. It meant so much to me to have them there. I was really keen to impress them. After our years and years of disagreements about where my life was going, it felt like this was when I finally got to show them what it had all been for. They didn't follow MMA in the media, so they weren't really aware of how big things were getting. This was their opportunity to see it for themselves; to see that I hadn't wasted years of my life after all.

It was appropriate that it was Paddy Holohan who kicked things off in the first fight of the night. I'd nicknamed him 'Berserker' – a type of old Norse warrior. Berserkers were fearless and they were always the first ones into battle, leading the rest of the army behind them. That's a pretty fitting description for Paddy. As an unbeaten fighter who often fought first on the card, he never failed to lay the foundations for a successful night.

Since he became a member of the SBG team, Paddy has been like a little brother to me. MMA is his life, and Brazilian jiu-jitsu in particular. We have that, among many other things, in common. He also shares my passion for coaching. I can never envisage a day when he won't be involved in the sport. Paddy was just a young novice from Tallaght when he started training under me, so it was a special moment for me to be able to walk out behind him in such a famous arena just a few miles from where he was born, as he made his debut on the biggest stage in the world before a live audience of nearly 10,000 and millions more watching across the globe. In the changing rooms you could sense that a special atmosphere was brewing in the arena, but I couldn't have been prepared for the noise that greeted us as Paddy emerged. Veteran journalists who had been covering the sport for years later described it as the loudest UFC event ever. Paddy was the first one to get a taste of it. I don't even know what song he walked out to, because the noise of the crowd completely drowned out the music. Around the octagon, UFC staff exchanged knowing looks. I imagine they were asking themselves, *Why the hell did we wait so long to come back here?*

'The crowd here is like nothing anybody has ever seen before,' Dana White said afterwards. 'I've been doing this for thirteen years and I've never seen anything like it. The fighters have never seen anything like it. The media guys who cover UFC fights all the time have never seen anything like it. It's so crazy here. It's just such a different level.'

Paddy's opponent was a guy named Josh Sampo, from the USA. Having already fought in the UFC twice, Sampo had the edge when it came to experience. Ultimately, however, that counted for little. Paddy is a passionate and patriotic Irishman. There was no way he was going to disappoint in his UFC debut in front of that crowd. Usually for the first fight on a UFC card, the arena would still be mostly empty. That night in Dublin, though, the place was absolutely packed by the time Paddy and Sampo got things started.

It would have been very easy for Paddy to get swept away and caught up in the occasion to the detriment of his performance, but he tapped into that positive energy perfectly. He was having fun in there and Sampo was a little spooked by it. Just over a minute into the fight, Paddy dropped him with an uppercut. While seeking to pass Sampo's guard, Paddy was able to avoid an armbar attempt before taking Sampo's back and forcing him to tap out to a rear naked choke. The perfect start. One down, three to go.

It wasn't quite so straightforward for Cathal Pendred but, then again, Cathal was never interested in doing things the easy way. Halfway through the first round of his middleweight bout against Mike King, Cathal was knocked down with a right hand and King followed up with flurry of strikes on the ground. Cathal was in trouble, no doubt about it. However, Cathal just doesn't quit and I was confident that he'd be able to weather the storm. King continued to unload, then he tried a rear naked choke. When Cathal withstood that, his opponent attempted an armbar. With forty seconds left in the round, Cathal managed to escape and the crowd nearly lifted the roof off the arena. At that point, King's demeanour was telling. He had emptied his tank by trying to put Cathal away when he appeared to be on the verge of victory. But when Cathal got back to his feet, King was baffled. As he stared back at Cathal, he wore a look on his face that said: *What on earth do I have to do to beat this guy?*

As Cathal walked back to his corner at the end of the first round, King was slumped with his hands against the cage, breathing heavily. The guy was absolutely exhausted. Out on his feet. On the other hand, Cathal felt like he hadn't even started yet.

There are times between rounds when, as a coach, you have to deliver specific instructions. Sometimes it's technical advice. On other occasions it's emotional advice. It can also at times be a mixture of both. Here, I had a simple message for Cathal.

'Look over at him, Cathal. He's done. He expended every bit of energy in his body in that round. He's beaten in his own head already. You've been here many times before. Just go out there, take the opportunity when it presents itself and show everybody else that he's beaten too.'

I'm often asked how I know what the right advice to give a fighter is in a particular situation. The end of that first round is a good example. On that occasion, even though he was quite fresh physically, Cathal was still recovering from a tough first round and trying to clear his head, so there was no point in bombarding him with technical information that his mind wasn't in a position to process. It would have gone in one ear and straight out the other. In a scenario like that, it's best to connect with a fighter's emotional side. You've been here before, there's nothing to fear, you've got the upper hand now – that's the kind of thing that will strike a chord in those circumstances. Those lines of communication between coach and fighter don't just develop overnight. You can't fake or force it. If Cathal had been a fighter from another team in that scenario, I wouldn't have been any good to him. The level of trust and understanding needed to make a difference between rounds takes a long time to grow. It's sort of like a relationship with a partner: when you reach the stage where you're so familiar and comfortable in each other's company, a nod or some other similarly minor gesture can communicate a message that you may have once needed words for. In recent years, a lot of fighters have been coming to train at SBG from gyms all over the world. A lot of promising and enthusiastic fighters come through the doors and they're all welcome, but I always explain to them that it's going to take about a year before I'm of any real benefit to them. Of course, I can demonstrate some technical things, but the fighter/coach relationship cannot be manufactured overnight. It will come if it's supposed to, but it takes time.

Cathal bided his time in that second round, before scoring a takedown, taking his opponent's back and submitting him via rear naked choke. Given that it was his lack of a track record for finishing his opponents that had prevented Cathal from earning a UFC contract previously, it was very satisfying to see him win his debut via submission. Not for the first time, Cathal was rewarded for his determination and relentlessness. As he soaked in the adulation of an ecstatic crowd, I couldn't have been happier for him. Nobody deserved it more.

That win over Mike King must surely go down as one of the

most profitable debuts in UFC history. Cathal earned $8,000 to fight plus another $8,000 for winning. On top of that, both he and Mike King picked up an additional $50,000 each as a 'Fight of the Night' bonus. It didn't stop there for Cathal. A few weeks later, the UFC revealed that King had tested positive for performance-enhancing drugs, so he was stripped of his bonus and the money was surrendered to Cathal. The most important win of his career – against a guy who was bigger and on steroids – and $116,000 in the kitty? I'd call that a pretty good start to life in the UFC.

Soon afterwards, Cathal repaid me the €1,000 I'd loaned him to go to *The Ultimate Fighter* – with significant interest.

'Thanks for believing in me, coach,' he said. 'That was a wise investment you made.'

My next duty at UFC Fight Night 46 was to coach Gunnar Nelson in the co-main event against Zak Cummings. Gunni had been training intermittently at SBG for years so the Irish fans already knew that he was worthy of their support, but this was a turning point. This was a night when they truly embraced him as one of their own. Dublin had been his second home for a long time, and it was great to see how the fans got behind him so passionately. He was blown away by the reception, and for the first time ever I saw him display some emotion around a fight.

As for the fight itself, it was classic Gunnar Nelson. A mature, patient build-up, followed by slick jiu-jitsu and a beautiful submission which came near the end of the second round, as Gunni moved one step closer to becoming a title contender.

Finally, the main event. The walk from the changing room to the octagon with Conor McGregor for his fight against Diego Brandão will go to my grave with me. To the Irish people, Conor was no longer just a sportsman. He was an icon. A symbol of national pride. The walk-out was proof of that. In such a scenario, the noise is so loud that your ears don't even hear it any more. It's a very strange feeling. You know you're being engulfed by thousands of screams but it's somehow still peaceful. For a long time, MMA fans in Ireland had been waiting for the chance to shout for one of their own on the biggest stage. Now that the time had come, they were making the most of it. The noise during Conor's introduction was like nothing I had ever heard before. It was officially registered as III decibels – louder than the sound of a jet taking off.

When the contest began, Conor looked superb. It was as if the injury had never occurred. Brandão sought to use his jiu-jitsu, but Conor had little difficulty in subduing that threat. When his left hand came into play, it was game over for Brandão. Just over four minutes into the fight, Conor had made a winning return from injury, dropping Brandão with a punch before swallowing him up on the ground for a first-round TKO.

'I said I was going to put him away in the first round and I put him away in the first round,' Conor said afterwards. 'It would have to be something special to come over here to my home town and take this away from me. There's not a man alive who can come on this soil and beat me. I said it last year: We're not here just to take part. We're here to take over.'

Even though we've had plenty of great nights since then, and I know there are a lot more still to come, I still sometimes daydream and wish I could transport myself back to that night just to experience it all again. It was absolutely amazing.

After each of our fights I made a beeline for my parents and enjoyed a brief moment of celebration with them. Four fights, four victories. That day when I brought them to see The Shed and my mam was in tears seemed like a distant memory now. In many ways, as someone pointed out to me afterwards, the entire event – enormous as it was – had grown from what I had started in that tiny shed thirteen years earlier. My parents were so proud.

When the people around them in the crowd saw me with my mam and dad, they'd ask them: 'How do you know John?' After they told them who they were, fans were asking for selfies; and at the end of the night, my mam and dad were nearly carried out of the arena on the shoulders of the crowd. My father told me it was the proudest day of his life. I really can't put into words how important that was for me. Having had a rocky relationship with him when I was growing up, receiving that level of approval from my dad meant more to me than I could ever explain. Every son probably craves his father's approval. Now, I finally felt like I had it. If I had become the best engineer in the world, it could never have had the same impact as this.

After the fight, Conor went out of his way to thank me publicly: 'John has changed our lives. He's been an inspiration to us all. He is a master of human movement. He's a genius at this game.'

It was kind of funny that he said I was changing my fighters' lives, because the way I saw it was that they were changing mine. I guess that's when you know you're doing things right as a team.

13

If I seemed particularly upbeat around the time of that UFC event in Dublin, it was not solely because things were going well for the team. It was also around that time that I realized I had met the woman I wanted to spend the rest of my life with. Three days after the UFC event, I'd asked that woman to marry me – not a bad week.

As you might expect, I get a lot of social media and e-mail messages from people enquiring about taking up martial arts. One message I received in July 2013 was from a girl from Belfast who was interested in doing kick-boxing lessons. I recommended that she check out Jamie Crawford, a good friend of mine up there who's an excellent Muay Thai and kick-boxing guy. I usually leave it at that when somebody contacts me looking for that kind of information, because I don't have the time to strike up friendly conversations with everybody, but for some reason, when the girl from Belfast replied, I wrote back. She replied, then I replied again, and so on. That went on for quite a while and developed into a regular correspondence that lasted a few weeks. We shared the same sense of humour and just clicked right away.

At the end of July she hopped on a train down to Dublin and I went to Connolly Station to pick her up. That was the first time I met Orlagh Hunter. I brought her to Pintxo's in Temple Bar, one of my favourite tapas places, and we've been together ever since. In June of the following year, after finishing university, she relocated to Dublin and moved in with me.

Orlagh is a massive sports fan with an encyclopaedic knowledge, particularly when it comes to football. She played from a young age and is a big Liverpool fan. When I introduced her to my parents, my dad was delighted: a stunningly beautiful Liverpool supporter who could spend hours talking about football! In his eyes I had met the perfect woman. When we go to meet up with my family on Sundays down at our local pub, Orlagh and my dad will be there yapping on about some game that was on the day before or earlier that afternoon. They could be speaking a different language for all I know. Thankfully for me, she has a similar passion for mixed martial arts. When one of my fighters has an opponent confirmed for their next bout, Orlagh will often be the one giving me the lowdown.

Given how rapidly things had grown at the gym, I needed extra help, and Orlagh began working there full-time after moving to Dublin. We share an office and she takes care of all the membership enquiries and logistical stuff like that, which removes a massive weight from my shoulders. We're in each other's company all day, every day, and I think it takes a special kind of relationship to make that work. But Orlagh's my best friend and I wouldn't have it any other way. She was actually born on 12 November 1991 – exactly two years to the day before the first ever UFC event took place. It's fitting that the true loves of my personal and professional lives share the same birthday.

Gunnar Nelson's win in Dublin was his fourth in the UFC. He was now ranked twelfth in the welterweight division and people were finally beginning to regard him as a legitimate contender.

Eleven weeks after the event in Dublin, the UFC had a big show scheduled for Stockholm. They needed a headliner and, as a popular Nordic fighter who was rapidly on the rise, Gunni was the man for the job. Just over a fortnight after he overcame Zak Cummings, the UFC announced a main event between Gunnar Nelson and Rick Story for UFC Fight Night 53 on 4 October 2014. Story was going to be Gunni's most experienced and highly regarded opponent to date.

It was going to be SBG's second UFC main event in the space of just a few months. Even better, we had fighters competing on separate UFC cards that night in two different parts of the world. Just a couple of hours after the Stockholm event, Paddy Holohan was set to compete at UFC Fight Night 54 in Canada. Unfortunately we haven't mastered human cloning yet, so I couldn't be in Paddy's corner in Nova Scotia. Artem Lobov and Ais Daly were with Paddy instead. With Cathal Pendred also on the Stockholm card, we were aiming to secure three victories in two different places in one night.

For obvious reasons, people usually seem to associate me most with my Irish fighters. However, I've always been closest socially to Gunnar Nelson. Having been with him from such a young age, there's been a very strong friendship between us. He's renowned for never showing any emotion but I can always tell if something's not right with him.

With a lot of momentum behind him and being at the top of the card, the spotlight was on Gunni in a big way during the build-up to that fight. There was much more publicity than he was used to, but he seemed to take it all in his stride. Going into the fight, everything seemed fine. We had a huge amount of respect for Rick Story, who is a great professional and a very dangerous opponent, but I was very confident. Story had previously struggled against top jiu-jitsu guys – Demian Maia ran through him a couple of years earlier – so I felt this would be an ideal opportunity for Gunni to showcase the extent of his ability. I was convinced that he would get the win and make a statement.

But that feeling suddenly changed when we began to go through the pre-fight warm-up. Gunni is probably my only UFC fighter who I still warm up personally. I certainly don't do it with Conor any more, after he chipped one of my teeth before one of his early fights. I leave that to people who enjoy being punched in the face, like Artem Lobov.

As I helped Gunni to prepare, there was a deadness to him that I had never noticed before in all my years of training him. He was completely flat and breathing heavily.

'Gunni, are you okay?' I asked.

'Yeah, I'm good,' was his unconvincing response. But I could tell that he wasn't there. I knew Gunnar Nelson better than any fighter I've ever worked with and this wasn't him.

It was time to walk to the octagon for Gunni's first UFC main event and we were in trouble. I could sense it. To the naked eye, Gunni looked the same as he always did: relaxed and showing no emotion. As Dan Hardy said in his commentary when the fight was about to begin: 'You wouldn't know it was the main event. Gunnar Nelson standing in his corner, he looks like he's waiting for a bus.'

His demeanour may have been the same as it always was, but the performance that followed was nothing like Gunni. He actually started well and looked lively early on. Just under two minutes in, he took Story down with a beautiful inside trip. But then the alarm bells began to ring. Within seconds, Story was back on his feet. I had never seen anybody do that to Gunni, either in the gym or in a fight. Gunni usually just needs one takedown, then it's game over. And that's how it should be.

When Rick Story scrambled back to his feet almost immediately after Gunni got that first takedown, it confirmed my feeling that Gunni wasn't himself. He actually hit his opponent with some really heavy shots, but Story just kept coming forward and putting the pressure on, like the tough bastard that he is. By the end of the second round, Gunni's tank was almost completely empty. What could we do? I knew Story wouldn't submit him, but I was worried that Gunni might get knocked out. I just wanted him to make it to the finish line, but I wasn't sure if he had enough energy left. I kept a very close eye on him as the fight progressed, and I've never been so close to literally throwing in the towel on a fighter's behalf.

After the fight, I received a lot of criticism for the advice I gave to Gunni at the end of the fourth and heading into the fifth and final round.

'Five minutes left. Last round . . . and recover. Last round. All you've got to do is do what you've been doing for the last few rounds. When he skips in, just put those hands up. He knows he's losing the decision so he's going to go wild with his hands in this round.'

I knew my comments would be picked up on the TV broadcast and that I'd probably be slated for them. Of course I didn't believe

Gunni was winning the fight. As far as I was concerned, the fight had already been lost. My priority at that stage was just for him to get through it without being finished, which was why my advice was geared towards encouraging him to play it safe and be careful. That was the best we could hope for now. There was no point in having him risk taking extra damage in pursuit of a finish that he was not capable of getting. As a coach, you have to weigh up what you'd like to see happen versus what you believe the fighter can manage to do. I believed he could last five more minutes of running out the clock for a decision loss. Then we could get out of there and find out what had been the problem. A five-round fight is no joke. I had to take my hat off to Rick Story because he came in and looked much better prepared than he had done for his previous fights. Gunni had prepared well too, but something was obviously amiss.

After the fight, people kept asking me why I didn't tell Gunni to shoot for a takedown going into the fifth round – as if just saying it could have made it happen. This isn't a video game, it's real-life competition against the best fighters in the world. I could see what other people couldn't. Gunni didn't have a takedown left in him because he was absolutely exhausted.

He lost a decision on scores of 50–44, 49–46, 47–48 – oddly, one of the judges had it in Gunni's favour, but even we couldn't agree with that.

Gunni's reaction was the same as it always was. This was the first defeat of his career but, as is the case when he wins, all he was concerned about was getting some food and some rest.

Earlier that night, Cathal Pendred had won a decision against Gasan Umalatov, in spite of a below-par performance. And later that night, in Nova Scotia, Paddy Holohan lost a decision to Chris Kelades. It wasn't our most memorable or successful night but, as always, we took plenty of lessons away from it.

Later, when we sat down to discuss what had gone wrong with Gunni, he admitted that his head wasn't in the right place beforehand as he had been dealing with a personal issue. He'd tried to shake it off and put it to the back of his mind for the sake of the fight, but clearly he hadn't been able to do so and it had had a detrimental impact on his performance.

Professional athletes' personal lives are very rarely taken into account by the audience in the event of a defeat or a bad performance. The fans expect to see the best version of their favourite athlete or team every time they compete. It doesn't enter their minds that those involved may be enduring difficult times in their private lives, just as anybody can. They expect them to operate on autopilot every single time, but it's much more complicated than that. If you're having a bad day in the office because of a personal issue, you can probably get away with it and come back the next day in better form without anyone noticing. But when your workplace is being scrutinized by a global audience of millions, it's not quite so easy to disguise.

Not even a day had passed since the defeat of Diego Brandão before Conor began to hound the UFC about setting up his next fight. Having been out of action for so long owing to the knee injury, Conor felt eager to catch up on lost time and he didn't want to wait too long for his next chance to compete. He has always been driven by competition and he was desperate to get back in there. Dana White was bombarded with text messages, with Conor offering to take any fight from featherweight to welterweight at the drop of a hat. The messages stopped when we were contacted with details of Conor's next assignment just three days after he had beaten Brandão. After that fight in Dublin, Dana had said that Conor's next fight was likely to be in Las Vegas. The UFC knew they needed to bring him to the fight capital of the world and the home of their biggest pay-per-view events. It would be there, at UFC 178 at the famous MGM Grand Garden Arena on 27 September, that he would face his highest-ranked opponent yet.

Dustin Poirier was fifth in the featherweight division, while Conor had moved up to ninth. Although Poirier was six months younger than Conor, the American fighter was much more experienced, with ten fights in the UFC already under his belt, compared to Conor's three. By now it was becoming a recurring theme that

Conor's next opponent was being billed as the guy who would prove to be a step too far for him, and although Poirier was definitely the most experienced one yet, I genuinely had no concerns. In fact, I thought he was less dangerous than Brandão and I was supremely confident about the fight. Poirier is a good fighter, don't get me wrong, but he had been around for a while and been through many wars, and he seemed like the kind of guy who had left his best fights in the gym.

Just ten weeks would separate the Brandão and Poirier fights a pretty quick turnaround – but that didn't seem like a big deal for us. My guys like to remain in fight-shape all the time, which allows them to stay more active than most. We sometimes use Ricky Hatton, the former world champion boxer, as an example of what not to do in that respect. He used to put on an enormous amount of weight between fights by completely abandoning his diet and training, but if you stay fit you can then be ready to seize any opportunity that might arise. This one made perfect sense.

Fighting in Las Vegas for the first time really felt like a big deal. Nothing will ever top the show in Dublin, but Vegas is where you want to be competing when you're involved in combat sports at the highest level. When I was a kid, staying up late to watch Mike Tyson fighting in the early hours of a Sunday morning, Vegas was where it happened. This felt like it was the beginning of Conor's run at the big time in America. And when the event's headliner, UFC light-heavyweight champion Jon Jones, was forced to withdraw from his title defence against Daniel Cormier due to an injury, Conor became an even bigger attraction on the bill.

After earning $32,000 (plus a $50,000 'Performance of the Night' bonus) for beating Diego Brandão, Conor was taking a significant leap forward in the financial stakes for his Vegas debut. Before any of the several sponsorship endorsements he could now boast were even taken into account, Conor was on a guaranteed $75,000 from the UFC per fight, as well as an additional $75,000 to win. That made him the second-highest-paid fighter at the event, behind only UFC flyweight champion Demetrious Johnson, whose flyweight title bout against Chris Cariaso would now headline the card. There were a lot of other top fighters on the UFC 178 card – Donald Cerrone, Tim Kennedy, Dominick Cruz – who had been around for a lot longer than Conor, but who weren't earning that much. Some of them might not have been too pleased, but Conor's earnings were an indication of the scale of the impact he'd had on the UFC as a company in such a short period. The days of queueing for his unemployment benefit at the post office in Lucan were a distant memory.

As UFC CEO Lorenzo Fertitta said at the time:

> At the end of the day, it's a business. [The] guy can literally drive numbers from an entire country. When Conor fights, the entire country of Ireland shuts down. He moves the needle on pay-per-view. He headlined his first event in Ireland, did a $1.4 million gate. Of course we're going to reward guys that are successful in the octagon and have a lot of wins and things like that, but when a guy is bringing the kind of excitement that Conor is bringing, then you're going to have the ability to potentially drive a little bit harder of a negotiating bargain because you do bring that to the UFC.

In order to get acclimatized, we decided to leave for Las Vegas about four weeks out from the fight. Conor was due to meet Artem Lobov and me for our flight, but after we arrived at the airport he called and said he was struggling with a cold and didn't feel like flying.

'I'll be fine,' Conor said. 'I'll just give myself a few days to get better. You go ahead and I'll follow you out later in the week.'

I wasn't sure about flying out without Conor, but if he was feeling unwell then he wasn't going to be training anyway, so we decided to proceed and wait for Conor to recover while we soaked up some Nevada sunshine. And I'm glad we did, because Artem and I enjoyed that few days. A lot.

My only previous trip to Vegas was the few days we had spent there while Conor was sorting out his visa for the fight in Boston a year or so earlier, but we didn't get the chance to do much and the hotel we stayed in was a bit of a dump. This time, we were met at the airport and taken to the Red Rock Resort. It's a very plush hotel on the outskirts of the city, about a half-hour's drive from the main strip. It is owned by the Fertitta brothers, Frank and Lorenzo, who also own the UFC. We had no idea where the UFC were putting us up when we landed, so we were quite excited when we ended up at the Red Rock. When we were shown to our room, it blew our minds. The place was incredible, with a cool balcony and a massive refrigerator that was stocked full of snacks and drinks.

'Conor's going to be disgusted when he sees what he's missing out on,' Artem said.

'There must be some mistake,' I responded. 'Surely there's no way they're putting us up in a place like this for the next month. Maybe we're just here for the first night as a bit of a treat and they'll turf us out into the most basic room tomorrow night. This is a bit too good to be true.'

We figured that we might as well make the most of the hospitality while we could. For the first couple of days, whenever we had any drinks from the room we replaced them with drinks we bought at the supermarket, because we assumed that would be much cheaper. We didn't want to be charged an arm and a leg for a tiny can of beer. We took a cab downtown, but it was a $100 round trip so we decided to just stay in the hotel from then on as that was a bit too expensive. That was until Artem got talking to a Russian girl who worked on reception.

'Are you guys going out downtown tonight?' she asked.

'Nah,' said Artem. 'It costs too much to get there and back.'

'Well, why don't you just get Dave to take you?'

'Who's Dave?'

'Your driver.'

'We have a driver?'

'Yes, he's on call for you 24/7. He'll take you anywhere you want to go.'

'Free of charge?' I chimed in.

'Of course. Everything is complimentary for you guys,' she replied.

'Even the food and drinks?'

'Everything.'

She also told us that the room we were in cost $1,500 per night. Artem and I just looked at each other and tried not to giggle. We spent a lot of the time over the next few days being driven around by Dave in a limousine. Most of the time we didn't even need to go anywhere. We were just like two kids who were getting a kick out of being chauffeured around Las Vegas in a limo. We also didn't hold back on the food and drinks, building up an enormous bill. We'd empty the fridge but the hotel would have it stocked up again almost immediately. It was pretty juvenile, but what else do you expect from two guys with a lot of free time on their hands in Las Vegas?

When Conor finally arrived, feeling fresh and healthy again, we playfully taunted him about missing out on all the fun.

'Sorry, Conor,' I said. 'We've already taken the good room. You'll have to settle for a standard single room, I'm afraid.'

As it turned out, our room was nothing in comparison to what had been set aside for Conor. He was upstairs, one floor from the top, in a $7,500-a-night suite with two butlers. The only superior suite to that one was on the very top floor, and Alicia Keys was staying in that. Being afforded such luxury by the UFC was an indication of how highly they were beginning to value Conor. It was something he'd quickly get used to.

Artem and I had a good time for a few days, but we got down to business once Conor arrived. Thankfully he was showing no effects from his illness, so he was able to put in a really strong last few weeks of work. Lorenzo Fertitta has a private gym in the basement, which is a very cool facility, so that's where we worked out. Conor looked in great shape during the final stages of the training camp, which merely added to my confidence that an emphatic victory was on the cards.

As the fight approached, it seemed clear that while there were a lot of big bouts on the UFC 178 bill, none was generating anywhere near the same kind of hype as McGregor versus Poirier. According to the UFC, 11 per cent of the 10,500 tickets for the event had been purchased from Ireland, but in the days beforehand, the Irish presence in town suggested that was a conservative tally. Vegas was mobbed by Irish fans. It was hard to believe that so many had travelled so far for the fight. The support and goodwill were unbelievable. We couldn't go anywhere without being stopped and wished well. It wasn't just Irish people either. Americans too, people from all over the world, were behind Conor – passionately so. Conor doesn't seem to have any casual fans. The people who support him do so almost religiously. We had seen already how things were taking off in Dublin, but this was when we realized Conor McGregor was truly a global phenomenon.

A couple of days before the fight, we moved from the Red Rock to the hotel at the MGM Grand in order to be closer to the arena. On the day before the fight, the morning before the weigh-ins, while Conor was going through the final stages of his weight-cut, I had to dash downstairs from our room to the lobby to ask for more towels. While I was making my way across the casino floor, I heard my name being called.

'Hey, John! Coach!'

I turned and saw a group of Irish lads waving at me from one of the bars. I assumed they just wanted to wish us luck so I waved back and said, 'Thanks, guys.'

But they were gesturing for me to come closer. 'Get over here, coach!'

'For what?' I asked, as I was in a bit of a hurry.

'To drink some shots with us.'

'Guys,' I replied. 'It's eight o'clock in the morning.'

'So?'

I guess that's Vegas for you.

Conor's ability to get inside his opponent's head long before the fight takes place is often spoken about. We had seen evidence of that for the Diego Brandão fight, and there was plenty more with Dustin Poirier. Even prior to the fight being announced, Poirier had been calling Conor out for quite some time via the media. Clearly envious of the amount of attention – and financial rewards – he was receiving, despite being new on the scene, a lot of guys didn't like Conor. Poirier in particular seemed to have a bee in his bonnet. He claimed that he would win the fight easily, while Conor was predicting a first-round knockout: 'Dustin thinks it's all talk, but when he wakes up with his nose plastered across the other side of his face, he's going to know it's not all talk.'

They traded insults at press conferences, and the build-up allowed Conor to put his personality on display to his biggest audience yet. In America they call it 'trash talk', but for Conor, he's just telling his opponents what he really believes. Some people reckon it's disrespectful, and while he has overstepped the mark on a couple of occasions and ended up apologizing for things he has said, that aspect of his character is something I would never try to moderate or influence. In fact, I enjoy watching his verbal exchanges with opponents. It's part of the fight game and it has always been a big part of Conor's arsenal. It's all good fun for him, and it's a Dublin thing: I think you can trace it back to Crumlin, where there is real wit and edge to the way young lads talk. If you can't give and take a bit of ribbing, you're going to be in for a tough time.

If we can agree that one purpose of prize-fighting is to make as much money as possible from your career, then what Conor is doing – being entertaining outside the octagon as well as in – makes sense. It sells tickets, it sells pay-per-view, it raises the profile of MMA. As Muhammad Ali used to say, half the people wanted to watch him kick ass, the other half wanted to watch him get his ass kicked. It's the same for Conor. We're talking here about a sport where the athletes are risking serious injury and careers are short. Conor understands this, and he makes no bones about wanting to make as much money as he can, while he can.

My own involvement in martial arts stemmed from my passion for the sport, not a desire to make money, but I recognize the importance of being rewarded for the risks you take. At professional level, athletes compete – first and foremost – to earn a living. There are significant dangers involved in MMA. If your fighting career lasts several years, you're putting your body – and particularly your head – on the line. When someone tells me that they want to fight professionally, I'm careful to ensure they appreciate the gravity of the decision they're about to make. People can take up MMA training to improve their lifestyle and health, but it's another thing entirely if they're opting to compete. They have to understand the dangers involved, especially when it comes to the risk of brain injury – one of the reasons we discourage heavy sparring. In my own fighting days, I probably didn't fully understand the risks. I want to make sure that every fighter at SBG knows exactly what's involved before they decide to step into the cage. If and when they do, I'll do everything I can to make sure they get the most from their career. In an ideal world, they'll earn enough money to set them up for life. That won't always be the case, but it's most certainly the aim. Of course, only a select few are going to earn as much as Conor McGregor. But as long as the fighters are making the kind of money that allows them to create a comfortable living for themselves and their families, that's all you can ask.

If ever I feel that someone is sustaining too much damage in pursuit of success I'll intervene and communicate my thoughts, and they'll usually call it a day. I've done it before and I know I'll have to do it again. As a coach, that's my responsibility.

The weigh-ins before UFC 178 were similar to the Brandão fight, with Conor being restrained while he did his best to antagonize Poirier, who was clearly already on edge. As we waited behind the door, I thought I could hear loud chants of 'Olé, Olé, Olé'. When we entered, I saw that the room at the MGM Grand was packed with Irish fans, who erupted when Conor emerged.

I turned to Dana White and said: 'Are we in Las Vegas or Dublin here?'

'It's unbelievable,' he said. 'I've never seen anything like this before.'

Poirier lost it after he weighed in. He began shouting and aggressively pointing at the crowd as they jeered him. He just seemed to be full of negative energy. Ten weeks on from the Brandão fight, there was definitely a sense of déjà vu. I guess it was pretty surprising to see these experienced UFC fighters being so wound up psychologically by this cheeky young lad from Dublin who was still very much a newcomer on this stage. Conor seemed to have the entire roster in a bit of a tizzy. You assume that these experienced fighters have seen it all before, but I suppose there had never been anyone like Conor. Watching how the likes of Brandão and Poirier handled it – or failed to handle it – I realized that most of the guys in this game were novices in that particular area. When Conor came in and raised the tide, most of them drowned.

Walking out for a fight at the MGM Grand was a surreal experience. I had watched so many fights there over the years and now I was about to be a part of one. What made it even more surreal was the number of Irish fans in the arena. Yet again, Conor was going to have the majority of the support despite fighting an American guy in the US.

Conor continued to taunt Poirier as the referee, Herb Dean, brought the fighters together beforehand to give them their final instructions. Once the contest began, he charged straight out and threw a big hook-kick which narrowly missed Poirier's head. You could see the look on Poirier's face change immediately and he barely took another step forward for the remainder of the fight.

Conor controlled the dynamic of the fight and chipped away with punches that were visibly rocking Poirier, who wasn't able to counter with much more than a couple of harmless leg-kicks. Conor hurt Poirier with a big left about ninety seconds in, which left him unsteady on his feet. Seconds later, Conor connected again – this time at the back of Poirier's right ear – and the American went down. After a couple of extra shots to seal the deal, Herb Dean stepped in to confirm Conor's fourth win in the UFC. Officially, it took him one minute and forty-six seconds. A first-round knock-out, just as he had promised.

'I don't just knock them out, I pick the round,' Conor said in his post-fight interview in the octagon. 'You can call me "Mystic Mac" because I predict these things. These featherweights don't understand, it's a whole other ball-game when they get hit by me. I wanted to come over here to America and show the American public the new era of "The Fighting Irish" and I brought my whole country with me. If one of us goes to war, we all go to war.'

The UFC had known for a long time that they were on to something special with Conor, but each fight just raised the hype to the next level. He had now done it under the bright lights of Las Vegas against one of the leading contenders in the division. Just twelve months on from undergoing surgery on an injury that could easily have kept him out of the octagon for a couple of years, Conor had worked himself into a position where the very top was now within touching distance.

'Wow! That's the real deal, ladies and gentlemen. Make no mistake about it, Conor McGregor is for real,' said Joe Rogan afterwards. 'He really did just make it look easy. That's the real deal. That was just glorious. No one has ever done that to Poirier before.'

After the event, Conor entertained the watching world at the post-event press conference in a brand-new ivory suit. He was awarded a $50,000 'Performance of the Night' bonus, which took his payout for the fight to $200,000. Designer suits had become a staple of his newly acquired wealth and I pinched one of them for the celebrations that night.

14

With women's MMA growing thanks to the likes of Ronda Rousey, the UFC decided to create a second weight division for women. It would be launched through a season of *The Ultimate Fighter* in 2014, with the winner becoming the inaugural UFC strawweight champion. When Aisling Daly was offered a contract to compete, it was the perfect opportunity for her to achieve what she had always aspired to.

On her full UFC debut, in Vegas on 12 December 2014, she submitted Alex Chambers with an armbar in the first round. The win was overshadowed a bit by the fact that she failed to make weight. That was a first for SBG in the UFC, and hopefully we won't see it happen again. But the win was a special moment for Ais, who had finally got thc chance to perform on the biggest stage.

While Ais was becoming the latest SBG fighter to win in the UFC, Conor was busy preparing for his next fight. We were maybe a little disappointed not to have been offered a bigger name than Dennis Siver, but we'd never turned down a fight yet, and we weren't going to start now. As we had been saying all along, the opponents didn't matter. Each of these guys was just another minor obstacle between Conor and the champion, José Aldo. I believed he was already too good for them all, so it didn't make much difference who he fought. Conor could beat them, regardless of their name, record, attributes or anything else.

After the win against Dustin Poirier, we felt Conor had done enough to earn a shot at the featherweight title. The UFC didn't necessarily disagree, but the problem was that Aldo was already scheduled to defend the belt against Chad Mendes, four weeks after the Poirier fight. If Aldo won, which we fully expected him to, there would likely be a long gap before his next title defence, because he wasn't renowned for staying active. During his three and a half years in the UFC, Aldo had fought just six times. Conor had already spent enough time out of action owing to his knee injury, so he had no interest in sitting out and waiting to see what happened. He wanted to go again — ideally before the end of 2014 — and harassed the UFC about arranging another fight. There were no openings for him to compete again before the end of the year, but with an event scheduled for Boston on 18 January 2015, who better to headline in the home of Irish America than Conor McGregor? He had moved up to fifth in the featherweight rankings, while Dennis Siver was down in tenth. Sure, it would have been nice to fight one of the top contenders, but the reality was that in spite of what they said in interviews, very few of them put their hands up for the opportunity.

Dennis Siver was a veteran of over thirty professional fights, and he had first joined the UFC way back in 2007. I knew quite a lot about him from his days of competing on the European circuit. In fact, Arni Isaksson had submitted him in the final of an eight-man Cage Warriors welterweight tournament in 2006. Siver had also only recently returned from being suspended for using performance-enhancing drugs — something Conor regularly reminded him of in the media during the build-up to the fight: 'He's a midget, German, steroid head.'

I respected Dennis for his ability and experience, and while anything can happen on any given night, a short, stocky, thirty-six-year-old veteran wasn't going to cause Conor any major headaches. I was sure of that.

As Ireland gradually came to terms with its status as the home of the biggest male star in mixed martial arts, the amount of press coverage of the sport increased dramatically. It was a famine-to-feast journey in the space of less than two years, given that MMA had previously been completely ignored by major Irish media outlets.

One consequence of the increased public interest in Ireland was to focus attention on the question of whether MMA is too violent. I took part in a few debates in the media and they usually seemed to follow the same pattern, with me putting forward the facts and the person on the opposing side stating an opinion along the lines of: 'I just don't like it.' I had been having the same debate for years – with friends, family or anyone else who asked – ever since I first became involved in the sport. The difference now was that a lot more people were listening.

The question of whether MMA is too violent ultimately comes down to definitions. Violence, to me, suggests an altercation in which one party doesn't actually want to be involved. I don't understand how that word can be used to describe a sporting contest – whether it's MMA, boxing or something else – in which two consenting adults are participating willingly. In fact, I believe it's quite an honourable thing for two individuals to agree to compete against one another under a specified set of rules, on a particular date, at an agreed weight, officiated by a referee and judges.

In the run-up to the Siver fight, an Irish politician, Senator Catherine Noone, called for 'this vile so-called sport' to be banned in Ireland, while adding that she had never actually watched a fight. The senator quickly backed down, admitting that she had 'jumped the gun'. Unfortunately, she received a lot of nasty verbal abuse from MMA fans as a result of her comments, which didn't exactly help to improve the reputation of the sport and those involved in it. I've always found that the most effective way to change someone's opinion for the better is to encourage them to attend an event or visit a gym. It gives them an opportunity to see at first hand that the individuals involved are just everyday people who enjoy competitive sport, not bloodthirsty savages. We invited Senator Noone to the gym and she took us up on the offer. Following her visit, far from calling for MMA to be banned, she was now calling for it to be recognized by the Irish Sports Council. She's an extremely nice lady who made some ill-informed comments while speaking from a position of ignorance, but that soon changed when she had a chance to see what the sport is really about.

I absolutely accept that MMA is not for everybody and I have no problem with that. If you don't like it, you don't have to watch it.

We live in a free society where we're fortunate enough to have a large variety of activities to choose from. If you dislike one of them, that's not a justifiable reason for it to be banned. I find it odd that so many people are fascinated by seeing a little guy whipping a horse around a track, but I just turn over when horse racing is on TV and I don't think any more about it. In terms of danger, statistically speaking, MMA falls around the same level as other contact sports. There is a perception that MMA is more dangerous than boxing, but a long-term Canadian study showed that boxers sustain more serious damage than MMA fighters. Competing in MMA, you end up shipping the same kind of bumps and bruises that you see in rugby, but the rate of serious injury is low.

I've never fallen out with anybody over the MMA debate, but I was definitely red-faced from discussing it so often throughout my twenties. I tried to convert people to my way of thinking, like a vegan or a CrossFitter who's so into what they're doing that they constantly talk about it and can't fathom how others aren't equally passionate. I definitely went through periods when I'd call into radio shows and have heated back-and-forth arguments if the issue was up for discussion. I guess I'm a lot more mellow now.

MMA has garnered an enormous number of new fans in Ireland and there's an onus of responsibility on them to represent the sport well. In that regard, it's important to acknowledge that without its most passionate fans, MMA might not have survived. In the dark ages of the early noughties, the UFC was struggling. It was the rabid fans on the internet forums who kept it alive by spreading the word to their friends and trying to convert anybody they could. The premiere of *The Ultimate Fighter* in 2005 marked the dawn of a new era, but the UFC – and by extension, the sport of MMA – probably wouldn't have made it that far were it not for the fans and how much it meant to them. It's always important to remember that. But at the same time, I do often cringe when I see the behaviour of some fans online, particularly when it comes to how cantankerous they become when defending the sport if it's coming in for criticism. Instead of berating somebody because they don't like MMA, fans should take a more positive approach by seeking to introduce them to it in an amicable manner. That's the best way an MMA fan can fly the flag for the sport.

If someone comes to SBG, they'll probably see a kids' jiu-jitsu class and meet intelligent people like Owen Roddy and Peter Queally. It's no different from what you'll find in any sporting environment. Of course, that's not to say that there aren't any dickheads involved in MMA. As in any sport, the law of averages dictates that there'll be a few bad eggs.

Obesity is a far greater concern for society than the aggression involved in some sports. I once heard a former Gaelic football player, when asked if soccer was the enemy of his sport, respond that the only enemy is inactivity. The most important thing is to encourage kids to be physically active, whether it's through martial arts, ball games, gymnastics or something else entirely.

Growing up, I spent all day, every day, running around outside, but I never, ever remember being tired. Nowadays, during their first session in my gym, some kids are on their knees and out of breath after doing a lap or two of the mat. That's worrying. Our children are becoming less and less mobile, and that's going to put a massive strain on our health service in years to come, when it's asked to care for a generation of people with weaker bones, more fat, little lean muscle and weakened immune systems. All these things are going to cause serious problems, so I'll support any movement that gets kids active.

Then there's the fact that we now live in a society where everyone's afraid of being sued. Councils are reluctant to build playgrounds for fear of being taken to court if a child is injured while using one. Kids fall and suffer bumps and bruises; sometimes they break bones. So what? It's part of growing up. Inactivity is far more dangerous long term than a scratch on the knee.

I'm sometimes asked if I'd like to see any changes made to the rules of MMA in order to make it more palatable to a wider audience, but the answer to that is always an emphatic no. What I would like to see in fights is a ten-minute first round, like in the old days of the Pride promotion. Or, better yet, fifteen-minute fights with no breaks, i.e. no rounds at all. In that instance I believe we would see very few fights going the distance to a decision. It would test fighters' ability to last the pace, which would then provide a much clearer examination of their skills as they'll be required to perform while combating fatigue. I'm tempted to run a show on these lines at local level to see how it would work. Somewhat paradoxically, I believe this would actually reduce the amount of unnecessary damage that fighters occasionally take. Removing that one-minute rest between rounds would change the entire dynamic. Sometimes a fighter may be close to being stopped at the end of a round, but then he has sixty seconds of respite, paving the way for him to possibly receive even more damage in the next round. The UFC Fight Night 85 bout between Neil Magny and Hector Lombard is an example of this. Lombard shipped a huge number of unanswered strikes in the latter stages of the second round, before he was finally stopped after twenty-six seconds of the third. With no breaks, I believe more fights would be stopped at the right time and fighters would therefore actually receive less damage.

The standard of judging in MMA is often criticized. Pretty much every UFC event throws up at least one controversial decision from the judges. People have suggested other methods of scoring a fight than having three guys sitting cageside and calling it as they see it, but the reality is that no system will ever be perfect because it's ultimately a matter of opinion. Judging could be done by simply counting takedowns and strikes, like the system used in amateur boxing in which the judges press a button on a machine whenever a scoring punch is landed, but that wouldn't work in MMA: the sport is far too intricate and judging must inevitably be subjective. Judging MMA fights is like tasting two different varieties of the same soup. Even if they're similar, you're going to prefer one over the other and there's no scientific reasoning for that. I also think it's impossible to have a judge who doesn't bring his own emotions into the equation. Maybe he has a connection to one of the fighters – he might be a friend of the fighter's coach or a teammate – or perhaps he doesn't like what he's seen from the fighter in the media (in which case Conor might be in trouble if he ever goes the distance again!). A judge from a grappling background might score a fight differently from one whose background is in kick-boxing.

The bottom line is that there are always going to be grey areas when human beings are involved, and, to be honest, I'm okay with that. You might see a strange decision now and again, but surely that's to be expected. I think judges get it right the vast majority of the time, even if the loser's fans on social media often try to convince us otherwise.

Conor put in another really good training camp for the fight against Dennis Siver. The way he manages to improve between fights is remarkable. Just when you start to think he can't get much better, he proves you wrong.

A couple of weeks before the fight, Dana White announced that Conor would be rewarded for a win over Siver with a title shot against José Aldo, who had successfully defended the belt against Chad Mendes in October. Dana's revelation was big news at the time, but it didn't really change anything for us. It was what we had been expecting. No other fight made sense at that stage. So here we were, just two years on from Conor's last fight with Cage Warriors, and he was officially one win away from fighting for the biggest prize in the sport.

One obstacle we encountered for the fight against Siver was that Conor's weight-cut was trickier than normal. The fight was scheduled to take place three weeks after Christmas, and being extremely strict with your diet can be very challenging over the festive period. In addition to that, cutting weight is always more difficult in cold weather, and Boston in January is pretty damn cold. When we arrived there a fortnight before the fight, the set-up was a lot more basic than what we had enjoyed in Vegas. At that stage in the process, it's essential to eat the right food because your portions are pretty small. It's mostly salads and stuff like that. The selection on the menu at the hotel wasn't great, however, so that posed another little challenge.

The weight-cutting process has become much more sophisticated over the years — we've gradually worked out the right way of doing things — but it took me quite a while to learn. I remember doing a same-day weigh-in for one of my own fights and I really pushed myself to the limit to make 145lb. After the weigh-in, with the fight itself just a few hours away, how did I refuel? By immediately scoffing down a massive pizza! I hadn't a clue what I was doing. Thankfully, nowadays we've acquired the knowledge from years of experience to do things a little smarter.

The weight-cutting process is different for every fighter, but it generally involves weeks of strict dieting, several days of water-loading on fight week, followed by an intense twenty-four hours of draining fluids from the body — usually via a sauna or a hot salt bath. Conor favours the latter, although it's fairly arduous. I had to laugh once when I returned from helping one of my fighters to cut their last few pounds in the bath and Orlagh said she'd like to try it some time — as if it were a case of putting on some music, lighting a few candles and chilling out in a nice, relaxing bath for an hour! In reality, you're spending hours in a hot bath, with Epsom salts drawing the fluids out of your body.

In the weeks leading up to the fight, you're reducing your calorie intake in stages while simultaneously trying to maintain your levels in training. It requires a lot of discipline because there's always temptation. Then, usually on the Sunday before a Saturday-night fight, the water-loading phase starts. That involves drinking as much as eight to ten litres of water a day, to the point where it can make you feel physically sick. Those few days result in the fighter piling on water-weight. Then Thursday afternoon comes and the cut begins in earnest with the baths or the sauna. The heat draws the moisture from the body and the pounds fall off, but it's long and it's arduous and it's bloody unpleasant. Getting those last few pounds off can be pure torture. It's both a physical and mental test, and a lot of people break.

Because I work with fighters, I sometimes get people asking for advice on how to lose weight. Often it's women who are trying to slim down for a wedding. They've heard of an MMA fighter who cut ten pounds in twenty-four hours and want to know what the secret is. But there is no secret. Cutting weight and losing weight are very different things. If a fighter completely drains their body in order to get to a certain weight for a couple of hours for a weigh-in, they'll put that weight back on again in the following twenty-four hours as they take on fluids and refuel their body for the fight. The whole painful process is geared towards gaining as much of a size advantage as you can on fight night.

It's funny that for the majority of the week, fighters are forcing water down their throats until they get to a point where they feel like they never want to drink again, yet by the time Friday arrives, they'd do anything for a drink. It's a weird, lopsided cycle. During that last twenty-four hours, food and water are out of the question as it's all about becoming as light as possible. It's a massive relief when they've stepped on the scales and made the weight, but the responsibility to be professional doesn't end there. Refuelling and rehydrating is a very delicate process. You can't just flood your body with food and fluids immediately, despite the urge to do so. It's about getting minerals and electrolytes in at the right times so that your system is given time to recover. Eating small portions of good carbohydrates – pasta, mashed potatoes, etc. – at regular intervals is the way to go.

Artem Lobov used to make life difficult for himself when cutting weight. Instead of slowly bringing his weight down as the fight approached, he usually left it to the last minute so that he had a huge amount still to cut in a very short period of time. When I'm there to help him, we sail through it; but if he's left to his own devices it's not so straightforward.

For one of his fights, Artem still had about thirteen pounds to cut on the evening before the weigh-ins, i.e. just shy of one stone in under twenty-four hours. He decided that he'd cut half that night and do the other half the next morning. After a few intense hours, Artem had managed to get rid of seven pounds before going to bed to get some rest. He woke shortly afterwards, feeling a bit delirious. He was extremely thirsty, and he remembered that there was a two-litre bottle of Fanta in his refrigerator. *I'll go down and have a little sip just to quench my thirst*, he thought. Ten minutes later, he was sitting at his kitchen table, staring at an empty bottle of Fanta. He had consumed every last drop – and put back on all the weight that he had spent the evening torturing himself to cut. He was back up at dawn and spent the entire morning in the bath to make up for his mistake, with his mother holding him down to make sure he couldn't back out. Artem still managed to make the weight, but that's a good example of how not to do it.

Weigh-ins usually begin at 4 p.m. With Conor on weigh-in day, I'm in his hotel room by 9 a.m. and I don't leave until 2 p.m. It's a long, difficult five hours of hot bath after hot bath after hot bath. It's well publicized by now that Conor cuts a significant amount of weight to make the featherweight limit of 145lb. He doesn't look healthy when he steps on the scales. We've taken some pictures while the weight-cutting process is ongoing and it's not pretty. I'm sure he'll treat you to those when he writes his own story. It's difficult to watch, particularly for Dee, his girlfriend. Fighters subject themselves to severe dehydration and overheating in order to make the weight and it's everyone's least favourite part of the game. At his lowest ebb while doing it, it evokes a 'never again' type of feeling for Conor. But when he arrives on stage to step on the scales, with the Irish tricolour draped over his shoulders and thousands of fans going berserk, the adrenaline kicks in and it ignites a fire in his belly that makes the suffering seem worthwhile.

That evening, after Conor has had several hours to replenish his system, I'll be in my room and he'll send through some pictures of himself looking human again. I still worry that he might get stomach cramps during the night, but then a text message will come through the following morning: 'Feeling great. Slept like a baby.'

That's always a massive relief. At that stage – bar a few minor little things that are to be said and done – my job is over. There's not much more I can do. He's made the weight and it's time to fight, and that's a satisfying feeling because that's what we're here for. We're involved in mixed martial arts to become the best fighter, not the best weight-cutter. The weight-cut is just a necessary evil that has to be dealt with before the fun can begin.

Extreme weight-cutting has become a hot topic in the world of MMA recently, particularly following the deaths of fighters in the run-up to fights in Brazil and the Philippines. It almost got to a stage where fighters were competing with each other to see who could cut the most weight, but I'm pleased to say that culture seems to be changing. The UFC's ban on intravenous rehydration has helped, while other promotions are beginning to monitor their fighters' weight over an extended period instead of for just one moment on the day before the fight. I welcome any move that changes the practice for the better. I'm in favour of anything that discourages fighters from putting themselves in danger by pushing their bodies beyond the limit with dehydration.

In an ideal world, cutting to that extent wouldn't be required, and I'm always conscious of ensuring that it doesn't become such a chore that it ends up taking the enjoyment out of the entire sport for a particular fighter. They're also less likely to make improvements in their last few weeks of training if the weight-cut is starting to interfere with the amount of work they're capable of putting in.

Eventually I think Conor will leave the 145lb division behind, but with someone as experienced as him, it's ultimately his decision. Nowadays with my newer fighters, I use my own experience to decide which weight class is best for them. But for the likes of Conor, it's a case of discussing what's on offer for each fight and weighing up whether it's worth another cut to 145lb. Despite winning his last pre-UFC fight as a 155lb fighter, Conor was signed by the organization as a featherweight because the contract offer had come via Sean Shelby, who matches all UFC fights from 145lb and below. From lightweight upwards, Joe Silva is the orchestrator. Had Joe made the initial offer, things would probably have been different. That was just the luck of the draw.

Weigh-in day for Conor's fight against Dennis Siver was 17 January, a date that had a real resonance for me – and not just because it's my dad's birthday. It was on 17 January 2009 that Tom Egan lost to John Hathaway at UFC Dublin. As a team, that was our first taste of the big time. That introduction to the highest level of the sport had shown us exactly what was required.

When Conor weighed in, he made 145lb for the first time in the UFC. That was a statement. He'd come in at 146lb for all his previous fights, because an additional one-pound buffer is allowed for non-title bouts. The belt wasn't on the line just yet, but Conor wanted to let the world know that he was ready for it.

To build up the hype, the UFC brought José Aldo to Boston to sit cageside for the fight. Their plan was to bring him into the octagon afterwards if Conor was victorious. However, Aldo refused, saying that he only enters the octagon when he's fighting – which was odd, because I remember seeing him in there playing football with Kenny Florian when they were promoting their bout in 2011.

On fight night, Paddy Holohan – the 'Berserker' yet again – got us off to a positive start in front of an attendance of just under 14,000 at the TD Garden. Paddy bounced back from the first defeat of his career three months earlier by turning in an utterly dominant performance against Shane Howell to win via unanimous decision.

Cathal Pendred was next out and he also went the distance before securing his third consecutive win in the UFC at the expense of Sean Spencer. There was plenty of controversy in the aftermath, with many observers of the opinion that Cathal was fortunate to be given the decision. Two of the three judges actually gave Cathal all three rounds. While I felt that he probably lost the first round, I thought he definitely did enough in the second and third to swing it.

I thought a lot of the debate surrounding the result stemmed from Joe Rogan's commentary on the fight. When Joe starts to see one guy getting the upper hand, his mind seems to be made up and he can't see it any other way. Sean started well, so that seemed to settle it for Joe, but there's more to a fight than the first round.

Finally, then, it was time for Conor to seal the fight he had building towards ever since that very first call came from the UFC: a title bout against José Aldo. I'd describe the fight with Dennis Siver as straightforward, although Conor's crystal ball was a little faulty on this one. He predicted another first-round knockout, but it was just under two minutes into the second round before the contest was brought to a halt. It followed a similar pattern to his previous outings, with Conor looking calm and relaxed as he overwhelmed his opponent with pressure and vastly superior striking and movement. Siver was tough, but it was simply a matter of time before he caved. Conor dropped him with a straight left to the body, then moved into full mount with a beautiful pass before forcing the stoppage due to strikes after one minute fifty-four of the second round. Conor was disappointed not to have finished it inside the first five minutes, but afterwards he said he felt like he was operating at a maximum of 40 per cent of his ability.

At the end of the fight, I went to shake hands with Siver's coach. But when he turned and saw me, he just started shouting angrily at me in German. Conor had antagonized Siver's camp beforehand with some of the things he had said and obviously they weren't going to let go of that. Siver himself was absolutely fine, but the coach didn't seem to take defeat well. I've been on the losing side many, many times. Irrespective of the outcome, or of what's been said in the build-up, I believe it's important to recognize that once the fight is over, respect should come to the fore and differences should be left in the past. I just don't understand any other way of doing things. It's a game, albeit a very intense one. As long as you've worked as hard as you can, you should be at peace with the result, whether it goes in your favour or not. Luck also plays a bigger part than we'd all care to admit, so don't be too hard on yourself when you lose and don't go overboard with patting yourself on the back when you win. That's been my approach from the start and it will continue to be until the end.

Conor, meanwhile, had other things on his mind once the fight ended. He laid eyes on José Aldo in his seat cageside, then scaled the cage and made a beeline for his next opponent. With the champion smiling back at him, Conor roared into his face: 'Eire! Eire!'

Aldo looked like he was enjoying it. In an interview afterwards, he said he was excited about the fight because it was going to make him a lot of money and it would be an easy defence of his title. *You're right about one part of that*, I thought.

The cageside confrontation between Conor and José made for great television and it kindled the rivalry that was to develop between them. No date for the fight had even been agreed yet, but you immediately got the sense that this was going to be very, very big. It was an exciting way to round off another monumental night for SBG. Three UFC wins, one of which secured a shot at a world title. I couldn't imagine a better way to celebrate my thirty-eighth birthday.

15

While Conor McGregor's win against Dennis Siver attracted most of the publicity from that night in Boston, it was also very satisfying to see Paddy Holohan return to winning ways. Having lost for the first time in his career in his previous bout, Paddy was eager to get back in there again as quickly as possible in order to right the wrongs from his defeat to Chris Kelades in October 2014.

Paddy didn't perform as well as he's capable of against Kelades, but we still extracted positives from it. Perhaps the main one for me was that Paddy, having been unbeaten in his first eleven professional contests, now knew what it was like to lose. Nothing illustrates the value of winning quite like a loss. That's not to say that Paddy didn't fully appreciate the taste of victory until that point, but it certainly left him more motivated and focused than he had ever been before. That manifested itself in a superb performance against Shane Howell in Boston.

It was an exciting time in Paddy's life. He was finally competing – and winning – in the UFC, which had always been his aim, but there was also something else on the horizon that was perhaps even more important to him.

Within a year of opening the new gym on the Naas Road, membership had grown to the point where it was already time to think about expansion. We would end 2015 with 700 members. I was interested in the idea of opening a second premises in Dublin, and we agreed that Paddy would spearhead the project. At the time of writing it's still a work in progress, but we hope SBG Tallaght will be up and running before the end of 2016.

Paddy is a proud native of Tallaght, so to be in a position to open a gym there meant the world to him. He still has many years of fighting at the highest level left in him, but it's been clear to me for a long time that Paddy will also go on to become a very good coach – a process he has already begun with us at SBG. I believe people are either born to teach or not. Paddy has got what it takes.

Owen Roddy has got it too. Paddy is still an active fighter, so he's balancing both commitments for now, whereas Owen has already retired from fighting, so coaching is his sole focus. As Conor McGregor's striking coach, Owen is deservedly beginning to receive a lot of recognition. In my opinion, he's way ahead of the majority of his peers in terms of what he's doing. Both Owen and Paddy will be successful coaches for a long time to come.

In order to be a successful coach, you require first and foremost the ability to communicate effectively with a wide variety of personalities. More often than not, the biggest mistakes I see coaches making can be traced back to communication. Some coaches may have been great fighters and they might find it difficult to comprehend that their students are unable to do things the way they could. The student may simply have a different style, but a coach might insist on forcing their way on to everybody.

You need to be able to adapt. I believe I'm quite flexible: I can work with different personalities and styles. When it comes to high-level athletes, you often encounter big egos, so you need to find a way to communicate your ideas in a manner that suits them.

Patience is also vital. If you're a strength and conditioning coach, for example, you might have an image in your head of coaching a bunch of Olympic athletes. However, the reality is that most of your clients will probably be Joe Soaps who are just trying to stay fit and healthy. The point is that you must be patient when you're teaching people with different levels of skill and competence. Not everybody is going to turn out to be a UFC-level fighter.

If you're only pretending to enjoy coaching, people will see through that very quickly. You either love and embrace it or you don't. There's no middle ground. If you open a gym solely to make money, it'll be destined to fail. You need to be able to appreciate the thrill of what I call the '*wow* moment' – when you explain to somebody how a certain technique works and their eyes light up after they manage to put it into practice. Moments like that probably give me more satisfaction than a big UFC win for one of my fighters.

Some athletes insist on training with a coach who also had a successful career as a fighter. Others just want to know that the coach has the ability to demonstrate to them what they need to do to keep improving. Take Greg Jackson in New Mexico, for example. He's regarded as one of the best coaches in the game – and he was never a fighter himself.

Ultimate success or failure depends on the athlete in question, of course, irrespective of the coach's record in the octagon, and I believe it's probably a sign of immaturity and lack of self-confidence when someone wants to be trained only by a coach who was a great fighter too.

As a coach, you also have to be prepared to put up with a lot of shit. You're constantly dealing with narky fighters who are trying to make weight while arguing with their girlfriends, teammates and seemingly everyone in their lives. In my case, you're also often semi-managing their careers. From the outside, people might see me as a guy holding pads or shouting at someone to do five more reps, but it's certainly much more complicated than that.

Taking the helicopter view is essential. You need to rise above everything and see what your fighters don't, that a certain sparring partner or perhaps a nutritionist needs to be brought in, for example. There are many layers involved and they're being added to all the time. I'm still learning myself. No matter how long I remain a coach, that journey of education will never end.

With people like Paddy Holohan and Owen Roddy, I can only hope that I have inspired them in the same way that coaches like Kieran McGeeney, Eoin Lacey and John Connor have influenced me. All three of those guys have taught me so much from their own experiences about striving for the highest standards.

Eoin and John run the Irish Strength Institute in Dublin, and they've been working with my fighters on strength and conditioning since 2009. Kieran first came to SBG in 2009, when he was the manager of the Kildare football team. He brought the Kildare play-ers in – out of curiosity as much as anything else – to do some Brazilian jiu-jitsu as part of their pre-season training. Seven years later, Kieran isn't just a member at SBG, but he's also one of our BJJ coaches. He competed at the highest level of his own sport for years and I've learned so much from him about having a competitive mindset. Kieran is obsessive regarding the pursuit of success and perfection. He's been a massive influence for me.

I've often been told that I have a methodical approach to coach-ing, in that everything is broken down concisely into parts. Cathal Pendred likened me to his school rugby coach, who was also a maths teacher. It may not be a complete coincidence that, if I had been forced to use my engineering degree to earn a living, I probably would have looked into teaching maths. People sometimes assume that my coaching methods stem from my academic background in engineering, but I think it's a reflection more of my personality than of my education. Even though it was my mother who pushed me in the direction of the engineering course in DIT, I had the right kind of personality to be enthusiastic about it.

In college, I always loved working in the labs because there was a rational and logical pattern to everything we did – A led to B, B led to C and so on. Following a set of steps in order to reach a definitive solution, basically. That's why maths and science always appealed to me in school more than other subjects. It wasn't like English, where you might be asked for your opinion on *Macbeth*. I hated that. I just didn't see the point in me, some random teenager in a school in Dublin, trying to come up with something more interesting to say about *Macbeth* than the best English teachers and scholars already had. We used to get sample answers in our textbooks which were only to be used as a guide, but I just learned them off by heart and used them word-for-word. Trying to come up with some forced opinion just seemed like bullshit to me.

With maths, however, there was just one right answer and it was up to you to work it out. There was no doubt or uncertainty. If you couldn't find the one correct answer, you were just wrong. Follow the steps that have been explained to you and you'll find that right answer. I think you can apply that to sequences in grappling and striking too. It's not magic. For the vast majority of the time, there are only a limited number of positions you can find yourself in so you can work on deducing the right responses to those. That's the role of a coach; to ensure that the athlete has the right answers to the most common positions. Then it's up to the athlete to find the area in which they particularly want to express themselves. I want my guys to be rock-solid in the over-under clinch hold, the double-leg and single-leg takedown and on how to throw a jab. After they have that foundation, their personalities will lead them to specific styles of fighting.

After Conor McGregor's defeat of Dennis Siver, I was inundated for days with social media messages from fans who were planning to attend the title bout against José Aldo. There had been some idle talk about the fight taking place at Croke Park in Dublin, but I felt then – as I still do now – that the prospect of a UFC event there was unlikely. All the indications were pointing to Las Vegas and speculation in the media suggested that UFC 187, on 23 May, would be the date. However, what we were hearing behind the scenes was that the fight was being lined up for UFC 189 instead. Fans were so keen to be there to see Conor become the first Irishman to challenge for a UFC title that they went ahead and booked their flights and hotels for Vegas for the May date. They were even tweeting screenshots of their bookings to me.

A week or so after the Siver fight, I mentioned in a radio interview with Newstalk in Ireland – another one where the presenters seemed surprised that I wasn't bigger and scarier-looking when I came into the studio – that nothing had been confirmed as regards a date for the fight, so fans should not take the risk by booking. But some were unable to contain themselves, and I'm sure it unfortunately cost them a bit of money. Just a few days later, the UFC confirmed that José Aldo would defend his UFC featherweight title against Conor McGregor at UFC 189 at the MGM Grand Garden Arena in Las Vegas on 11 July.

Another subject of fascination for the fans was Conor's earnings. People asked if I was worried that the money would go to his head and distract him from the task at hand. *Will he start to slacken off now that he's rolling in the cash? Will you lose him to that?*

I'm sure that has happened on countless occasions in the past to athletes in many sports, but I had known Conor for long enough to realize that this wasn't a concern for us. Sure, now that he was earning the kind of money he could once only have dreamed of, he was certainly making the most of it. But Conor is astute enough to recognize that it could all disappear in an instant if he were to take his eye off the ball. Ultimately it comes down to what motivates you. If money is your only incentive, your determination to succeed in competition will fade as soon as you start admiring your bank account. Conor has stated publicly that money is a motivating factor for him, but only because it happens to be a consequence of learning, improving, competing and winning – which is what drives him, first and foremost. If an athlete is motivated solely by money, they'll come unstuck as soon as they start to make it in large amounts. It's happened many times before. Mike Tyson wanted money and fame, but he was never the same soon after he began to experience it. Some people said his decline was a result of the death of his coach, Cus D'Amato, but for me the problem seemed to be a lack of motivation.

Another question I've sometimes been asked is whether Conor will eventually leave SBG and join one of the big teams in America.

It's not something I've ever worried about. Conor places a lot of importance on loyalty, but even more so it's about intelligence. The relationship between a coach and a fighter does not develop overnight, and Conor knows that. As a younger fighter, with his boxing background, he has a lot of friends who would have travelled to places like the Wild Card Boxing Club in Los Angeles over the years. When you go to a place like that as a newcomer, you join the back of the queue for the attention of the coaches. That's also quite true for new fighters who join us at SBG. They're welcome, of course, but they'll need to work hard to move their way up the pecking order and prove that they're serious about becoming a permanent member of the team. I'm not going to compromise the time and effort I put into fighters who have trained under me from day one for somebody who could be gone again in a few months. If a professional fighter leaves their own team to join SBG, I have to wonder how long it will be before they decide to depart SBG for somewhere else? Particularly in recent years, we've had high-level fighters come to the gym to train from every corner of the world. The door is open to them and they'll be greeted warmly, but it'll take some time to build up the trust that's required to consider them as part of the team.

Conor saw that I gave him everything I had from the moment he first walked through the door, and he gave me everything in return. We rose up together and it has paid off for us both. If Conor had left to become just another sparring partner in some gym in America with a hundred professional fighters, I don't believe he would have been able to develop in the manner that he has.

Just from a practical point of view, Conor's timekeeping is so bad that it probably wouldn't have worked for him anywhere else! If you're in a big US gym and you miss the 1.30 p.m. team session, that's your problem. And that's pretty much the crack of dawn in Conor McGregor's time zone. I've learned that's just how he is, and I do whatever I can to accommodate him. He has his own key to the gym and often comes in to train after midnight.

Conor's title shot against José Aldo was being billed as the biggest fight in the UFC's history, as evidenced by the organization's decision to embark on a twelve-day media world tour in March 2015, with both fighters in tow. Beginning in Rio de Janeiro and ending in Dublin, the tour would take in ten cities across Brazil, the USA, Canada, the UK and Ireland. One of my first thoughts was that I felt slightly sorry for José Aldo, having to endure being tormented by Conor every day for nearly two weeks, but it sounded like a lot of fun for the fans and it was an indication of how important the fight was for the UFC. This was something they had never done before.

When Conor got in Aldo's face after the Siver fight in Boston, Aldo didn't seem too bothered. But over the course of the media tour, Conor poked and prodded, chipping away at Aldo. It was clear that Aldo wasn't enjoying himself. On the set of a TV show, Conor grabbed Aldo's neck and snatched his belt while it was unattended. Aldo's coach, André Pederneiras – asked Dana White to make sure that Conor didn't make physical contact with the champion. As soon as Conor found that out, he was never going to be able to resist.

The fighters had a hectic schedule over the course of the media tour, but I wasn't concerned about it placing too much stress and strain on Conor, especially as the fight was still nearly four months away. He had Artem Lobov with him along the way, so they were training as they travelled. We've learned over the years that there's always time to train, even if that involves moving the beds aside in a hotel room to create sufficient space for a session.

We also have to allow for the promotional requirements of the game. For Conor, in particular, it's an area in which he feels like he can gain an advantage. Is it the difference between winning and losing? I don't believe so. Conor has more than enough physical skills to beat his opponents without putting them under psychological pressure first. Still, it doesn't do any harm. I knew that being in Conor's company for that amount of time would wear on Aldo.

John, bad news. Can you take a phone call?

My stomach started doing somersaults when I read Artem's message. He and Conor were in Canada for the final North American leg of the UFC 189 media tour, before it made its way across the Atlantic Ocean for stops in London and Dublin.

When I got Artem on the phone, he told me news I didn't want to hear: 'Conor has hurt his knee.'

Artem explained that Conor and Rory MacDonald – a Canadian welterweight who was scheduled to take on the champion, Robbie

Lawler, in UFC 189 – had been training together that afternoon. Nothing strenuous, just a bit of grappling. But during their session, Rory landed awkwardly on Conor's left knee – the same knee he had injured against Max Holloway. The knee was already swelling up and Conor was having it looked at by a medic. I was almost afraid to pose the question out of fear that I'd inevitably receive an unpleasant answer. But I needed to know.

'Artem, how bad is it?'

'I'm not going to lie,' he said. 'It doesn't look good.'

16

I first came across José Aldo in 2008, when he began to make a name for himself with the now-defunct WEC promotion. He was only twenty-one at the time, but he was already being earmarked as a future world champion, and it was easy to see why. By 2015 he had become the pound-for-pound best fighter in the world, and arguably the UFC's most dominant champion. He had only ever been beaten once in his career, as a raw nineteen-year-old.

So it was a big deal when, as part of the tour promoting UFC 189, José Aldo came to Dublin. This was one of the modern greats of mixed martial arts, an icon, and he was coming to my home town to promote a world title bout against one of my own fighters. With the benefit of hindsight I can now appreciate how significant that was, but it's not something that really registered with me at the time. Then, he was just the next opponent. The final hurdle between Conor and the very top.

Unlike some of Aldo's previous opponents, we didn't make the mistake of putting him on a pedestal. Another reason I wasn't getting carried away by Aldo's presence in Dublin for the Irish leg of the UFC 189 media tour was that I wasn't even sure if the fight was going to take place as scheduled. A couple of days had passed since Conor hurt his knee while training with Rory MacDonald in Canada. We still weren't sure how serious the damage was. I had spoken to Conor on the phone, and the bad news was that his knee was painful and swollen. The good news was that he was certain it wasn't as serious as the ruptured anterior cruciate ligament he'd sustained against Max Holloway in August 2013. But I wasn't convinced. If the injury really were serious, I would expect Conor to be in denial about it.

Conor didn't tell anyone else about the injury until he returned home to Dublin. Once the media obligations were out of the way, we could decide on our next move.

According to the UFC, over 70,000 fans applied for tickets to attend the press conference – the final one on the media tour – with José Aldo and Conor McGregor at the Convention Centre in Dublin on the afternoon of 31 March 2015. Unfortunately, the venue only catered for 3,000 so there were a lot of disappointed fans. The lucky ones who managed to get inside the building certainly seemed to enjoy the occasion. Conor was given a hero's welcome while Aldo received an extremely hostile reception. I watched it all on TV back at the gym. Aldo looked like he had reached breaking point as Conor gave it one last push with his antics, which included snatching the belt again. I couldn't help but think that there were people looking at this from all over the world, none of them aware that the fight these guys were promoting might not even go ahead because of the state of Conor's knee. At the same time, I was slightly reassured by how he was able to jump around the stage like a maniac.

'I actually think it's fine,' Conor told me when we eventually got together. I was keen for him to have a scan in order to discover exactly what the problem was, but he was reluctant.

'Let me figure this out,' he said. 'I don't think this will need surgery. I can get by without it.' Given that he was about to begin a training camp for the biggest fight of his life, Conor wanted to avoid being operated on. Having to do so would immediately have forced the postponement of the fight and he was convinced that such a move wasn't necessary.

By now, Conor had mentioned the injury to Dana White, who recommended that Conor visit a clinic in Germany which specialized in stem-cell therapy. As a sufferer of Ménière's disease, Dana had undergone stem-cell treatment at the same clinic and found it to be very effective. Conor took his advice. He flew straight out to Germany and was given stem-cell injections into his knee. Within a few days, he was back in the gym.

'It feels good,' he insisted. 'It's not perfect but it'll get better over the next few weeks of training. Let's do this. I'm ready.'

And that was that. We were going full steam ahead for the biggest fight in UFC history in spite of a knee injury the seriousness of which was unclear. I still wanted Conor to have a scan. If we needed to push the fight back a few months, so be it. But he was adamant. There was no telling him otherwise. All I could do was take his word for it and devote myself to the task of preparing him accordingly.

Conor had plenty of physical therapy, and more stem-cell injections later on at a clinic in Los Angeles. As I observed him in training, I began to agree with his assessment that he could get by without surgery. What he needed was rest, but we didn't have the time for that with a world title fight on the horizon. Conor was able to train hard, but his mobility was restricted, which meant that his wide array of kicks was limited and he couldn't really do any wrestling at all. I was kind of okay with that. When the Aldo fight was first announced, I wrote in my column for The42.ie that I believed Conor would win inside three of the scheduled five rounds. That was a modest prediction: I could honestly picture Conor getting the job done in the first. I thought he was capable of getting an early knockout, so wrestling wouldn't even have time to come into the equation. My belief in Conor's ability gave me peace of mind that we could get through this despite the injury.

The situation reminded me of something former world boxing champion Steve Collins once said to some of my guys when he visited the gym: 'I'd rather be 75 per cent physically ready and 100 per cent mentally ready than 100 per cent physically ready and 75 per cent mentally ready.'

That certainly applied to Conor, because there was no doubting that his psychological preparation was spot on. There wasn't a single question in his mind about wanting to proceed with this, so the best thing I could do as his coach was get fully behind him. But I'd be lying if I said there wasn't any concern. As we prepared to launch the training camp, I had no idea how things would unfold.

★

Because this was our first world title bout, we wanted to leave no stone unturned in preparation for 11 July. The stakes had been raised so it felt like things needed to be done a little differently. We made the decision to spend the ten weeks before the fight in Las Vegas – the idea being that we'd become completely acclimatized to the heat and the time zone. By fight night, the place would feel like home.

The day before we left for Vegas, I was in my office at the gym when Orlagh walked in and handed me the phone: 'This is for you.'

'I'm really busy at the moment,' I said. 'Who is it?'

'I think you want to take this call. It's Royce Gracie.'

When Orlagh handed me the phone, I couldn't believe it was actually Royce on the other end of the line. I was speechless for a moment before I could actually utter a greeting.

'John, hello,' he said. 'My name is Royce Gracie, I'm from the Gracie family.'

'I know exactly who you are, Mr Gracie. You don't need to introduce yourself to me.'

It turned out that one of Royce's private students was in Dublin and needed a gym to train in. Naturally I was delighted to be able to accommodate him.

'While I have you on the phone,' I said to Royce, 'I can't allow you to hang up without telling you that you've basically given me this life. I saw you when I was a terrified nineteen-year-old kid who didn't know where he was going or what he wanted to do, but when I saw what you were able to do, it changed my life. I really can't thank you enough. You've given me an amazing life. None of us would be doing what we're doing now without you stepping into that octagon.'

He just laughed and told me that we're all standing on the shoulders of his father. He wouldn't accept the credit.

That was an amazing phone call to receive, especially just before departing for our biggest fight yet. Without Royce Gracie, I wouldn't be where I am today. For him to send one of his students to me was one of the biggest compliments I've ever been paid.

★

We secured the use of a luxury, seven-bedroom, 12,000 square-foot house in a private gated estate in Vegas for the duration of our time there; Conor christened it 'The Mac Mansion'. It was a big commitment for me to leave Dublin for two and a half months and I knew it would be challenging to lead a world title training camp on one side of the world while running a gym on the other. If there was a faulty toilet in the changing room back at SBG, I would get a call about it.

Conor wasn't the only SBG fighter preparing to fight in Vegas. Throughout the week leading up to UFC 189, the Amateur World Championships were also scheduled to take place and four of my up-and-coming fighters were set to represent Ireland. Sinéad Kavanagh, James Gallagher, Frans Mlambo and Kiefer Crosbie joined Conor, Artem Lobov, Owen Roddy, SBG wrestling coach Sergey Pikulskiy and myself at the house. Tom Egan flew in from Boston too, and Gunnar Nelson joined us later on. Gunni was ready to return following his loss to Rick Story, and a fight against John Hathaway – the man who'd defeated Tom Egan in Dublin back in 2009 – had been booked for the UFC 189 card. Owen, Tom, Sergey and I focused on coaching. As wrestling coach, Sergey was extremely limited in what he could do with Conor due to the injury. Nevertheless, he used his expertise to prepare him in that regard as well as he possibly could. A former member of Moldova's national wrestling team, Sergey had become a key element of our coaching ticket since joining SBG in 2008.

Artem Lobov was also gearing up for something big, having been selected to compete on an upcoming series of *The Ultimate Fighter*. At the Mac Mansion, we had a lot of like-minded people under the same roof working together, each with a target to aim for. It made for a very productive training environment.

Eager to play my part in ensuring that everybody remained on track for the duration of the training camp, I decided to subject myself to a strict diet. My nutrition is pretty good anyway, but here it became extremely rigid. It was all geared towards fostering a world champion mentality. Even Conor said it gave him a boost to see me rowing in behind him in that manner. To maintain a sense of discipline, we pinned a list of house rules to the door of the refrigerator. One of those was that no processed or sugary foods were permitted. Everyone in the house adhered to it.

In a house full of determined individuals, I felt everyone learned and improved substantially over the course of the ten weeks. We all made big leaps forward, myself included. But that doesn't mean that people didn't get under each other's skin from time to time. There was definitely an element of cabin fever at various stages, which I suppose is to be expected in a situation like that.

A lot of fun was had, too. We cooled off in the pool in the mornings and enjoyed barbecues for dinner in the evenings. Everyone chipped in with the preparation of the food – one person marinaded the meat, another took care of the salad, someone else would set the table, and so on. It all contributed to creating a family vibe, which was important when we were all so far away from home and for so long.

The build-up to Conor's fight with Aldo was generating an unprecedented amount of coverage for an MMA bout, and almost every social media post from those of us in the house seemed to be turned into an article by the media. The output of one Irish website in particular seemed to consist entirely of events inside the Mac Mansion. *You'll never believe what Conor McGregor ate for breakfast today, click here to find out* . . . that sort of thing.

I'm sure the pictures and videos we were sharing online made it seem like we were having the time of our lives, but they only captured the brief highlights of each day. For the most part, it was mundane and it was boring. Apart from the few hours that were spent at the gym each day, we were stuck in the house for almost the entire ten weeks. On a few occasions we tried to arrange to do something together away from the house, but it never happened. For example, on the way to or from the gym, someone might spot a billboard advertising one of the shows in Vegas: 'Let's go and see that on Saturday night.' It was usually Artem who ended up responding: 'Yep, let's add it to the growing list of shit that we're never going to do.'

I guess there were just so many people there that it never really suited all of us to get up and do something at the same time. While one group might be in the mood to go out, another preferred to rest and recover from training, and vice versa. Getting Conor out of bed for anything other than training is no easy task either, so that also didn't help matters.

This was my first experience of coordinating a training camp for a world title fight. I suppose I made the natural assumption that longer is better. But, as I came to realize in the latter stages, ten weeks was a little too long. It became difficult to sustain the intensity in training and the guys were getting a bit agitated towards the end. It was another lesson learned. No matter how long you're involved in this, or any other, sport, you'll never master it entirely. Anyone who claims otherwise is just not being honest.

Because the house was in a gated community, it was safe enough for us to keep the doors unlocked. But we were located at the back of the estate, and kids would often show up on the other side of the perimeter walls and shout Conor's name, hoping to catch a glimpse of him.

On a random Tuesday afternoon, we were chilling out at the house when the front door suddenly opened and a loud, distinctive, familiar voiced filled the hallway and living room.

'Ah . . . so this is what a world champion training camp looks like. Why is nobody lifting weights?' the visitor laughed.

Holy shit! It was Arnold Schwarzenegger. He had met Conor before, through his partner Heather Milligan, the physical therapist who had played such an important role in Conor's recovery from the ACL injury. Arnie was in Vegas and decided he wanted to stop by to show his support. He's a very cool guy and it was incredible to be paid a visit by someone of his stature.

Over the course of this journey, meeting people like Schwarzenegger, Sylvester Stallone, Jean-Claude Van Damme and Mike Tyson and discovering that they're huge admirers of Conor has been quite surreal. I am a child of the eighties, and these guys were all heroes of mine. Now they're fans of a fighter I train. It's crazy.

Around the time he first met Tyson, Conor had been thinking about buying a Lamborghini. Mike gave him some financial advice: 'If it depreciates, rent it. If it appreciates, buy it. That's all I've gotta say.'

Cristiano Ronaldo also got in touch with Conor after he wore a pair of the football star's CR7 brand underwear at the weigh-ins for the fight against Diego Brandão. When I look at Conor, even now, I still see the same guy who first walked into my gym all those years ago. But stuff like that does serve as a reminder that he's now a global superstar.

Midway through the training camp, I had to leave for a few weeks for Mexico City, where Cathal Pendred claimed his fourth straight UFC win, against Augusto Montaño. When I left, I was concerned that the routine we had established at the house in Vegas would collapse in my absence. The drill was that at 8 p.m. every evening, we all left together to go and train at the *TUF* gym, where *The Ultimate Fighter* is filmed. There were two reasons for training at night: because UFC fights take place at night, and because of Conor's body clock. We put the work in at *TUF* for a number of hours before heading back to the house, usually around 1 a.m. But while I was in Mexico, everyone just started doing their own thing: 8 p.m. quickly became 8.30 p.m., then 9 p.m., 9.30 p.m. and so on. From what I was told, that had a detrimental impact on the mood in the house. That little bit of structure had kept us on track and given everyone a sense of purpose.

Conor wasn't too bothered. He's the type of person who can get up at any time of the day or night and decide that he wants to train. From my experience, most fighters favour routine. They like to know the what, where and when of their training schedule. Conor is an exception. There's no pattern whatsoever to his desire to train, but the problem is that not everybody can function according to his body clock. On some evenings while I was away, it would get to a stage where it was so late and Conor still hadn't emerged from his bedroom that the guys would assume that he wasn't going to train that night. As they settled in for the evening to watch a movie, prepare for bed or whatever else, a message would then come down from upstairs: 'We're leaving in ten minutes.' That wasn't ideal, and I think everyone was relived when, with just under four weeks to go until Conor's fight against Aldo, I returned to Vegas and re-established the status quo.

When I got back, I also discovered that the guys hadn't been sticking to the strict dietary rules we had put in place. We used a minivan to transport us to and from the gym, and there was an outlet of In-N-Out Burger on the route. I hopped into the van one day and found a burger wrapper on the floor underneath one of the seats. I couldn't believe it. I asked for an explanation and Tom Egan admitted that they had slipped up, but it was 'a one-off'. But James Gallagher was a little more honest: 'Ah, we've been going all the time. Sorry, coach.' I pulled Conor up on it later.

'What's going on with the burgers?' I asked.

'We only went once, I swear,' he claimed.

'James said you've been going there most nights.'

'All right, fuck it, we have, but that's the end of it now. Honestly. No more.'

While I was in Mexico with Cathal, news emerged from Brazil that there had been some confusion over a drug test that had been administered to José Aldo. In early June, a tester from the Drug Free Sport lab, Ben Mosier, had seemingly been prevented from collecting a urine sample from Aldo at his gym in Rio de Janeiro. The tester, under instruction from the Nevada State Athletic Commission – who would be overseeing the fight in Las Vegas on 11 July – was challenged by a police officer who was a member of Aldo's gym. The police officer told the tester that he didn't possess a valid visa to carry out his duties in Brazil. Aldo's camp got the Brazilian MMA Commission involved, and the sample was collected by them the following day instead. According to the NSAC's report, the police officer had confiscated Mosier's passport, and the Brazilian tester asked Aldo for a picture and an autograph after collecting the sample. It all sounded like a very bizarre situation, but there wasn't much we could do about it. Conor had been tested a couple of weeks earlier while he was attending UFC 187 at the MGM Grand. A tester pulled him aside and Conor gave both blood and urine samples. It was as straightforward as that. They're called random tests for a reason. Being given twenty-four hours' notice is not random. When one of my fighters is subjected to a drug test, they do so without asking for paperwork or anything like that. We don't see the need to complicate what should be a simple process.

As a team, we take a hardline stance against performance-enhancing drugs. I believe there is a culture of PED use in certain gyms and certain parts of the world. There seems to be a pattern of guys from the same teams or countries being caught in recent years. It must be something that becomes a topic for discussion in the changing room. I know for certain that if somebody broached the subject with anyone in SBG, they'd be absolutely shredded. Of course, the coach has an important role to play in establishing that type of environment. It's something I'm very serious about. My first wave of fighters and I have been so vocal in our opposition to the use of PEDs that the younger guys coming up know it's not even to be considered. But if you're in a gym where there's a different attitude to it, it's probably only a matter of time before you get sucked in.

A week before the aforementioned incident with Aldo's drug test, the UFC announced strict new rules to combat PEDs in the organization by bringing the United States Anti-Doping Agency on board to police it. I believe that a lot of fighters who were previously using banned substances have since been forced to stop taking them as a result. Fighters don't take drugs because they want bigger biceps. It's all geared towards allowing them to work harder in training. A typical rhythm for a clean fighter might be to train hard for two days, then go easy on the third day. But with the benefit of PEDs, fighters were training hard three times a day, every day.

It has never happened so far, but if one of my fighters were to come to me, curious about sampling PEDs, I'd be absolutely devastated. It would almost be like being dumped by a girlfriend. I'd feel like I had failed as a coach in setting the kind of environment where it's never even thought about. If you're not good enough to train without drugs then you shouldn't be training at all. At SBG, you either fight clean or you go elsewhere. Thankfully we've never had to implement it but we have a zero-tolerance policy when it comes to drugs. And that goes for every single person in the gym.

With just over two weeks to go until the fight, Conor's knee was approaching 100 per cent again and we were glad to be coming to the end of a long training camp. The final two weeks are just about keeping the body fresh and loose, so we weren't going to use them for any last-minute cramming of the wrestling drills that he had missed out on over the previous couple of months. That wasn't a concern for me. He was looking so good that I was fully confident of an emphatic win against José Aldo.

One morning, Dana White and Lorenzo Fertitta arrived at the house. They're both based in Vegas – maybe they were just stopping by to see how everything was going? That's what we hoped. But the look on their faces suggested that there was bad news in the post.

'It looks like José is out,' said Dana. 'His rib. It seems there's a fracture.'

Fuck! Here we go again. We were well used to having Conor's opponents withdraw by now, and we were always relaxed about a change of opponent, but this was different. Other guys can be easily replaced, but not the champion. We wanted that title and the only way to get it was by beating Aldo.

Dana and Lorenzo explained that it would be a few days before there was clarification. Apparently Aldo was undergoing medical examinations to discover the extent of the injury so he hadn't yet officially pulled out of the fight. But it wasn't looking good. We began to discuss alternative options.

Part of me wondered if this was a good opportunity for Conor to pull out too, given that he had also been carrying an injury. But that idea was never going to get off the ground. Thousands of fans had already paid a lot of money to travel over for the fight. It was a massive pay-per-view event for the UFC too. Conor wasn't going to let that fall apart. Whether it was Aldo standing across the octagon from him or somebody else, Conor was going to be fighting at UFC 189.

As Dana and Lorenzo began to explore replacement opponents, I knew who I wanted to avoid. Conor had virtually no wrestling drills in the bank during this training camp, so the worst-case scenario here was a fight with Chad Mendes. An NCAA Division 1 All-American wrestler, Mendes was as good as they came in that department. Without any injury problems, I'd have no issue with Conor facing Mendes. But this was one time when he could be a bit of a banana skin. Mendes was ranked as the top contender in the division, so his name was obviously in the mix. Another possibility was Frankie Edgar. Nate Diaz's name was also mentioned, but Diaz seemed unlikely because he was a lightweight and the UFC were keen to keep this as a featherweight bout. Their plan was to put an interim title on the line in the event of a confirmed withdrawal from Aldo. The final say on a new opponent ultimately rested on their shoulders, but Conor let them know that he was ready for anyone they chose. It didn't matter to him.

The confusion surrounding Aldo's involvement in the fight dragged on for a week until I eventually received a call, eleven days out from UFC 189, from Dana. It had been confirmed. Aldo was definitely out. His replacement? Chad Mendes, of course.

It was around midday when the call came through, which is approximately dawn in Conor McGregor's time zone. I went upstairs and knocked on Conor's bedroom door until I was answered by a grunt from inside. I opened the door.

'Aldo is out,' I said. 'It's Mendes.'

Conor opened one eye, muttered, 'They're all the same,' then went back to sleep.

He wasn't perturbed by the fact that the goalposts had been

moved. I wasn't so relaxed. Against novice strikers, Mendes fancied himself as a boxer. But against Conor his game plan was going to be to look for the takedown and win the fight on the ground. A wrestler of his calibre was very capable of doing that. Conor's knee was much better than it had been, but his mobility was still very restricted. His sprawl and takedown defence are usually excellent, but that wasn't the case now. There wasn't much we could do in eleven days to prepare for the guy with the best takedowns in the division.

As I've noted, we don't train specifically for opponents, but that's not to say we don't take a look at them. With this change of opponent, we had gone from facing a kick-boxer to a wrestler. Aldo and Mendes occupied positions at either end of the MMA spectrum. I believed Mendes was a serious threat but, given time to process the situation, I was glad we were going ahead with the fight. When Jon Jones refused to fight Chael Sonnen as a last-minute replacement for Dan Henderson at UFC 151 in 2012, the entire event fell through. We couldn't allow that to happen again on our watch.

We had anticipated a massive following in Las Vegas for UFC 189 fight week, but absolutely nobody expected the numbers that actually turned up. There must have been at least 10,000 Irish people in Vegas for the fight. For such a small country, we certainly know how to make our presence felt. It doesn't matter how long we're in this game, I don't think that support will ever not be overwhelming. There have been times when Conor has been finding the weight-cut tough, wondering whether it's all worth it, but then you show him a video of fans around Vegas chanting his name and it reminds him of how big this really is.

'Look at these guys, champ,' we'll say. 'They've spent their hard-earned money to come all this way to support you. Let's put on a show for them.'

It's little things like that which give him the extra push when times are tough.

Over the past couple of years, I've heard so many stories from fans who say they feel like they've been given a new lease of life by the success of Conor and SBG as a whole. They may have been down in the dumps, struggling in life, but seeing what we have achieved on a global stage has made them proud to be Irish. It has inspired them to embrace life and make the most of every day.

The sacrifices they make to attend the fights are unbelievable. They're spending every penny they have just to be there. There have been plenty of times after fights in the US when Irish fans have told me that they have to go straight back into work once they get off the plane after the overnight flight home. It's remarkable dedication. We could never truly express just how grateful we are for the support.

A few days before the fight against Mendes, I was walking down the strip in Las Vegas when somebody stopped me to ask for a picture. While it was being taken, a big group of Korean tourists came over for pictures too. I must have taken at least twenty with each and every one of them. When they all had a photo, one of the tourists turned to me and asked: 'So, who are you?' I guess we haven't quite cracked the Korean market just yet.

People sometimes ask if having so many fans on our side adds to the pressure. The reality is that when you're preparing for fights, particularly at this level, you're just too busy to even let that enter your thoughts. It doesn't happen and we can never allow it to. If the coach is nervous then the fighter will be too. A novice might pull you aside before a bout to go through the game plan again for reassurance because they're a bit tense. They just want to hear you say: 'You're going to be okay. We're ready for this.' But I've never had that with Conor. By nature, we're both very relaxed.

That the prize was an interim belt instead of the undisputed title may have detracted slightly from claims that UFC 189's main event would be the biggest UFC fight ever, but the final few days before the show certainly had the feeling of something huge and unprecedented. For the first time ever, the UFC decided to open up the entire MGM Grand Garden Arena for the weigh-ins. Over ten thousand people were there to watch Conor step on the scales. Two and a half years earlier we could barely draw a thousand to watch him fight.

As expected, the staredown between Conor and Mendes was heated. It had been another taxing weight-cut for Conor, so he was a little bit narky. Mendes, on the other hand, seemed to be on a high. He had stepped in at short notice in an attempt to capitalize on a huge opportunity, for which he'd be paid more money than he had ever earned before. He had nothing to lose and his demeanour reflected that.

Before the weigh-ins, much was made in the media about an altercation Conor had in the hallway of the arena with Mendes's teammate Urijah Faber. The truth was that there was very little to it. They engaged in a bit of playful grappling, and it irritated Conor because he was already cranky from the weight-cut. But there were no hard feelings. It was just a bit of handbags. If you don't like Urijah Faber, there's probably something wrong with you. I think he's one of the nicest guys you'll ever meet and I know Conor feels the same.

I'm not sure if I'll ever experience a more hectic day as a coach than 11 July 2015. That night, Conor was going to compete for an interim world title. I also had two other fighters on the UFC 189 bill. John Hathaway had to pull out of his bout against Gunnar Nelson, so Gunni was going to take on Brandon Thatch instead, while Cathal Pendred – just four weeks after beating Augusto Montaño in Mexico – had stepped in as a short-notice replacement to fight John Howard.

But my duties for the day began even earlier, because the finals of the Amateur World Championships were scheduled for that afternoon at the Flamingo, just up the strip from the MGM Grand. Frans Mlambo and Sinéad Kavanagh had both made it to the last stage of their respective divisions after a successful week. Sinéad unfortunately came up short in the women's featherweight final, but Frans looked superb as he became the men's champion at 145lb.

That gave us a good start to the day as I prepared to make my way across town for UFC 189.

Fight day for Conor involves – as usual – a late rise from bed, probably just after midday. He'll have a meal at lunchtime and again at around 4 p.m. Between the weigh-in and the fight, you want to eat the kind of food that your body can turn into fuel right away: meat, fish, pasta, rice and mashed potatoes. Slow-burning carbohydrates such as vegetables aren't much good. Eat what you can't eat while cutting weight, basically. After the two meals, Conor will have something small, like a banana, at 6 p.m. or so, and then it's time for him to head to the arena.

I had stayed at the MGM Grand instead of the Mac Mansion the night before the fight, and with Cathal slotted in early on the card, I was already at the arena by the time Conor arrived. His recovery from the weight-cut had been smooth and he had slept well. That's always music to my ears. At that point, I feel like my job is mostly done. Now it's just time to fight. Some people place a bit too much importance on what's going on in the corner during a fight, but there's not really a whole lot involved. Sometimes I've received a lot of praise for things I've contributed during fights but, in my mind, it's not going to change the outcome. Maybe you can provide a little bit of guidance and it's comforting for the fighter to know that their coach, someone they know and trust, is there for them. But there's not much more to it than that.

When Cathal took on John Howard, he was aiming to become the first fighter in UFC history to win five fights within the space of their first year with the organization. Unfortunately it wasn't to be as he was edged out on a split decision. It was bitterly disappointing for the entire team in the SBG changing room, but we've learned over the years on smaller shows never to allow one result to dampen the mood. The fighters know what's expected of them as teammates. Regardless of the result, when you return to that changing room you grab your bag and go, allowing colleagues to focus on the fights that are still to come. That might sound cold or callous, but it's the same when they win. They've all experienced both sides of the coin and they appreciate it when someone else does it for them. Cathal wished Gunni and Conor all the best, and then he was gone. As always, we'd all get together again later in the evening once business was taken care of. That's the policy and it has been from the very start.

When Gunni was rematched to face Brandon Thatch, people said we were crazy to accept the fight. Thatch is a big, devastating striker and Gunni needed to get back to winning ways after the disappointment of losing to Rick Story. But the old Gunni was back during the warm-up and he submitted Thatch in the very first round. The fight lasted just under three minutes, but that was enough time for Gunni to remind the world of what he can do. It was an immaculate performance.

Then it was Conor's turn. There were people all over the world tuning in to an MMA fight for the first time in their lives, which summed up just how big this was. But the atmosphere in our changing room was incredibly laid-back.

There were a lot of celebrities in the arena for the fight, including Arnold Schwarzenegger, Mike Tyson, pop star Bruno Mars and Neymar, the Brazilian footballer. I also bumped into Anthony Kiedis, the lead singer from the Red Hot Chili Peppers, in the corridor.

'Hey Coach Kavanagh, how's Conor feeling?' he asked. 'Big fan of you guys. Good luck!'

That was amazing, but I knew there was somebody else in our changing room who'd appreciate it more than I did. When I told Chris Fields, who was there as a warm-up partner for Cathal, he ran out and went looking for Kiedis, screaming like a teenage girl at a One Direction concert. Chris is a huge Chili Peppers fan so this was a big deal for him.

Conor didn't have a clue who Anthony Kiedis was. When Chris came back in, Conor asked: 'Who's that? Guns N' Roses or some fella, is it?'

Conor likes to warm up for his fights with Artem. You almost have to restrain him as the walk-out approaches, like a dog on a leash. It's become a bit of a running joke that Artem has left his best fights in the changing room when he's getting Conor ready.

Then there's a knock on the door from one of the UFC's staff. It's time. The security guys come in to walk you out. You hear the crowd – for each fight they get louder but it's just a soundtrack of background noise. As UFC commentator Mike Goldberg said: 'It's like a rock concert in here.' But all I hear is the same silence that always allows me to focus on the task ahead. Sinéad O'Connor's haunting voice is carrying Conor to the octagon. It's an iconic moment, reminiscent of the spectacular walk-outs that became synonymous with boxers like Prince Naseem Hamed during the 1990s. Even when we appear in the arena and it seems clear that the vast majority of the crowd is on our side, the colour of the occasion doesn't become a distraction.

Going into this fight, there was little doubt in my mind that Mendes would be successful with his takedowns. His ability as a wrestler, coupled with Conor's lack of work in that area over the past few months, meant that it was inevitable. Our game plan was focused on what would happen when the takedowns came. There was no need to panic when it happened, because Conor had the jiu-jitsu to take care of himself on the ground. We focused on making sure that the action on the ground was always busy and active, which would prevent Mendes from grinding out a boring decision over five rounds.

Just as Conor was about to enter the octagon, we had our customary embrace and I said, 'All day,' which he repeated back to me. The message was that Mendes might get his takedowns, but that's okay. Conor could go for as long as was necessary to get this win. When Artem, Owen and I took our places in the corner and Mendes began his walk to the octagon, it really hit me that we were about to face the best wrestler in the division without sufficient preparation. *Oh well*, I thought. *There's no turning back now. What will be, will be.*

Part of our strategy was to target Mendes with shots to the body, and that worked well from very early on. Going to the head too enthusiastically against a small, stocky wrestler like Mendes would be a recipe for disaster, as he'd see that as an invitation to change levels and hit big takedowns. We knew the takedowns were coming, but we didn't want to invite them. When aiming for the body, if the opponent does level-change, there's always a chance of connecting with the head instead. Conor used his eight-inch reach advantage well and the shots to the body also helped to take the wind out of Mendes's sails. Each one that connected drained a little more gas from his tank.

Conor didn't seem to be showing any ill effects from the knee injury until midway through the first round. Mendes shot for his first big takedown and Conor wasn't able to sprawl as well as I knew he was capable of. However, there was no sense of panic. This was exactly what he expected. When Mendes secured that takedown, two things went through my mind. First of all, what an absolutely beautiful takedown! Secondly, I thought that it had to take a lot of energy for him to pick up a big guy like Conor and dump him on the ground like that. Just over two minutes into a potential twenty-five-minute fight, he invested a lot in that manoeuvre physically. If you watch my guys, they tend to get small takedowns against the fence because I like to focus on the most efficient way of moving. This one looked great, but it took so much effort that he needed to make it count. Conor was comfortable with Mendes in his guard and, even though he ate some shots, he was back on his feet just seconds later.

Conor continued to control the fight on the feet but another takedown for Mendes with just a minute remaining was probably enough to give him the first round on the scorecards. Still, we were very satisfied at the end of that first round. Mendes already looked exhausted, whereas Conor – in spite of a deep gash over his right eye thanks to an elbow from Mendes – looked fresh.

'Let's stick with the long shots,' I said, encouraging Conor to work the range, although I wasn't keen on the spinning kicks he had been using due to the risk of being taken down. 'The left kick to the body is beautiful and the straight to the body as well with the left hand. He's very tired now.'

When the fighters returned to their feet for round two, Mendes was breathing heavily while Conor beckoned him on with a maniacal smile on his face. Conor hit Mendes with some beautiful shots early in the second round and it seemed like a stoppage might be on the way if things continued in that vein. But Mendes countered with a takedown with fifty seconds on the clock. Mendes spent the next three minutes in top position on the ground but Conor maintained a strong guard. At one point he landed a flurry of devastating elbows to the top of the head, which Mendes protested as illegal shots, but referee Herb Dean was quick to let him know that they were fine. One of the cameras cut to me at that point and I was laughing because that's exactly what we had worked on as a means of staying active if Mendes was on top. I felt it would be a suitable tactic to make Mendes uncomfortable on the ground, and that proved to be the case. The ideal scenario for Mendes was to hang out in guard, but Conor's success in countering with the elbows would eventually force Mendes to rush a guard-pass attempt. With forty-five seconds left in the round, he stepped over and tried to advance the position. However, that's a scenario Conor has spent a lot of time on in the gym. As Mendes sought to lock in a guillotine choke, Conor slipped out using a move we call 'The Heartbreaker' and, all of a sudden, they were back on their feet.

It's easy for anyone to say, with the benefit of hindsight, that they knew what was coming. But when Mendes failed to make anything from that sequence on the ground, I was certain he was done. The look on his face suggested as much too. As soon as they were upright, Conor went to work with some beautiful combinations. To give Mendes credit, he was unbelievably tough and kept battling as he was being hit with big kicks and punches. But he was on borrowed time. He eventually went down under a left cross from Conor and the stoppage came with three seconds remaining in the round.

In the corner, I leapt to my feet and breathed a huge sigh of relief.

Conor's injury hadn't been made public so nobody was aware of how truly significant this win was for us. He had taken on a dangerous opponent at short notice without being at full capacity, yet still emerged victorious. As Conor climbed on to the octagon perimeter to celebrate with his team, I was a very proud coach. There were tears of elation. Conor was more emotional than I had ever seen him after a fight and I think we all felt the same. The world hadn't seen that side of him before. Conor is always supremely confident, but he knew he had been at risk facing a guy like Chad Mendes in those circumstances. The risk had paid off and it felt really, really good.

The team and Conor's family gathered in the octagon as Dana White wrapped a UFC belt around his waist. Margaret McGregor beamed as she embraced her son, the interim UFC featherweight champion of the world. That phone call she made to me back in 2008 had paid off for us all.

'I just honestly want to say thank you to my team, my family, everyone that has come up with me, because it's a tight, tight circle,' said Conor in his post fight interview in the octagon. 'People since day one are here with me now, I just want to thank everyone that has been with me.'

The undisputed title would have to wait for another day, but there was now a UFC belt coming back to Ireland. It took a while for that to sink in.

Afterwards, I went backstage to find an empty room so I could carry on my tradition of taking a few private minutes to myself after a fight. The first room I went into seemed to be hosting a little private party for the likes of Arnold Schwarzenegger, Mike Tyson, Dana White and Sinéad O'Connor.

'John, come in, have a drink,' Dana said. But I politely declined. I needed a chance to let it all sink in before getting the party started.

When we did get stuck into the celebrations, that first cold beer in ten weeks was perhaps the most satisfying thing I've ever consumed. We had a lot of fun for a couple of days, making the most of the rare opportunity to check out the bars and nightclubs of Las

Vegas. In one of them I ended up having a little wrestling match with Artem Lobov because he refused to leave! When there's beer and dancing involved, Artem can't be stopped.

By the time we headed back home to Ireland, however, attentions were already beginning to turn to a featherweight title unification bout. We had a belt, but the one in José Aldo's possession was what we had been chasing from the start. It was time to resume that pursuit.

17

For a long time I had aspired to have fighters competing regularly in the UFC in different parts of the world. When I arrived back from Las Vegas on the Wednesday afternoon after UFC 189, jet-lagged and emotionally drained, I was slightly regretting the fact that those goals were coming to fruition.

I had twenty hours back home in Dublin before returning to the airport to head for Glasgow, where Paddy Holohan was scheduled to face English veteran Vaughan Lee at UFC Fight Night 72 on Saturday, 18 July 2015. Not long before the fight with Paddy was announced, Vaughan had actually been planning to join SBG. He came over for a while and even did some training with Paddy. But Vaughan was planning to move down to the flyweight division from bantamweight, which put him on a potential collision course with Paddy, so nothing more came of it. Now they would be up against each other in Glasgow.

Vaughan is a great competitor, very durable and experienced, and he had already faced top guys like TJ Dillashaw and Raphael Assunção. However, having trained with him, Paddy was supremely confident, and so was I. I expected Paddy to finish him and he was close to doing so on a couple of occasions, but in the end we had to settle for a very comprehensive win on the scorecards, with the judges calling it 30–27 across the board. The win took Paddy to 3–1 in the UFC. He had responded brilliantly to the first defeat of his career the previous October and there was now a real sense of momentum behind him.

When I returned home from Glasgow, I finally felt like I had a chance to take a little breather and assess everything that had taken place in the previous fortnight. After each UFC win, the popularity and visibility of MMA in Ireland just got bigger. It was particularly noticeable on the back of Conor's win against Chad Mendes. Ireland was officially the home of a UFC belt. Only three other European countries – Poland, the Netherlands and Belarus, thanks to Joanna Jędrzejczyk, Bas Rutten and Andrei Arlovski – have been able to say that.

It's a little family tradition now that we all meet up at the Glenside pub in Rathfarnham on Sunday afternoons. I'd really missed those occasions while I was away in Vegas, so it was great to get back from Glasgow in time to join the family there, with Conor's belt in tow. Everybody in the pub came over to extend their congratulations, as they offered to buy us drinks and took pictures with the belt, and the owner brought us in behind the bar for a photo; but for me the reaction of my mam and dad was possibly the most satisfying part of the victory. They were just incredibly proud. Being able to enjoy an achievement with your family is priceless.

For Conor, simple things like making a shopping trip to Dublin city centre had already become complicated undertakings which required a driver and bodyguards. Now even I was being recognized often on the same streets where I had been completely anonymous for most of my life. That took a while to get used to, but it's always nice to receive people's support wherever you go throughout the city and country. It was becoming common to hear a 'Howya, John?' as I walked down the road, or a beep from a passing car. On the short walk between my apartment and the gym, I pass a primary school. After the Mendes fight, the kids in the schoolyard began to shout their encouragement when they spotted me on the way in: 'Go on, Coach Kavanagh!'

It made me laugh the first time it happened. The positive vibes are always appreciated, but being recognized on the street can be strange. In your head, you always expect that you're a stranger to people who are strangers to you. It took a while to get my head around the fact that that was not necessarily the case – another example of how life was beginning to change for us all.

★

While Conor enjoyed an enormous amount of support, there were also a lot of people who, even after he beat Mendes for the interim title, still remained unconvinced by his credentials. For a long time he had been subjected to claims that he was being protected by the UFC: they were supposedly deliberately keeping him away from top wrestlers. As I saw it, stopping a guy like Chad Mendes in the second round was as emphatic an answer as anyone could give to the question of whether Conor could overcome a high-class grappler, but apparently it still wasn't enough. Excuses were made on Mendes's behalf: he took the fight on short notice; he won the first round; the fight was stopped too early.

I struggled to agree with any of that. It was a short-notice fight for Conor too, given that he had been preparing for a completely different type of opponent. And from what I could see, Mendes was in very good shape. He would have known that, given José Aldo's history of withdrawing from fights, there was a strong chance he'd be getting a call-up. When that call came, I'd suspect that it didn't come as much of a surprise to Mendes. He would have been ready for it. At this level, guys are always in shape for at least three rounds anyway.

He may have had the better of the first round, but that counts for little if you can't even make it as far as the end of the second. When Chael Sonnen outwrestled Anderson Silva for four rounds in 2010, I don't recall anybody claiming that it diluted the significance of Anderson's victory, which came via submission in the fifth and final round. In fact, Silva was praised for having the ability to dig out a seemingly unlikely win.

As for the criticism of referee Herb Dean stopping the fight with just three seconds of the second round remaining, it's worth noting that there wasn't a single complaint about that from Chad Mendes. I'm sure he was grateful to Herb for intervening and preventing him from taking any further punches while he was clearly concussed.

After the fight, there were claims that Conor's lack of grappling ability had been exposed. Sure, he had given up a few takedowns, but he actually withstood more takedown attempts than he conceded. And even when he was taken down, he was doing damage from the bottom.

Still, the questions and criticism kept on coming. A lot of people were extremely reluctant to admit that he was winning simply because he was a great fighter. I soon realized that this was no bad thing. As long as there are questions to be answered, there'll be big fights to be made. Can he beat a wrestler on a full training camp? Can he beat a champion? Can he beat a champion in a heavier weight class?

Questions are good for business. If questions aren't being asked, people will be less interested to see him fight. Critics may never run out of questions, but we'll do our utmost to answer as many of them as we can.

In an ideal world, Conor would have taken some time off after his win against Mendes. After returning from the injury he sustained against Max Holloway, he fought three times in six months to seal his title shot and then went straight into a hectic promotional tour for UFC 189, before embarking on a challenging training camp while dealing with a knee problem and the change of opponent. It had been draining for us all, but especially for Conor. I felt he could have done with a holiday. However, lying on a beach for a week is not his style.

Shortly before the Mendes fight, Conor had agreed to be a coach on a series of *The Ultimate Fighter*. It required an additional six weeks in Las Vegas, during which he would guide a team of up-and-coming European fighters against their counterparts from the USA, who were under the stewardship of Urijah Faber. Filming was scheduled to begin just a few days after UFC 189, so Conor was heading straight from one big commitment to the next without taking a break. I was concerned that he might be pushing himself too far, but I also understood him well enough by now to know that his mind always needs to be occupied: he gets bored on the rare occasions that he takes even a couple of days off. Perhaps this was going to be the perfect solution. It was six weeks of work, but he was observing fights and training sessions instead of taking part.

The day before filming began, he tried to back out of it. At that stage he just wanted to come home. The only thing that convinced him to go ahead was that Artem Lobov was involved. Artem had been striving to earn a UFC contract for a long time and, unlike many other fighters, he refused to take the easy route to the top. He regularly took fights at short notice against top opponents, competing from featherweight to welterweight. He took risks and they didn't always pay off. That left him with as many losses on his record as wins, but there was no doubt in my mind that he was good enough to compete in the UFC. He just needed an opportunity to prove it. That finally came when he was selected for *The Ultimate Fighter* after impressing at the tryouts.

In order to secure a place in the show for the duration of the series, fighters are first required to come through a preliminary fight against a fellow contestant. Artem's fight was scheduled to take place on the Wednesday after Conor had beaten Mendes. As always, Artem had played an important role in Conor's training camp, so the plan for him once UFC 189 had finished was to have a massage, get some rest and prepare for what was likely to be the most important fight of his life. But that's not quite how things played out.

We all got a bit carried away with the jubilation of Conor's achievement, and the celebrations went on for a couple of days. Artem was at the heart of it all. He was due to report for *TUF* filming on the Monday morning, but he woke up late that afternoon nursing a dreadful hangover as a result of a two-day bender. Forty-eight hours from his fight, he could barely get out of bed.

Artem managed to report to the *TUF* crew on the Monday evening and spent Tuesday cutting weight. He had been drawn to face Mehdi Baghdad, who was one of the favourites going into the season. Artem was still suffering the effects of the hangover by the time he entered the octagon so he subsequently didn't show what he was capable of. Mehdi Baghdad won via majority decision and Artem's dream of earning a UFC contract was seemingly over. He was devastated: it looked like he had blown his chance.

That's when Conor's influence came into play. In spite of the loss, he was able to arrange for Artem to receive a wildcard spot in the competition. It was a second bite at the cherry for Artem and no one was more deserving of that break. He certainly grabbed that opportunity with both hands, picking up three consecutive wins, all by knockout, making him the first fighter to do so in the history of *The Ultimate Fighter*. Artem eventually lost a decision in a frustrating final fight against Ryan Hall, but it was a case of 'mission accomplished' as he had done enough to convince the UFC to offer him a contract.

I was over the moon for Artem. He'd grown up in Russia, but his family had moved to Ireland when he was a teenager. Artem had never practised any martial arts until he took up self-defence classes at Dublin City University at the age of twenty-one, while studying for a degree in Business Studies and Spanish. That led him to Straight Blast Gym. For a number of months after Artem joined the gym, I actually thought he was Brazilian. I have no idea why. I tried to use my few words of Portuguese with him whenever we spoke, but he just smiled back at me awkwardly. Eventually he corrected me discreetly: 'Sorry, coach. We speak Russian in Russia, not Portuguese.'

Watching that season of *The Ultimate Fighter*, it was particularly intriguing to observe Conor's approach to coaching other professional fighters. After a couple of days of filming, he sent me a message: 'I'm glad I went ahead with this. I'm chilling in the gym and watching fights. This is exactly what I want to do every day. It's perfect.'

Conor demonstrated the concept of light, flow sparring at an easy pace to the guys on his team and most of them were fascinated by it. Like the majority of fighters, they were only familiar with full-throttle sessions that mimicked a fight. It didn't surprise me that flow sparring was a completely new idea for so many of them. It's something I had been preaching for a long time but it was often met with scepticism from outside SBG.

As for Conor's overall performance as a coach, I was very impressed. I don't think his future lies in coaching, but that has nothing to do with his ability to teach. It's because he's bloody incapable of showing up for anything on time! When Conor coached striking classes at SBG, he was absolutely excellent. Even nowadays in the gym, he's always helping his teammates. It comes naturally to him. But if you're scheduled to teach a 7 p.m. class, you can't turn up at 9 p.m. and act surprised when you find out that all your students have left. Punctuality is actually a hugely important part of coaching. If people are preparing themselves physically and mentally to train at a certain time, you can't keep them waiting. Maybe he'll rectify his poor timekeeping when he gets older and settles down, but it's hard to picture it now. I've worked with him for ten years and he's never been on time for anything. But if somebody asks Conor a question when he's on the mat, he could end up spending forty-five minutes explaining the answer. I've seen him do that many times in the gym, whether it's with a beginner or a fellow professional. The ability to teach is definitely there. The ability to arrive early is not. Conor has spent a lot of money on nice watches in the last couple of years. Some day he might actually start using them.

The fight we'd been waiting for, against José Aldo, was set for UFC 194 at the MGM Grand on 12 December. It would be a featherweight title unification bout – the reigning champion versus the interim champion.

There was universal agreement among Conor, his training partners, the other coaches and myself that while we had achieved the desired result against Chad Mendes, the training camp had been far too long and draining. For the next one, things needed to be different. We decided to scale things back by staying in Dublin until three weeks before the fight.

A lot had been invested in promoting and preparing for the fight when it was initially booked for July, so part of me wondered if we were about to go through all of that for a second time only for it to be postponed again. We were well accustomed to opponents pulling out, but this was different – this was Aldo, the long-time champion. We really, really wanted this fight.

When people referred to Conor as the 'interim' champion, he didn't like it. His view was that Aldo had gone running when the time came to fight, which made him the new champion. But Conor knew, as did everyone, that he couldn't legitimately claim to be the best featherweight in the world without beating José Aldo. Even if Aldo had been stripped of the belt and Conor had been crowned the undisputed champion after beating Mendes, he still couldn't claim to be the best featherweight in the world. That required a win over Aldo and nothing less. Aldo had become the best 145lb fighter in the world by seeing off the very best challengers on the planet for the past six years. In most cases he did so while in second gear. As nice as it had been to have a UFC belt in the gym, it was no more than a token.

After he concluded his duties as a coach on *The Ultimate Fighter*, Conor returned to Ireland in September 2015. He kept himself ticking over with some light training while he was away and I was curious to see how the knee had been holding up. Thankfully, it appeared to be as good as new. It was no longer restricting him at all. It hasn't been an issue since and I can only hope it stays that way.

People often ask me for a glimpse of the schedule for Conor's training camps, but the truth is that there isn't one. Some coaches like to organize camps into blocks – strength training in the first four weeks, turning strength into explosiveness for the second four weeks and so on – but I don't find that practical for MMA. With short-notice fights, opponents changing and stuff like that, the goalposts are always moving.

At SBG, our training doesn't really change, regardless of whether the athlete is preparing for a fight or not. We don't tend to do training camps in the same way that other teams do. In many gyms, fighters might take a few weeks off after a bout, during which they'll abandon their diet and do absolutely no training. Then they'll head back into a training camp for their next fight, starting from scratch, going from one extreme to the other. We prefer to keep ticking over at a similar, steady pace throughout the year. In Conor's case, he used to train twice a day but now he mostly does one long session – lasting three or four hours – each day. It's not intense from start to finish. Instead he maintains a steady pace all the way through. One day could be about sparring, the next might focus on pad work, another could be all about grappling. It's adaptable. There are no restrictions. He could wake up one morning and feel like he's not jumping out of his skin to train, so he might just come down and do a short session working on technique. The next day he might be on fire and you're lining up ten sparring partners for him. When that energy is there, it's important to capitalize on it. On the odd occasion that it's not, it's important to make allowances. Over the course of six, eight or ten weeks, you're going to have a few days when you're not feeling at your best. The content of the training changes every day. You go according to how you feel.

One side-effect of Conor being based in Dublin for the majority of this training camp was that we had to contend with people turning up at the gym looking for pictures and autographs. Conor has always been happy to accommodate his fans – he really appreciates the support – but we have a very strict policy about designating the gym as a place of work. Anybody who does come to the gym won't get beyond the front desk unless they're a member. People have shown up and said they've come all the way from America just to get a photo. They expect to march on through and ask for a selfie while Conor is in the middle of a session. People are sometimes shocked when we don't allow them to walk in and get what they want. But the gym is where we train and it's strictly off limits to the public. It's the fighters' place of business and it's important that they're not interrupted while conducting it.

*

It was full steam ahead for Conor's crack at becoming an undisputed UFC champion, but in the meantime there was another big night for SBG on 24 October: UFC Fight Night 76 at the 3Arena. Even though Conor wasn't involved, the tickets sold out in a matter of minutes. Once again there was a strong SBG presence on the bill, with Paddy Holohan, Aisling Daly and Cathal Pendred flying the flag. While Ais and Cathal were to feature on the prelims, Paddy had been given a main-card slot for his clash with American prospect Louis Smolka. It was a big fight and it became even bigger as the event drew nearer. With ten days to go, an injury to Stipe Miocic forced the cancellation of his heavyweight bout against Ben Rothwell. Paddy's fight was subsequently bumped up to be the penultimate fight of the night. But it didn't end there. On the Tuesday night before the event, we found out that Joseph Duffy was out of his fight against Dustin Poirier due to a concussion. That fight had been at the top of the bill, so with four days to go, Paddy was promoted to headline a UFC card in his home town, just as Conor had done fifteen months earlier.

In hindsight, it was too much, too soon. It had been a nice, low-key build-up to what was an important fight for Paddy, in which a win would have been rewarded with a place in the rankings in the 125lb division. Then, all of a sudden, a heavy weight of promotion rested on his shoulders. A lot of pressure accompanies the role of being an Irish fighter in a UFC main event on home soil, and Paddy felt it. He did his best but, as he confided in me afterwards, he just wasn't ready to handle it. His ultimate aim was to be involved in those high-profile occasions but he wanted to work his way into that position gradually. The expectation became extremely draining. Even the walk-out left him feeling tired. As soon as he stepped inside the octagon, his legs felt heavy. That's common for fighters — it's a natural feeling, a hormonal fight-or-flight response as blood rushes to the legs — but if you're cognizant of the magnitude of the situation, that can grow in your head and spread throughout your body, to the detriment of your performance. You can usually brush off that feeling of heaviness once the action begins, but if there's even a tiny seed of doubt in your mind, that seed will flourish and manifest itself in your physical output. That's exactly what happened to Paddy against Louis Smolka. He looked sluggish right from the start and he faded very quickly. That had never happened to him before. He has maintained a good pace in three-rounders before and against opponents that I'd rate as tougher than Smolka. But fair play to Smolka, who wasted no time in capitalizing. He scored a rear naked choke win in the second round. It was hugely disappointing, but Paddy learned so much from the experience, and I'm excited to see him putting those lessons into practice.

There were mixed fortunes for us earlier on the card, but the night really belonged to Aisling Daly. During the previous UFC show in Dublin, Ais had been stuck in filming for *The Ultimate Fighter* while her teammates were creating the biggest night in the history of Irish MMA. Missing out on that was really tough for her, so she was determined to make the most of this opportunity. She had been battling depression and was coming off a loss to Randa Markos the previous April, so Ais left no stone unturned in her preparation for this fight. Her opponent, Ericka Almeida, was a teammate of José Aldo's at Nova União in Brazil, so it was also a chance for Ais to draw first blood for SBG in that particular battle.

Everything that night went Aisling's way, from the walk-out to the fight itself. Before we went out, I told Ais to soak the whole occasion in. That's important for fighters. Sometimes we forget that. I want all my fighters to be able to look back on these moments some day with their grandkids and have great stories to tell. We can often be guilty of rushing through fights and ignoring the atmosphere, but you've got to create memories to cling to, which will remind you of why you put in all this effort when you reflect on your career in twenty, thirty, forty years' time.

However, I also said to Ais that when we got to the octagon, everything else was to be blocked out. That's exactly what happened. She looked me in the eye and I could see that she had flicked the switch. She was in the zone now. Ericka was good, but Ais was on fire. The unanimous-decision win was her reward for months of hard work.

It wasn't such a good night for Cathal Pendred. He'd had so many fights in such a short space of time – this was to be his sixth in just fifteen months – and I tried to steer him in the direction of taking a break. But he just wanted to keep going. His opponent, Tom Breese, had far less experience, but he's someone who I believe could go on to great things in the future. The difference in skill between them was enormous, as evidenced by Breese's first-round TKO win. Breese made it very one-sided. You could do nothing but tip your hat to him. He's definitely one to watch.

Cathal hadn't been his usual self in the build-up to that fight. The desire and determination that had taken him so far seemed to be lacking.

When Cathal told me a few weeks later that he had decided to retire from MMA, it didn't come as any great surprise. He had been going non-stop for a long time and I knew the hunger was starting to fade, as it eventually does for everyone. Other interests away from the gym were starting to enter his life, which is a healthy thing. I always encourage my fighters to make sure that they're working on an exit strategy for when that time comes. Cathal had a few things on the go, including potential movie roles, media work and opening a restaurant. As a result, he was starting to miss training sessions, which was extremely out of character for him. When you start seeing stuff like that, you know the fighter has one foot out the door already.

I'm pretty blunt with my fighters. Everything is black and white. They know they'll get all my attention if they're on the mat, but that won't be the case if they're skipping sessions. I have to put my energy into people who are in the gym. I've got forty fighters now, so I don't have time to chase them all if they're not showing up. The guys know that's part of the deal. Regardless of how big your upcoming fight may be, if you're not on the mat, you're not even in my head. If we're not having a lot of interaction on the mat, there's not much I can do for you as a coach. I know some coaches do it differently. Kieran McGeeney is great when it comes to monitoring his players all the time. If one of them is out on a Friday night, Kieran will hear about it and he'll be at the guy's door on Saturday morning. I can't imagine anything more terrifying than seeing Kieran at the door. But I've never really been that type. If you're at the gym, we're there together.

Cathal has always been very honest with himself, and he recognized that there was a substantial skill difference between himself and Tom Breese. After a loss like that, you have to take a step back and assess your situation. Do you want to be that guy who's just a journeyman and a stepping stone for other fighters? If your heart isn't in it the way it had been before, you could end up getting hurt. When he told me he had decided to walk away, I thought it was a very brave and wise decision. I was proud of him for making it himself, because most guys need to be told when they've gone too far. Cathal had done some amazing things in mixed martial arts. Winning four times in the UFC after being a Cage Warriors champion is something only one other Irishman has achieved. He left MMA with his head held high and rightly so, particularly given how late he came to the sport. He was an inspiration to many people, including myself. If you want something badly enough, never let anyone tell you that you're not capable of attaining it. You'll eventually reap the benefits of possessing that kind of attitude. Cathal Pendred is the proof.

Three weeks prior to the Aldo fight, we flew out to Los Angeles for the final stages of Conor's training camp. We were preparing for a UFC title fight, just as we had been at UFC 189, but things were so much more relaxed this time. On that occasion there had been a lot of focus on the knee and how it would hold up. Here, it was just about the fight. *This is where SBG is now*, I thought. *This is our level and it's time to make a mark. It's the best guy in Ireland against the best guy in the world. Let's see if we belong here.* Training had gone perfectly, so there was no need to be tense or apprehensive. All the bases had been covered. We were as ready as we had ever been.

The plan was to spend a couple of weeks in LA before driving up to Las Vegas for fight week. Conor had been admiring the expertise of a movement practitioner named Ido Portal for a while, and he invited Ido to join us for those final stages of training. By then, all the hard work was already done. Conor had been preparing for this fight for almost the entire year, so it was important to keep not only the body but also the mind fresh and loose. Ido's callisthenic exercises were perfect for that.

At the pre-fight press conference a couple of days before UFC 194, the media read a lot into how laid-back Conor was. They were even examining his attire. Instead of the usual expensive suit, Conor showed up in a pair of jeans and a polo shirt. Having barked and snarled at Aldo during their previous media encounters, Conor actually gave him a respectful nod at the end of this staredown. Reporters wondered if this was some sort of reverse psychology to engage Aldo further in the mind games, but I think they were probably overanalysing it. As I recall, Conor's new suits just hadn't arrived on time. In addition, I think everyone had grown tired of promoting the fight at that stage. Having invested so much in it, Conor had come to the end of that particular task. In his mind, Aldo had shown up and the fight was definitely, finally, going to happen, so the time for talking was over.

This was to be Conor's first time competing since the UFC introduced a ban on intravenous rehydration after the weigh-ins, so the weight-cut had the potential to be trickier than usual because he usually used IV. But thanks to the assistance of George Lockhart – a nutrition consultant and former fighter – this cut was as easy as it could possibly have been. The preparations had been absolutely perfect. There was nothing I would have changed. If the fight didn't go our way, there would simply be no excuses.

I expected the fight to unfold one of two ways. Either Aldo would be cautious and fight very defensively during a tentative first round, or else he would bullrush Conor early and try to get his hands on him as quickly as possible. I hoped it would be the latter, because I was sure that would play into Conor's hands. He's a brilliant counter-puncher on the back foot and would punish Aldo if he overextended.

Once again the Irish fans had travelled to Las Vegas in huge numbers. However, this fight wasn't quite so much about the occasion. We were used to that by now and knew that nothing at the MGM Grand could top what we had experienced at UFC 189. This was purely about going in, defeating José Aldo and taking that belt. Everything else was immaterial.

As we made the walk to the octagon and Conor stepped inside, there was a massive feeling of relief. Finally, this was it. It was almost as if we were at peace, as a team. The fight was going to happen. José Aldo against Conor McGregor: it was here for real now, and it wasn't going away until the debate over the best featherweight in the world was settled. Since Conor's time with Cage Warriors, I had been picturing their paths crossing. People laughed when Conor mentioned Aldo's name in an MTV documentary that was made just after he was signed by the UFC. No debuting featherweight had done that before. You had to earn the right to talk about Aldo, let alone fight him. But Conor was very serious. He wouldn't have seen any point in fighting in the UFC unless Aldo was his target.

Afterwards, many observers discussed Aldo's pre-fight demeanour and body language, claiming that he seemed tense and anxious during the walk-out and introductions. It's easy to be an expert in hindsight, but I'd be lying if I said I noticed anything different about him. He had his head down until the fight began, but that was normal for him. It had never failed him before.

Having given a deliberately restrained prediction of 'Conor to win inside three rounds' when the bout with Aldo was originally announced earlier in the year, I was more honest when writing my column for The42.ie just before the fight at UFC 194: 'Part of me can see it being over in sixty seconds.' I genuinely believed that could be the case, but that didn't make it any less shocking when it actually happened. After such a drawn-out build-up, the contest that transpired was the shortest title bout in UFC history.

Conor charged out of his corner and took the centre of the octagon. He opened up with a straight left which narrowly missed the target, followed by an oblique kick to Aldo's front leg. And then came the bullrush. Aldo pressed forward and faked a right to disguise a left hook, which actually landed. But Conor beat Aldo to the punch. He stepped back, countered with a beautiful left and the previously infallible UFC featherweight champion was chopped down like a pine tree. A year of preparation for just thirteen seconds . . . but we weren't complaining.

I watched on in amazement, my mouth wide open, as I tried to process the fact that a historic moment in MMA, in Irish sport, had just happened a few feet in front of me. There was pandemonium in the arena all around me and I was soon partaking in it, but it took a while to come to terms with the significance of what had occurred. It's never nice to see a fighter hurt like Aldo had been, particularly a legendary champion like him. But Conor's achievement was simply phenomenal. Has a bigger statement ever been made in the UFC? I doubt it. Conor wouldn't have to contend with that word he didn't like any longer. Now he was undisputed.

After the new champion had been officially crowned and we made our way backstage, I found a quiet room and lay down on the floor. Orlagh can be sneaky with her phone and captured the moment I lay on the floor. At a time like that, it's difficult to stop yourself from reflecting on the journey. I thought about being beaten up in Rathmines; about painting that tiny shed in Phibsboro on a scorching hot day; about Dave Roche and all the training partners from the days when we barely even knew what we were doing; about never having a penny to my name because I spent everything I earned on furthering my martial arts education; about the tough nights of working on the doors; about how I was in tears when the gym in Tallaght fell through; about being kicked out of the place in Rathcoole; about all the losses and the setbacks. For the vast majority of the journey, the most convenient move would have been to throw in the towel. But there's no easy route to any place that's worth getting to.

We enjoyed the celebrations, of course, but overall it had been a bittersweet night for SBG. Earlier on the UFC 194 card, Gunnar Nelson had suffered a comprehensive loss against Demian Maia. It wasn't long after Conor's win that my thoughts turned to Gunni. It's always been the case that I'll linger on a defeat even on our most successful nights. If there are nine wins and one loss, it's the loss that will consume my mind afterwards. I wasn't sure how Gunni would react to it – I was almost expecting him to tell me that he was done with the sport – but when we sat down together with the benefit of a couple of days to reflect on the fight, his words were music to my ears.

'I've never been more certain that I'm going to win that welterweight belt. I'm 100 per cent convinced about that. I love this. I don't want to do anything else. I'm going to be the champion.'

I was so happy to hear Gunni say that. He acknowledged immediately that the loss was a valuable lesson and he was already enthusiastic about putting what he had learned into action. It marked a real change in his mentality, because his response to losing to Rick Story hadn't been nearly so positive. Gunni could have reacted to the defeat to Maia by telling himself that his opponent was just so much better than him that there was no point in continuing to be a fighter, but instead he chose to focus on the fact that he had survived three rounds without being submitted by probably the best Brazilian jiu-jitsu practitioner in mixed martial arts. There were times when he could have looked for a way out, and most guys probably would have, but Gunni persevered. Sure, he had made physical errors in the fight, but none of them were unsolvable. And given that he's ten years younger than Demian Maia, Gunni has plenty of time to rectify his mistakes.

I hadn't had much of a Christmas in 2014, because Conor had been preparing for his fight against Dennis Siver. I made up for that in

2015 by spending ten days over the festive period with my family in Spain. Usually when I'm getting on an aeroplane it's for something MMA related, so this was a very welcome novelty. There was no talk of fights for the duration of the holiday and it was just what I needed.

I knew that as soon as I stepped off the plane back in Dublin, Conor would embark on a quest to do something that had never been done before.

18

I assumed it was a joke when I first saw the story. 'Oireachtas to discuss petition to put Conor McGregor's face on the €1 coin,' the headline read.

It sounded ridiculous, but seemingly there was substance to it. An Irish government committee was to examine the petition, which had been submitted by a member of the public. Unsurprisingly, it was eventually dismissed – but the episode was another example of how drastically Conor's place in Irish society had changed. For most of the time I've known him, he barely had a €1 coin in his pocket. Now they were talking about putting his face on it. It was absolutely crazy, but that's just the way things were going. He had become the biggest star MMA had ever seen, generating record revenue for the UFC and bringing the sport into the homes of people who had never paid attention to it before. Now, after each fight, you think there's no way he can get any bigger, but every time he proves that theory wrong.

The discussion regarding the outrageous coin proposal took place just twenty-four hours after Conor's next fight had officially been announced. Conor had already committed to fighting at UFC 200, which was going to be an enormous event – but that wasn't happening until 9 July. I knew that Conor – particularly given that the fight with José Aldo had lasted just thirteen seconds – would want to fight again much sooner. There was no way he was going to sit on the sidelines for seven months.

In the aftermath of the Aldo fight, a couple of options were being discussed in the media. One was a rematch with Aldo, which was unlikely in the short term as the knockout would have restricted him from returning to training for quite a while. Another possibility was a featherweight title defence against Frankie Edgar. A former lightweight champion, Edgar was on a solid run of five consecutive wins at 145lb – the most recent of which was a first-round knockout of Chad Mendes just twenty-four hours before Conor defeated Aldo. Conor was enthused by the idea of taking on Frankie Edgar. He was the only legitimate featherweight contender Conor hadn't yet fought. That was attractive, but Conor's preference regarding his next move wasn't in the featherweight division at all.

A move up to the lightweight division was something we had openly discussed; sooner or later, it was an inevitability. The weight-cut to 145lb was hard work for Conor, but 155lb would be far more straightforward. On top of that, there was an opportunity to make history. No fighter had ever been a UFC champion in two different weight classes at the same time. Following his quick win against Donald Cerrone in December, lightweight champion Rafael dos Anjos was in need of a new challenger and the chasing pack in that division hadn't exactly been setting the world alight. Conor saw an opening and when an idea forms in his head, there's simply no removing it until he follows through on it. He wasn't completely abandoning the 145lb division, but for now things looked more attractive in the heavier weight class. Conor was intent on replicating what he had achieved with Cage Warriors: he wanted a belt on each shoulder.

In spite of the protests of some members of the UFC's lightweight division, the fight made sense and it was officially announced on 12 January 2016. Rafael dos Anjos versus Conor McGregor for the UFC lightweight title at UFC 197 – which later became UFC 196, due to some reshuffling on the UFC's calendar – at the MGM Grand Garden Arena in Las Vegas on 5 March. A chance to do what had never been done before. Unprecedented events. Just weeks after a historic night in Las Vegas, the preparations began for another.

Stylistically, Rafael dos Anjos was nothing we hadn't seen before. To put it in simple terms, he's a bit like a southpaw version of José Aldo. Dos Anjos had been on a good run of form, during which he defeated the likes of Anthony Pettis, Benson Henderson and Nate Diaz. In terms of his status as a champion, I felt he had done well to capitalize during a stale period for the lightweight division. No fight is easy at this level, and we would train accordingly for the significance of the occasion, but my belief was that Conor's superior skills would result in one-way traffic and another first-round finish in our favour.

In a couple of columns I wrote as the fight approached, I discussed Conor's move up to 155lb, probably his most natural weight; and I mentioned that I wouldn't rule out a subsequent move up to the next division – welterweight, 170lb – either. Various media outlets interpreted this as Conor McGregor's camp issuing a call-out to the reigning welterweight champion, Robbie Lawler. Conor admitted publicly that he was considering a challenge at 170lb as a possible option in the future and the press lapped it up. We hadn't even fought for a second belt yet and already people were talking about a third. Conor had never fought at welterweight before. It was something we were open to, but it hadn't been discussed in any great detail. As it happened, that 170lb debut was going to come much sooner than expected.

With the fight just twelve days away, I learned the bad news via a text from Conor: 'Dos Anjos is out.'

This was late on a Monday night. By the Tuesday afternoon, the news that dos Anjos had sustained a foot injury was everywhere. Once again, Conor's opponent had withdrawn. It was the sixth time it had happened in his last twelve fights.

That left the UFC in a race against time to save the main event of a big pay-per-view card, because there was never any question of Conor pulling out too. We were ready to go. The onus was on the UFC to find a replacement. A few guys raised their hands, but I knew from the start who was going to get the nod.

When Conor first expressed his desire to move up to lightweight after the Aldo fight, there were actually two possibilities – one being the title shot against dos Anjos, the other a meeting with Nate Diaz, who competed at both lightweight and welterweight. We were very intrigued by the latter, to be perfectly honest, but the chance to make history was too good to turn down. Now, with dos

Anjos having pulled out, the situation was resolved within thirty-six hours. Diaz wanted to fight Conor, Conor wanted to fight Diaz, and the fans wanted to watch two of the most entertaining and popular fighters in the sport locking horns. It made perfect sense. Diaz was ranked fifth at lightweight, but that didn't accurately reflect his ability or standing in the game.

It was disappointing that the chance to win the second belt was gone, for now, but there was no point in complaining about that. A fight against Nate Diaz was a pretty good alternative. I've been a big admirer of the Diaz brothers – Nate and his older brother, Nick – for a long time. If you're a fan of MMA, there's just no way that you can possibly dislike those guys. They're already icons of the sport. Nate and Nick have unapologetically done things their own way for years; they don't care for conformity and I've got a lot of time for their attitude. They come to scrap every single time. Regardless of the outcome, there has never been a time when the Diaz brothers haven't delivered for the fans. Boring fights aren't in their arsenal and they actually seem to get stronger and better as the rounds progress. The Diaz approach is to walk through the opponent's shots and try to take him out. I believed that, up against Conor's own unique style, was the recipe for a captivating contest which would be a lot of fun for everyone involved – the fans and the media and the fighters themselves. I also believed that a win was well within Conor's capability. Diaz had looked impressive in his win against top-five lightweight Michael Johnson in December, but he had allowed himself to be hit very often. I expected Conor to expose that flaw.

The only obstacle in arranging this fight was weight. Owing to the short notice, Diaz didn't want it at 155lb. At first, a catchweight of 160lb was suggested, and Diaz seemed happy with that initially. But then he changed his mind and asked for 165lb. At that point in the negotiations, Conor was done with the back-and-forth.

'Tell Nate to get comfortable,' he said. 'I don't want him making any excuses. Let's do it at 170lb.'

And that was that. In the space of twelve weeks, Conor was going to fight in UFC main events at both featherweight and welter-weight, jumping right over lightweight. 'Unprecedented' was beginning to feature regularly in his vocabulary. His mind was in a place where he felt nobody could touch him. The who, where or when of the situation didn't matter.

The build-up to this new match-up was brief but enjoyable, as two witty guys exchanged insults during the press conferences. However, it was disappointing and quite baffling for me to observe Diaz's accusations that Conor had used performance-enhancing drugs. Considering that a couple of Diaz's own teammates had been penalized for PED use previously, it seemed particularly bizarre. It was probably little more than an attempt to get under Conor's skin. But if Diaz was hoping to wind Conor up, he didn't succeed. I've always thought that clean fighters recognize each other. I believe Diaz is a clean fighter and that, deep down, he knew there was no substance to what he was saying.

Conor had just arrived in the US, accompanied by Artem Lobov and Ido Portal, when he learned of the withdrawal of Rafael dos Anjos. Again, Los Angeles was the initial base before moving across to Las Vegas. I followed them out for fight week, landing on Monday. With nine SBG fighters competing on a show in Dublin for British promotion BAMMA on the previous Saturday night, I had been unable to travel out any earlier.

When I met the guys in LA, they were incredibly calm. Even compared to the José Aldo build-up, it was a very laid-back atmosphere. It felt like we were preparing for a fun exhibition fight, not a UFC pay-per-view main event. With no weight to cut, Conor was certainly enjoying a more flexible diet and that was reflected in his mood. I had never seen him in such good spirits in fight week.

Removing the need to cut weight actually made it a very strange time because those last few days are ordinarily focused almost entirely on the number on the scales. Without that, I found that I almost had to remind myself that we were actually preparing for a fight. That change to the routine really threw us off. When we were backstage, waiting to walk out for the weigh-ins, I realized that I didn't even have a bottle of water with me. We didn't need one, because Conor was fully hydrated and well under the weight limit at 168lb, but I searched around and found one anyway, because that's just how we usually do things.

I've always felt that having a relaxed mindset going into a fight is a positive, but maybe there's such a thing as being a little bit too relaxed. Both backstage and in the arena itself, it seemed like there was a party atmosphere at the MGM Grand for UFC 196. It didn't feel like any other UFC event I had been involved in. Even in the changing rooms beforehand it was difficult to process the fact that there was a fight ahead. From Conor's perspective, everything was fine. The warm-up was good and he was looking as sharp as ever. But this was our fourth time in these changing rooms in the space of eighteen months and this time it just felt different.

This was the first time at the MGM Grand that we walked out after the opponent. As we waited for our turn to go, I had my eyes on one of the TV monitors backstage. For a split second, I actually said to myself: 'Oh, cool. Look, Nate Diaz is fighting.'

I quickly checked myself and remembered that I wasn't sitting at home watching a UFC event from the comfort of the couch. Yes, Nate Diaz was fighting, but we were the ones in the opposite corner.

When we walked out and positioned ourselves beside the octagon, I was excited. These were two alpha male warriors going toe-to-toe. There were no belts on the line, no drama over weight-cutting. It felt like old-school prize-fighting. One martial artist testing his skills against another. This was purely about ability. As a spectator, I was eager to find out what would unfold. This contest was going to be a privilege to watch.

The first round played out pretty much as I expected. At the end of it I was relatively satisfied, but not completely happy. While Conor landed plenty of good shots, I noticed early on that he was winding up a lot on his left hand. He was sort of falling into shots, which is something he usually would never do. He connected well a couple of times and sensed that Diaz might be about to fade, which is what usually happens when he lands those punches. He felt that a finish was imminent, which only served to convince him to wind up that left hand more and more in order to pursue it. He was investing a lot of energy in those punches, instead of using the clean technique that he has become renowned for.

Late in the round, Conor gave up a single-leg takedown. However, he reversed it well by using the type of jiu-jitsu that he never seems to be given credit for. It was beautiful work against a BJJ black belt to finish the round on a positive note. That was one round in the bag, 10–9 to Conor.

I made my way into the octagon at the end of the round. When Conor sat down on the stool, I was taken aback. His mouth was wide open and he was breathing heavily. *Okay*, I thought. *I haven't seen that before.* That was a concern. He had put a lot of energy into searching for a knockout punch and it was evidently taking a toll on his gas tank.

Nate Diaz is not easy to put away. He had already proven that over the course of his nine years in the UFC, during which he had been stopped just once in twenty-one fights. I encouraged Conor to slow things down in the second round; to work his jab and fire off some leg-kicks while staying on the outside to reduce the intensity that we had seen so far. You can afford to do that against Nate Diaz. He won't look to maul you. There's scope to hover outside of range for a round to get your breath back, if necessary. That's what I wanted Conor to do. We weren't in any hurry to win this fight. With a potential twenty minutes still remaining, the opportunities for a stoppage would eventually open up.

Within the first few exchanges of the second round, however, Conor was loading up the left hand again, picking up where he had left off. Maybe he felt something in there that I didn't – I trusted him – but I knew that approach was taking a toll on his energy reserves. I could only hope that it wouldn't backfire.

Conor was still in the ascendancy early in the round, but the tide soon began to turn. Just beyond the midway point, Diaz landed a nice straight left square on Conor's face. Then I saw something I had never seen before: Conor's legs wobbled. I had never once seen him rocked by a punch. He was hurt. We've been working together for ten years and this was the first time I'd seen Conor hit so cleanly. Ordinarily, if he's hit by a punch, Conor's default response is to smile at his opponent, walk forward and send three or four back in return. But there was nothing to smile about here. He was in trouble and it startled me.

A situation like that is a challenging one for me. The coach in me wants to steer the fighter back into the contest in pursuit of the victory. But as for the friend, the brother, the guardian? His protective instincts are heightened and the priority is the safety of the fighter. For that side of me, when I see one of my fighters hurt like that, the result ceases to matter.

Conor did his utmost to keep himself in the fight, and he was able to catch Diaz with a couple of good shots in spite of the pressure he was now under. But with little over a minute remaining in the round, he put himself in danger with a laboured takedown attempt. Diaz was able to sprawl before attacking with a guillotine-choke attempt. Just as he had done against Chad Mendes, Conor sought to use 'The Heartbreaker' to squirm free, but he was unable to complete the roll – probably owing to fatigue – so he couldn't make it out. Diaz maintained top position and moved into full-mount, while landing heavy shots. It was an ominous situation for Conor. Exhausted and at the mercy of a high-level BJJ practitioner, he tried once more to break free but ended up exposing his back momentarily. Diaz needed no invitation to seize the opportunity. He locked in a rear naked choke and there was no way out. Conor tapped, referee Herb Dean stepped in to confirm the biggest win of Diaz's career, and a deafening silence at the MGM Grand greeted Conor McGregor's first taste of defeat in the UFC.

While the rest of the world began to come to terms with the implications of such a shocking outcome, the result was the furthest thing from my thoughts at that moment. I needed to know that Conor was okay. That straight left had hurt him and he'd taken a few more after that too. Even if he had won, my initial thoughts would have been the same. He had shipped his fair share of damage. It was much later, when I thought about the impact of the defeat, that I said to myself: 'I'll do whatever I have to do to make sure I never see him hurt like that again.'

When I entered the octagon in the aftermath of the fight, I was relieved that he seemed okay physically, but the emotional pain he was enduring was written all over his face. I hugged him and delivered a message.

'Who else is doing what you're doing? Who else would move up two weight classes and fight a top guy on less than two weeks' notice? You could have backed out of this when dos Anjos pulled out and nobody would have said a negative word, but unlike what everybody else would have done, you didn't even give it a thought. You hold your head up high and speak positively when you're on that microphone. Be proud of what you're doing because I know I am. Remember what Fedor Emelianenko said: "Only those who never stand up, never fall down."'

Next, Conor spoke to Joe Rogan. For the first time, he was doing so as the defeated fighter. It was a bitter pill for him to swallow but he handled it with grace and humility. People appeared to be surprised by that afterwards, but I expected nothing less. He had experienced losses earlier in his career. He had been here before. This time, the difference was that the entire world was watching.

'I took the chance going in at 170lb but Nate came in and I felt I took him in the first round, but I was inefficient with my energy. But I'm humble in victory or defeat. I respect Nate. He came in, he took the fight at short notice and he done the job. He was efficient, I wasn't efficient. That was it, I feel. It is what it is. I'll face it like a man, like a champion, and I'll come back and do it again.'

In spite of the outcome, Lorenzo Fertitta continued what had become a tradition afterwards when he brought a bottle of Midleton Very Rare whiskey into the dressing room. There was no win to celebrate this time, but we all had a drink to toast a memorable contest. Having said that, Conor wasn't paying much attention. He already had his head stuck in a phone, watching the fight back.

What people seem to forget about this whole thing is that Conor just loves to fight. Everything else – money, belts or fame – is just a bonus. It's important that people understand that. He puts himself in dangerous, risky situations by accepting late changes of opponent and exploring different weight classes. Who else would do that in the same way he does? He keeps doing it because it's all just so much fun to him. He takes those chances because he knows he'll end up regretting it if he doesn't, irrespective of the consequences. A strategy error in round two was the difference between victory and defeat on this occasion. Nevertheless, the sun still rose the following morning, just as it would have done if he had won.

We took a gamble and this time it didn't pay off. That won't change how we go about our business. We will, however, continue striving to make sure that we're as well prepared as we can possibly be. That's what gives us the confidence to face any challenge. We'll take that risk again if we need to.

Lessons were learned and changes will be made. Two weeks isn't quite long enough to spend in the US before a fight like that. We need at least three, ideally four.

Many fans bizarrely pointed the finger at Ido Portal for this loss, just as some of them had credited him for the win against José Aldo. The reality is that Ido wasn't responsible for either result. While I was still back in Dublin preparing my other fighters for BAMMA, the fans were watching a lot of footage of Conor going through some light movement exercises with Ido. They couldn't understand why he wasn't sparring and working with me, even though we've said many times that the final fortnight before a bout is just about staying fresh and loose. When we got to Vegas, people were stopping me in the hotel and asking why I wasn't Conor's coach any more. It was ridiculous. Conor's work with Ido is just something fun for him to do at the end of a long training camp. Unlike some camps, we don't spar during that period. Late sparring is one of the reasons why there are so many injury pull-outs in other camps. For us, the intensity of the eyes watching us increases during the final two weeks, but the training levels decrease. People didn't see the eight-to-ten weeks beforehand when we had done some big sessions.

Frankie McConville, an excellent Muay Thai coach in Belfast, once said to me: 'Nothing is as boring as training for a fight because you know exactly how many miles you have to run and how many rounds of sparring to do. It's mind-numbing.' Every once in a while, you introduce something new and enjoyable to freshen things up. That's been Ido's role for those last couple of fights and I believe it has been a success.

Not having to cut weight for the fight against Diaz was supposedly helpful, but in hindsight it was undoubtedly a hindrance. Cutting weight may not be much fun, but it does serve as a reminder that you're preparing for a fight. It focuses the mind and has been an enormous part of what we've been doing. Without that ritual, things were just weird. It left us all in an unusual state of mind. The routine we had established was suddenly absent. The need to cut weight gets the fighter in the zone and lets them know that a fight is on the horizon. If a person is starving, they're in survival mode. It focuses the mind and taps into the reptilian part of the brain. When Conor is cutting weight, he views his opponent as an obstacle in the way of his next meal. It's a primal thing. On the other hand, when you've eaten a good dinner, all you want to do is relax in front of the TV. The fire in your belly is replaced by food. Being stuffed isn't conducive to maintaining a competitive mindset.

Even for his next welterweight fight, Conor's diet will be strict. We've accepted now that it's an important element of his preparation, so you can expect him to come in on weigh-in day at around 165lb. No cheesecakes this time! It will be nutrition geared specifically towards performance.

Conor's loss was a lesson and it's one that our next wave of fighters, in particular, will be able to learn from. He's blazing a trail for the younger fighters coming through. They can study his journey and benefit from every step.

There were mistakes made and, as the coach, I'll take ownership of them. We should have travelled out sooner. We should have maintained the same level of meticulous preparation and competitive mindset that we had become accustomed to. We won't be tucking into desserts, driving around in flashy cars and fucking about. Well, maybe there will still be nice cars, but anything that negatively impacts our usual level of preparation will be knocked on the head. It has to be, and I know it will be, because nobody is more critical of Conor than Conor himself.

In the aftermath of the defeat to Nate Diaz, it was difficult to sit back and observe what Conor was going through. It wasn't because so many of his detractors celebrated the result and revelled in the fact that, for once, he was unable to back up his cocky predictions. That kind of public reaction didn't come as a surprise. Conor wasn't bothered by it so neither was I. What I found tough was that I was familiar enough with Conor by now to know that the loss, the errors that were made, would be eating him up inside, keeping him awake at night and occupying his mind every minute of every hour of every day. But there was substantial consolation in the knowledge that Conor would emerge stronger and wiser. One of the great things about this sport is that even after you've reached the top, you don't stop learning. In fact, the lessons just become more valuable than they've ever been before.

Epilogue

Shortly before this book was completed, one of my fighters was involved in a contest which resulted in a man losing his life. My fighter, Charlie Ward, was victorious by TKO in the third round of his bout against Portuguese opponent João Carvalho at Dublin's National Stadium on Saturday, 9 April 2016. It was a very tight contest that could have gone either way. João came close to stopping Charlie on a couple of occasions but the balance tipped marginally in Charlie's favour in the final round. After knocking João to the ground with a right hook, he followed up with strikes before the referee stepped in to bring the fight to an end.

Later that night I learned that João had been taken to Beaumont Hospital after complaining of feeling unwell in the changing room after the fight. João ended up in a critical condition and underwent emergency brain surgery. He was dead within forty-eight hours.

Given that I was in the opposite corner, João's death hit me hard. The night after I discovered the tragic news, I didn't sleep a wink. I was in a bad way. João had travelled to Ireland to do something he loved; something he had devoted his life to. Thinking about what his family must have been going through just tore me apart.

Having given the whole scenario plenty of thought, I'll openly admit that I wondered whether this was something I wanted to continue doing. But when I asked myself that question, walking away never felt like it would be the right course of action.

Your emotions constantly alternate in the aftermath of something like that. I found it tough, but for Charlie it was particularly difficult. Sometimes you can think rationally and accept that you merely competed within the rules of a sporting contest. But there are other times when you're an emotional wreck and you start to question – incorrectly – whether what happened was your fault. That's something Charlie has to endure, but he's doing so with the benefit of whatever support he needs from his coaches and teammates.

There was some peace of mind for him a few days later when João's brother gave a TV interview in which he insisted nobody was to blame, that João loved the sport and nothing would ever have stopped him from pursuing his dream of making a successful living from MMA. Both fighters entered the cage with the very same intention. Charlie knows that with another flip of the coin, he could have been the unfortunate one.

I've cornered for nearly a thousand fights and I can honestly say that this one didn't stand out as being more punishing than any other. There was a lot of grappling involved and it did look like quite a tiring contest. When I heard afterwards that João had collapsed in the changing room, I immediately assumed it was due to exhaustion. Even though he had won the fight, Charlie was also quite fatigued. There didn't seem to have been a huge amount of heavy shots landed by either fighter. There were probably fewer punches landed over the course of the entire bout than you'd see in one round of a professional boxing match. I certainly wouldn't describe it as particularly brutal.

The finish actually reminded me of Conor McGregor's fight against Chad Mendes. With João in the turtle position, Charlie pounced and threw nine additional shots, most of which landed on João's shoulder and forearm. Recalling Conor's victory against Mendes, people bemoaned what they believed was an early stoppage. Yet on this occasion, critics said the referee stepped in between João and Charlie too late. It's easy to complain about the stoppage with the benefit of hindsight, but the reality was that it didn't look out of place at the time. The referee gave João a chance to recover when he went down. As soon as a couple of those shots connected with his head and it was clear that João wasn't fighting back or defending himself intelligently, the ref intervened.

I didn't see João backstage afterwards but others who did said he initially seemed okay. He even asked Conor for a picture. There didn't appear to be anything out of the ordinary about the situation, which added to the sense of shock over such a tragic outcome.

João's passing became a huge news story globally, which tells you just how rare and unforeseen a death in MMA is. For days afterwards I was inundated with calls and messages from the biggest media outlets around the world. Eventually, I had to change my number because the phone just didn't stop ringing. Much of the media's reaction focused on calls to ban mixed martial arts, with journalists keen to get my response.

You're in a weird place at a time like that. It was difficult for everyone connected to SBG. Every fighter and coach in the gym was hounded by the media. It was almost as though we didn't have a chance to mourn because we were trying to put on this public front in an attempt to represent the sport in a positive manner as it came under fire.

In every sport there are tragedies and there's not always somebody to blame. I read an article recently which said that for every ten successful ascents of Mount Everest, there is one death. Yet there never seems to be any outcry for banning mountaineering. There have been deaths in many sports – cycling, rugby, boxing, etc. – yet people claim MMA is different because it involves striking your opponent. My belief is that if a sport is to be banned, that decision shouldn't be made based on its perception or intent. The sport should be banned only if it can be proven to be disproportionately dangerous in relation to other sports. The statistics show that, in terms of injuries and fatalities, MMA is by no means the most dangerous sporting activity. If there are no calls for other sports to be banned, why should MMA be any different?

Banning a sport because of a death would result in the world being left with few – if any – sports at all. If that's your process of reasoning, you're better off staying indoors and watching TV for the rest of your life. But that's not the safest option either. Having no sporting activity in your life whatsoever is far more dangerous to your health than competing in sport. It's human nature to want to test your physical limits. Some people like to kick a ball or climb a mountain, others prefer to compete in martial arts. That's the way life has been for a long time and it's not going to change.

At the time of writing, an inquest and investigation into the exact causes of João Carvalho's death is ongoing. Was there a pre-existing issue or was the damage done by one of the shots he took? I don't know the answer to that, but I'm sure there will eventually be one.

One of the main talking points in the media after the fight was the fact that mixed martial arts is not recognized by Sport Ireland (formerly the Irish Sports Council), the state's sporting body. Without government recognition or regulation, there are no standards that MMA must adhere to in Ireland. Currently, any person can run an MMA event in this country and there are no minimum requirements pertaining to officiating, medical care or anything else. That should not be the case. A promoter is generally a businessman whose priority is to make a profit, so the level of care they provide for fighters shouldn't be at their discretion. No one can stop you from hosting an MMA event with the lowest of standards if you so wish. Gym owners like myself can choose not to cooperate with such a promoter, but they'll always find willing fighters elsewhere.

Total Extreme Fighting was the promotion which hosted the bout between Charlie Ward and João Carvalho. Straight after the fight I had to dash backstage to prepare another one of my fighters, Luka Jelčić, who was due to compete later in the evening. Therefore, I wasn't in a position to scrutinize comprehensively the medical procedures that were in place on the night. However, to the naked eye, everything appeared to be of a high standard. In fact, the doctors present were performing head injury assessments between each round in every fight, which is something I had never seen before at any level. It seemed to me that things were being done correctly, but having said that, I'm not in a position to evaluate the doctors' track records or determine whether the correct protocols were completely followed. I wasn't overseeing every single aspect of the show, but things appeared to be in order from what I could see.

João Carvalho's death has served as a reminder that, while these occurrences are extremely rare, there are still risks and dangers involved in MMA. That's something I've never shied away from. I'm passionate about defending my sport and its safety record, but my head isn't buried in the sand either. That's why regulation for MMA in Ireland is so important. We can't eliminate the risks involved, but with government assistance we can certainly minimize the possibility of such a terrible tragedy recurring.

There's no silver lining to be taken from any person's death but we still have to make sure that we react to this in the right way. Regulation for MMA in Ireland is something I've been striving for, and while it is absolutely regrettable that it took a man's death to act as the catalyst for the powers-that-be to share in the desire to achieve that goal, at least we now appear to be heading in the right direction.

In my role as president of the Irish Amateur Pankration Association – an organization that represents MMA in Ireland – I have entered preliminary discussions with government and Sport Ireland officials. I'm keen to follow the model in Sweden, where they've had a national governing body to regulate all aspects of MMA since 2007.

Securing recognition for MMA in Ireland remains a significant challenge. There's still much work to be done. However, getting to that point would be a more important step for the sport here than any world title or UFC event.

Unfortunately we cannot guarantee that there will never be another fatality. But what I do know is that I want to do everything I possibly can to ensure that every individual who competes in mixed martial arts in Ireland – and all over the world, for that matter – returns to their family afterwards in good health.

Whenever I tell people about the most difficult parts of my journey, they always seem to assume that the only thing that kept me going was the thought that I'd eventually coach a UFC champion and the biggest superstar the sport has ever seen. As if I knew when

I was taking out a loan to rent a shed at the back of someone's house in Phibsboro that I was on my way to being involved in some of the biggest occasions in the history of mixed martial arts. That was the dream, of course, but only a tiny percentage of people ever get to experience the very pinnacle of their profession. Given the recent success that SBG has had, I can understand why people will look at me today and conclude that this was how it was destined to be. But that really isn't the case.

This has been a rollercoaster ride. There were as many low points as there were highlights along the way. At times it might have made more sense to get off and try something else, but I'm certainly glad I never did. My long-term involvement in this sport didn't hinge on UFC success. To be completely honest, that has been nothing other than a bonus, albeit a pretty huge one. All I've ever wanted was to do enough to ensure that MMA paid the bills. As long as that was the case, I was in this for life. There are a lot of other coaches in Ireland who have been involved since the early days. They haven't had successful UFC fighters, but they're as enthusiastic about the sport now as they've ever been. It could very easily have been me in the same position.

I'm extremely grateful to have become involved with a golden generation of fighters from our little island, who happened to be led by one of the most remarkable athletes and characters in the history of mixed martial arts and, indeed, all Irish sport. I've been told that it was a coincidence that so many fighters with so much talent happened to arrive at the same time, but I don't think this is really about talent. As I see it, the coincidence was that so many fighters with such an incredible work ethic and appetite for learning all came along at once.

I've been Ireland's first MMA fighter, first Brazilian jiu-jitsu black belt and first coach of a UFC champion. Sure, they're significant achievements to reflect on, but that's not what I'll take the most satisfaction from when I call it a day. The overriding theme when I look back will be that I spent my life doing something I love. There's no greater satisfaction than that.

The pinnacle for an MMA coach is to train a UFC champion. I've already achieved that, yet it still seems like we're just getting started. I genuinely feel like a beginner at this level of the game. Conor McGregor is my first world champion. He's leading my initial wave. But I believe the hardest work is still to come. Let's get the teenagers, fourteen, fifteen and sixteen years of age, and mould them into world-class athletes. I know so much more than I knew when Conor made his debut in the UFC. I'm learning every day and, with my fortieth birthday approaching, I expect to continue that cycle of education for at least another twenty years. You'll never master everything about this game, because there's simply too much involved. I'll be a student of the game until the day I die.

It's not all about competing, either. SBG caters for people at all levels who have a wide variety of goals. The vast majority of our members don't train to fight. For them, the training is part of their lifestyle. We've had some great success stories over the years of people who had been enduring difficult times but found a new lease of life after becoming a part of SBG. I take as much satisfaction from seeing somebody achieving a long-term fitness goal as I do from big wins for my professional fighters.

For many years, my family weren't keen on my involvement in mixed martial arts. However, it's important not to mistake that for a lack of support. The fact of the matter is that without their backing, I simply wouldn't have made it this far. In the early days they felt my time would have been better spent using my degree to find a 'normal' job instead of fighting people in sheds, and who could blame them? It would have been remiss of them not to give me that advice. Abandoning a good career in favour of training full-time was sheer lunacy, in hindsight, but it was an obsession for me. My family appreciated that. Considering how well things have worked out, nobody is happier for me than my dad, Alan, my mother, Margaret, my sister, Ann, and my brother, James. Their support means more to me than I could ever convey. Without the encouragement I've received from my parents, the help I've had from Ann over the years and the inspiration I take from James, that success wouldn't have occurred and this book wouldn't be in your hands.

At its birth, SBG Ireland was a few beginners in a small, damp, smelly shed. Now, we have over 700 members in a state-of-the-art gym. In order to cater for the ever-growing demand, we're expanding to additional facilities in Swords, just north of Dublin, and Tallaght, to the south-west. We've gone nationwide too, with ten satellite gyms throughout Ireland that are affiliated to SBG. Today, a person can join SBG and acquire in six months a level of knowledge that I needed six years to attain.

We're home to a UFC world champion and several contenders, plus a bunch of promising youngsters who are rising rapidly through the top shows on the European circuit. The numbers are always increasing, but the overall philosophy remains the same.

Perhaps it's fitting that this tale of success against the odds has ended with a setback. At Straight Blast Gym, sometimes we win, sometimes we lose, but every time we learn. That attitude was with us when we were a tiny outfit that nobody in the UFC had ever heard of. We persevered and have travelled all the way to the top. Now that we've arrived, we're staying loyal to the same mantra that got us here. It's now more important than ever, because one loss isn't going to send us back to the drawing board. There are challenges ahead that will test our capacity to absorb the lessons that are dealt by sport at the highest level. I know that some of those challenges will result in victory and others will end in defeat. But I'm enthusiastic about them all. Regardless of the outcome of any contest, the real winners are those who learn the most.

Acknowledgements

John Kavanagh

There are so many people I could thank for making this story a possibility: I'm afraid if I start listing them all individually, I'll forget someone. So I'll simply say that I'm thankful to every single person who has played a part in this journey. I think you all know who you are by now. Special thanks to Conor McGregor, who took the time to write the foreword for this book. I'd also like to thank Paul Dollery for investing his time and expertise in helping me to put this story into words, as well as Tommy Lakes and Dolly Clew for contributing their photography. Finally, I need to extend a special thank you to my beautiful soon-to-be-wife Orlagh Hunter, who has the unenviable task of putting up with my obsessive mind every day.

Paul Dollery

To my wife and best friend Sinéad, without whom I wouldn't have been able to balance the biggest professional and personal commitments of my life; to my colleagues at The42.ie, especially Adrian Russell, whose patience, support and encouragement made my involvement in this book possible; to Niall Kelly, Fintan O'Toole and Jackie Cahill for their advice; to Artem Lobov, Cathal Pendred and Conor McGregor for their contributions; to Orlagh Hunter for filling in the gaps in John's memory; to Brendan Barrington, Michael McLoughlin and the team at Penguin for imparting their knowledge, experience and guidance; to Ciarán Medlar for his assistance; and to John Kavanagh for giving me the honour of telling his inspirational story . . . Thank you all.

Index